I0889366

Shrubs and Vines of Iowa

A BUR OAK GUIDE

Holly Carver, series editor

Shrubs and Vines of Iowa

Peter J. van der Linden and Donald R. Farrar

UNIVERSITY OF IOWA PRESS, IOWA CITY

University of Iowa Press, Iowa City 52242

www.uiowapress.org

Printed in the United States of America

Design by April Leidig

The University of Iowa Press is a member of Green Press Initiative and is committed to preserving natural resources.

Printed on acid-free paper

Library of Congress Cataloging-in-Publication Data

Van der Linden, Peter J., 1953– author.

Shrubs and vines of Iowa / Peter J. van der Linden and Donald R. Farrar.

pages cm. — (Bur Oak guides)

Includes bibliographical references and index.

ISBN 978-1-60938-397-8 (pbk), ISBN 978-1-60938-398-5 (ebk)

1. Shrubs — Iowa — Identification. 2. Climbing plants — Iowa — Identification. I. Farrar, Donald R., 1941– author. II. Title. III. Series: Bur Oak guide.

QK160.V37 2016

582.1709777 — dc23 2015028382

CONTENTS

ACKNOWLEDGMENTS

WE ARE INDEBTED TO the many Iowa scientists, past and present, whose work has contributed so much to our knowledge of Iowa's flora. Among our contemporary colleagues, we are especially grateful to Mark Widrlechner, who generously shared his knowledge of the genus *Rubus* by providing the key and distribution information; Deb Lewis for being such a gracious host at the Ada Hayden Herbarium; and John Pearson and Laura McCormick for their assistance in the field.

Many others contributed to this work through the support they provided. We thank staff at the Brenton Arboretum for permission to collect specimens; Jimmie Thompson for providing material for photography; Judy van der Linden for help in measuring specimens; Holly Carver, Karen Copp, and the staff of the University of Iowa Press for their excellent editing and design; and Eugenia Farrar, Dave and Sue Benson, and John van der Linden for their hospitality during author van der Linden's travels.

Finally, we thank the Iowa State University Publication Endowment Fund for funding in support of this project.

INTRODUCTION

TREES DOMINATE Iowa's forests while grasses predominate in our prairies and roadsides. Shrubs and vines receive much less attention, though they, too, are important elements of our natural landscapes. This book is a guide for those who want to know more about these interesting and useful plants.

Like trees, shrubs and vines are woody plants that are easy to observe year round. The first part of this book will help you identify them. Illustrated keys take you through the process one step at a time and are followed by images and descriptions of all but the rarest species. Summer and winter features are covered separately to facilitate identification at these two very different times of year.

Information about the distribution, ecology, and uses of each species native and naturalized in Iowa is provided with the descriptions. We hope this information will enhance your appreciation of shrubs and vines and help you use these plants effectively in your outdoor spaces.

The book continues with brief chapters about the culture and natural history of shrubs and vines. These offer tips for selecting, planting, and caring for these plants in your landscape and explain why the plants grow where they do in nature.

While complete in its coverage, this book is not meant to be a flora or taxonomic treatise. Synonyms are provided when botanists differ on how to name a species, but the reasoning behind the differing opinions is not explored. Nomenclature mostly follows Eilers and Roosa (1994) because that text has been widely used and quoted by Iowa botanists; other sources are listed in the bibliography.

Readers will note that this book does not include many exotic shrubs and vines that are cultivated in Iowa. Insufficient space precluded the illustration and discussion of these varied and attractive plants, although we acknowledge their value for landscaping here.

Unless otherwise credited, photographic images are the work of author Donald R. Farrar. Most drawings in the keys were created by John van der Linden. Other drawings in the keys and the illustrations in the first chapter were prepared by Carol Jacobs and first appeared in our previous work, *Forest and Shade Trees of Iowa*. Carol Jacobs also assembled the winter twig plates in this book.

Shrubs and Vines of Iowa

How to Identify Shrubs and Vines

TO BEGIN, what is the difference between a shrub and a vine? Like trees, both shrubs and vines have woody stems that survive the winter and from which new shoots grow in spring. The main difference is that shrubs can stand unsupported, while vines cannot. Vines need a tree, shrub, fence, wall, or other upright object on which they can climb.

The stems of vines are adapted to hold fast to their support. Some grow tightly against tree bark or walls using aerial roots. Others climb more loosely, using slender, curly tendrils that either twine around the support or grasp it with adhesive disks at their tips. In a few vines, such as clematis, the leaf stalks twist around the supporting structure.

The most conspicuous feature of shrubs is their multiple upright stems. In many species of shrubs, these sprout from a single crown. In others, they arise from underground stems that grow horizontally through the soil, sprouting at intervals to create colonies of aboveground stems. Some species produce both clumped and colonial stems.

In a few kinds of shrubs, for example, the pagoda dogwood, the initial stem that develops from the seed often remains dominant over the others and grows much larger. Over time this dominant stem may become the size of a small tree. Individuals exhibiting this form are said to be arborescent or treelike.

Other kinds of shrubs are natural dwarfs, with clumped or colonial stems growing no more than knee- or waist-high. Some of these stay small because their stems die back every winter, for example, some species of wild roses. Others, such as the dwarf raspberry and bunchberry, have only their underground stems woody. Still others, including the blueberries, are diminutive in all their parts with relatively short-lived stems (although the colonies themselves may survive for many years).

For purposes of this book, a small shrub is one growing up to 1 meter in height (approximately 3 feet). Medium-size shrubs grow 1 to 2 meters tall (3 to 6 feet), while large shrubs are more than 2 meters tall.

The difference between large shrubs and small trees isn't always clear. A tree is usually defined as a woody plant with one or only a few main stems whose diameters are greater than 10 centimeters (about 4 inches). A shrub is a woody plant with several to many stems that are mostly less than 10 centimeters in diameter. As mentioned above, some species such as pagoda dogwood may occasionally fit into both categories. Another example is choke cherry, which sometimes becomes a small tree. Both these species are included in our *Forest and Shade Trees of Iowa* as well as this book.

THE FOLLOWING MATERIAL will help you identify the shrubs and vines growing wild in Iowa. Because these plants have woody stems, you can study them year round. No special equipment is necessary, other than a small magnifying glass to examine the surfaces of leaves and the features of winter twigs.

Vines are especially easy to identify because only a few species are native in Iowa and their characteristics are so distinctive. Identifying species in some groups of shrubs can be challenging, but for the most part shrub identification is straightforward, too.

You can use this book in two ways to identify an unknown shrub or vine. First, try comparing it to the illustrations and descriptions in the genus and species accounts, which cover Iowa's most common species. If you don't find it there, use one of the three keys, which are more comprehensive.

What to Look For

Before you can identify shrubs and vines, you need to know something about the structure of their leaves, stems, flowers and fruits. What are some basic features you need to look for?

LEAVES

Leaves are the most visible parts of shrubs and vines and thus particularly useful for identification. Figure 1 illustrates leaf characteristics. Three of these features are especially important.

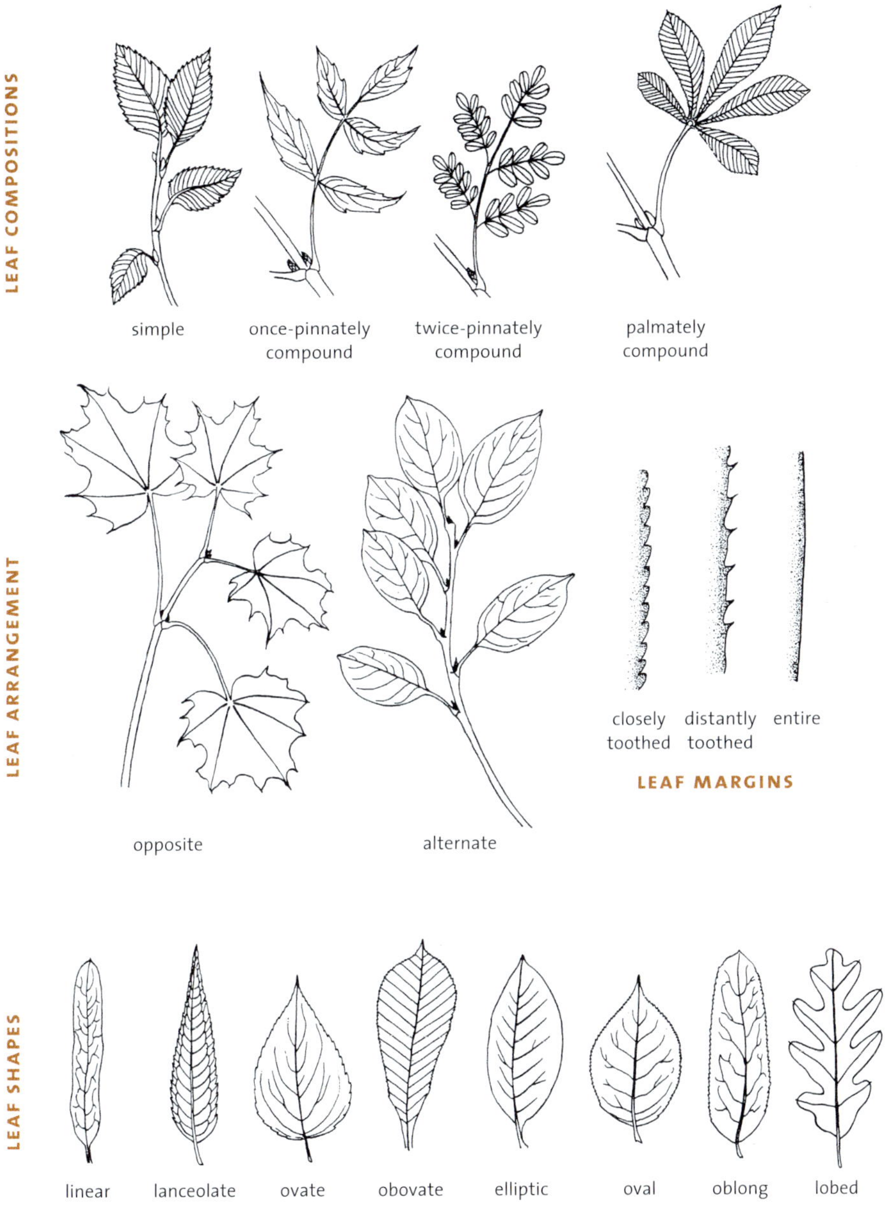

FIG. 1. Leaf characteristics.

Composition. A leaf can have one blade or be divided into several blades called leaflets. Leaves with a single blade are simple, while those with leaflets are compound. Compound leaves are pinnate if the leaflets are arranged along the side of an axis or palmate if the leaflets radiate from a point like the fingers of a hand.

Arrangement. The area where a leaf and a bud are attached to the stem is called a node. "Arrangement" refers to how many leaves are growing at each node: alternate if one, opposite if two, and whorled if three or more.

Margins. The edge of a leaf is toothed if it has small toothlike projections and entire if these projections are absent.

Other distinctive features of leaves are their shape, including whether or not they are lobed; the presence or absence of hairs on their surfaces; and the branching pattern of their veins. Some species have distinctive stipules, which are small, paired, leaflike appendages attached to the leafstalks or nodes.

STEMS

The terminal, leaf-bearing portion of a stem is called the shoot; after it has hardened and developed its winter features, it is called a twig. Twigs bear several distinctive structures that help you identify species, especially in the winter when leaves are absent.

A leaf scar is a small mark left on the twig when the leafstalk breaks off in autumn. In many species it is somewhat semicircular in shape; in others it is rounded or shaped like a heart, crescent, shield, or the letters U or V. Within it are one or more dots or marks called bundle scars that show where the vascular bundles of the leaf entered the twig. Leaf scars are arranged in the same way as leaves: alternate, opposite, or whorled. Figure 2 illustrates leaf scars.

A bud is a partly developed shoot or flower cluster. Most buds are enclosed by one or more scales, whose number and arrangement are consistent within a species. A bud without scales is said to be naked. Buds are usually solitary or borne singly above each leaf scar, but in some species two or more are either located side by side (collateral) or lined up one above the other (superposed).

In some shrubs, the buds that produce flowers are quite different from the buds that become shoots. In the birch family, the flower buds are elongated and covered with many tiny scales, forming a distinctive sausage-shaped structure that helps identify members of that family in winter. Both the buds and the flower clusters they eventually produce are called catkins. Figure 3 illustrates bud shapes.

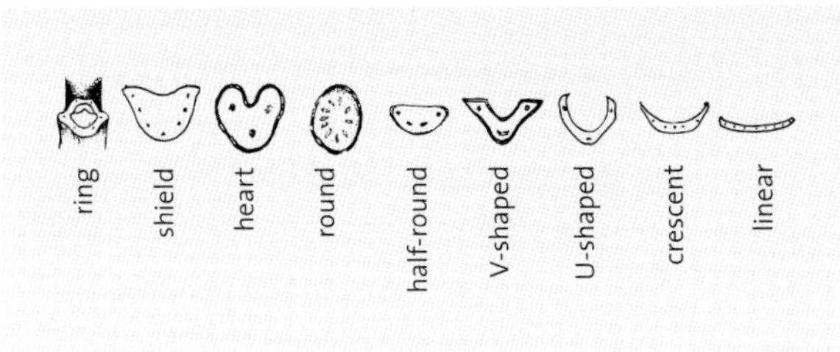

FIG. 2. Leaf scar shapes.

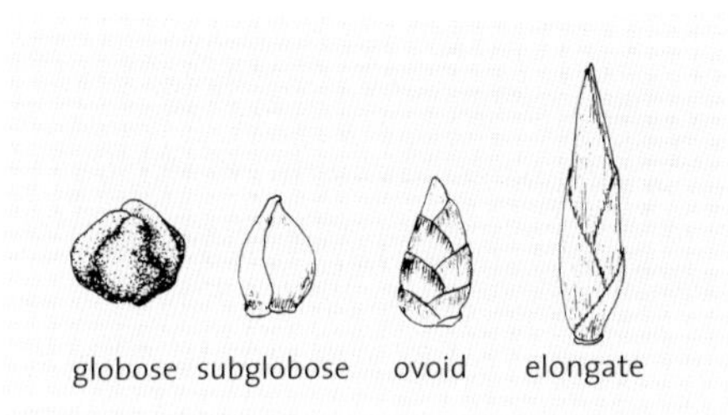

FIG. 3. Bud shapes.

Thorns, spines, and prickles are often used interchangeably in everyday speech, but in botany they have distinct meanings. Thorns are modified twigs and are thus found in the same positions you would expect to find twigs, immediately above the leaves or leaf scars. Spines are modified leaves or stipules; when stipules they are usually found in pairs at the nodes, one on either side of each leaf base or leaf scar. Prickles are outgrowths of the stem and are typically arranged somewhat randomly along the twig between the nodes. (In roses, prickles can be associated in pairs at the nodes as well as scattered between the nodes.)

FLOWERS

Flowers are ephemeral but useful for identification when present. A complete flower has four groups or whorls of flower parts, which from the outside toward the center are called sepals, petals, stamens, and carpels. One or more of these are lacking in some flowers, for example, those of willows that have only stamens or only carpels.

Sepals are usually green and leaflike. The sepals in an individual flower are referred to collectively as the calyx.

Petals tend to be colorful and showy, serving to attract pollinators. They are absent in most wind-pollinated flowers. The petals in an individual flower are referred to collectively as the corolla.

Stamens produce pollen. They consist of slender stalks called filaments and pollen-bearing sacs called anthers.

Carpels enclose tiny structures called ovules that eventually become seeds. In many species, the carpels are aggregated into a flask-shaped structure called the pistil that has three parts: a bulbous basal portion called the ovary, a slender neck or style, and a swollen tip or stigma. Superior ovaries have the sepals, petals, and stamens at their base, while inferior ovaries have these structures at their summit.

A flower may have both stamens and carpels or either of them. When a flower has both, it is bisexual or perfect. A flower with only one is unisexual or imperfect. Unisexual flowers bearing stamens are staminate, while those bearing pistils are pistillate. A monoecious species has staminate and pistillate flowers on the same plant, while a dioecious species has them on separate plants. Polygamous species have both bisexual and unisexual flowers on the same plant.

A cluster of flowers is called an inflorescence. The arrangement of flowers in an inflorescence differs among species and can be helpful in identification. See figure 4.

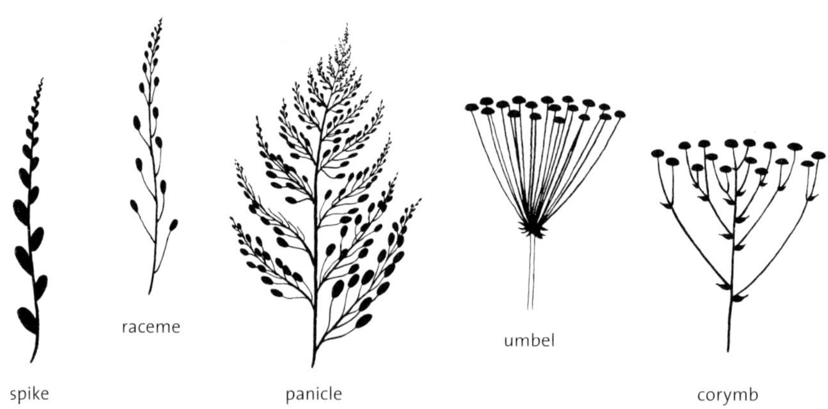

FIG. 4. Types of inflorescences.

FRUITS

"Fruit" is a much broader term in botany than it is in the kitchen or grocery store. Defined as the ripened ovary of a flower, it thus includes anything bearing seeds — dry pods and capsules as well as fleshy fruits. For identification purposes, fruits are commonly divided into two groups referred to as fleshy and dry.

Dry fruits include one-seeded achenes such as those of the dandelion and sunflower, winged fruits or samaras like those of maple trees, legumes like beans and peas, and follicles such as milkweed pods, all of which develop from a single carpel. Dry fruits that develop from more than one carpel are called capsules. Typically capsules have two or more compartments and split open along two or more seams.

Fleshy fruits include the applelike pome, which develops from an inferior ovary and has the seeds confined to compartments in the center; the drupe, which has a single large stone in the center, as in cherries and plums; and the berry, which has small seeds distributed through its flesh.

Using a Key to Identify Plants

A key is a device that helps you identify something through a step-by-step process, much like a treasure hunt where one clue leads to another. Each step offers two alternatives that are mutually exclusive, for example, "leaves simple" or "leaves compound." After deciding which one applies to the specimen at hand, you are referred to the next step in the key, where the process is repeated. As you progress through the key, the possibilities become fewer and fewer until you find the specimen's identity.

Keys are constructed in different ways. Some keys offer three or more alternatives in a step, for example, "leaves alternate," "leaves opposite," or "leaves whorled." Other keys consider multiple features at a time, for example, the leaf shape and fruit type in one step. In this book, you normally have to consider only one feature and select between two alternatives in each step.

Species, Genera, and Families

Living things are classified according to a hierarchical system that includes species, genera, and families. What do these terms mean?

Most people have an intuitive understanding of what a species is: a particular kind of plant or animal. Defining it scientifically is a more complicated matter, and biologists do not always agree. The noted botanist Arthur Cronquist defined species as the "smallest groups that are consistently and persistently distinct, and distinguishable by ordinary means" (Cronquist 1978), which leaves some room for interpretation but explains the concept very well.

A group of closely related species is called a genus. Among woody plants, the genus is often a clearly recognizable group with a familiar English name. Some examples are *Cornus* (dogwood), *Acer* (maple), *Vitis* (grape), and *Salix* (willow). The plural form of genus is genera.

The next level in the hierarchical system is the family, a group of closely related genera. As an example, the Salicaceae or willow family includes *Salix*, *Populus* (poplar, aspen), and one other genus not found in Iowa. Note the ending -aceae, which by convention is used to designate a family of plants.

These and the higher levels of classification are based on the presumed evolutionary relationships of plants. In recent years our understanding of some relationships has changed because of research using modern techniques. Thus the maples, which were once placed in their own family, Aceraceae, are now considered part of the Sapindaceae. The viburnums, long considered part of the Caprifoliaceae, are now included in the Adoxaceae.

Botanical Names

All plant species have a two-word botanical name or binomial that is used by scientists around the world, even though they may know the plants by more familiar names in their home countries. The assignment of these names is based on rules that have been developed by international agreement. The names are always italicized or underlined in print.

The first word of the binomial represents the genus to which the species belongs and is always capitalized. The second word, called the specific epithet, designates the species and is never capitalized, even if based on a proper name. Thus the name *Acer spicatum* tells you two things about the species: the plant is a maple, and which maple it is.

In formal botanical writing, a binomial is followed by the full or abbreviated surname of the botanist who proposed it, for example, *Acer spicatum* Lam., referring to Jean Lamarck. The abbreviation "L.," used behind so many names, stands for the Swedish scientist Carolus Linnaeus, who developed the system of binomial nomenclature in the eighteenth century.

In some cases it is helpful to name a variant of a species that occurs in a particular geographic region. These variants are called varieties or subspecies and are designated by an italicized, uncapitalized name following the specific epithet and botanist's name. An example is *Juniperus communis* L. var. *depressa* Pursh, with the abbreviation "var." indicating the name is a variety and the word "Pursh" indicating the botanist who proposed the name.

Botanical names normally don't change over time — one of their main values — but on occasion further study will result in a plant receiving a different name. When a plant is transferred to another species or genus, the abbreviated name of the botanist who originally described it is retained in parentheses as part of its new botanical name. In some cases, botanists disagree about the appropriate name for a species, and two or more names continue to appear in print; such synonyms are listed in this book as an aid to readers.

Key to Shrubs and Vines

THE FOLLOWING KEY identifies shrubs and vines that are native or naturalized in Iowa. Most are identified to species, either in the main key or the genera keys immediately following. Some naturalized shrubs are identified to genus only, for example, the honeysuckles (*Lonicera*) and privets (*Ligustrum*).

The key is based primarily on characteristics of the foliage, supplemented with fruit and twig characteristics where necessary for accurate identification. Separate keys identify shrubs and vines based on their fruits and winter features.

To use the key, read the two descriptions in step 1 and select the one that matches your specimen. The number at the end of that description will tell you the step to go to next. Proceed this way, step by step, until the key gives you a name.

Once you have identified a specimen with the key, we suggest you check your identification by comparing the specimen to the descriptions and images of that species. If you do not know the meaning of a botanical term, see the previous chapter or the glossary.

General Key

1. Shrub: 2
1. Vine: 60

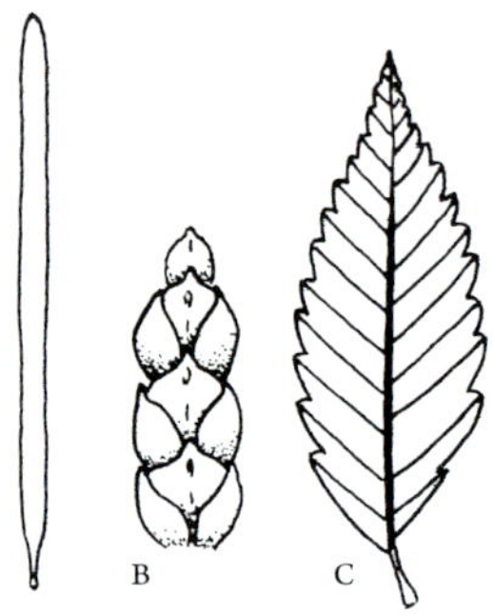

A B C

FIG. 5

2. Leaves scalelike or needlelike (fig. 5a, b): 3
2. Leaves broad (fig. 5c): 5
3. Leaves opposite or whorled: juniper, *Juniperus* (see page 21 for key to species)
3. Leaves alternate: 4
4. Leaves needlelike, more than 5 mm long, pointing away from the twig: Canada yew, *Taxus canadensis*
4. Leaves scalelike, overlapping and flattened against the twig, 1 to 3 mm long: beach heath, *Hudsonia tomentosa*
5. Leaves alternate: 6
5. Leaves opposite, subopposite, or whorled: 44
6. Twigs and branchlets with spines, prickles, or stout bristles at the nodes or between nodes: 7
6. Twigs lacking these structures (some twigs may be short with thorny tips): 11
7. Leaves simple: 8
7. Leaves compound: 9
8. Leaves lobed: gooseberry, *Ribes* (see page 24 for key to species)
8. Leaves not lobed: Japanese barberry, *Berberis thunbergii*

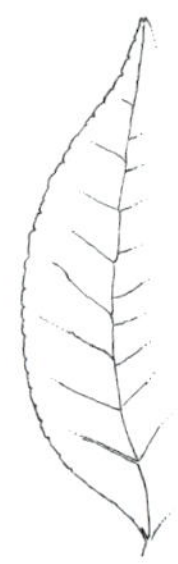

FIG. 6

9. Leaflets appearing entire, on close inspection with tiny widely spaced teeth (fig. 6); twigs with 2 spines at each node and none in between: prickly-ash, *Zanthoxylum americanum*
9. Leaflets conspicuously toothed; twigs with prickles or bristles at and between the nodes: 10

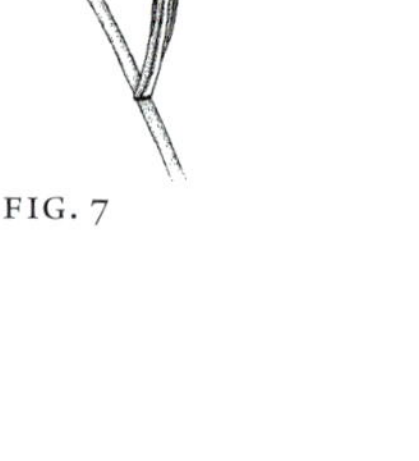

FIG. 7

10. Stipules forming a narrow wing along the base of the petioles (fig. 7): rose, *Rosa* (see page 24 for key to species)
10. Stipules not forming wings on the petioles: raspberry, blackberry, and dewberry, *Rubus* (see page 26 for key to species)
11. Leaves compound: 12
11. Leaves simple: 18
12. Leaflets 7 or more: 13
12. Leaflets 3 or 5: 15
13. Leaflets sharply toothed: sumac, *Rhus* (see page 24 for key to species)
13. Leaflets entire: 14
14. Rachis (axis) of leaf winged with green leafy tissue: winged sumac, *Rhus copallina*
14. Rachis not winged: leadplant and indigo bush, *Amorpha* (see page 19 for key to species)
15. Leaflets very small, the terminal ones 1 to 2 cm long: cinquefoil, *Potentilla* (see page 22 for key to species)
15. Leaflets larger, the terminal ones 3 or more cm long: 16

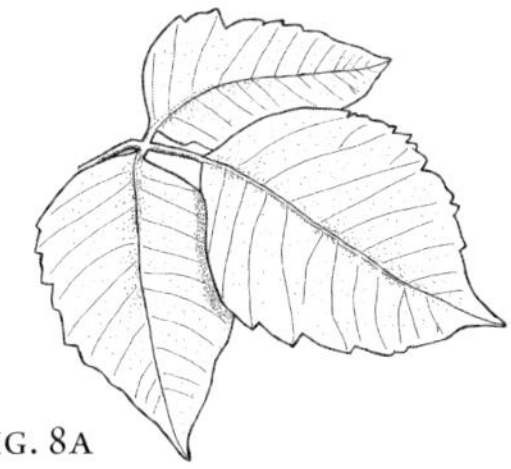

FIG. 8A

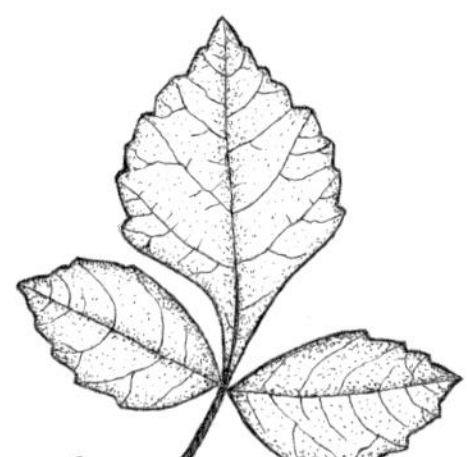

FIG. 8B

16. End leaflet with a much longer stalk than the other 2 (fig. 8a): poison ivy, *Toxicodendron* (see page 32 for key to species)
16. End leaflet short-stalked or not obviously stalked (fig. 8b): 17
17. Leaflets conspicuously toothed (fig. 8b): fragrant sumac, *Rhus aromatica*
17. Leaflets with tiny inconspicuous teeth, appearing entire on casual inspection: hoptree, *Ptelea trifoliata*
18. Leaves lobed: 19
18. Leaves not lobed: 20

FIG. 9A

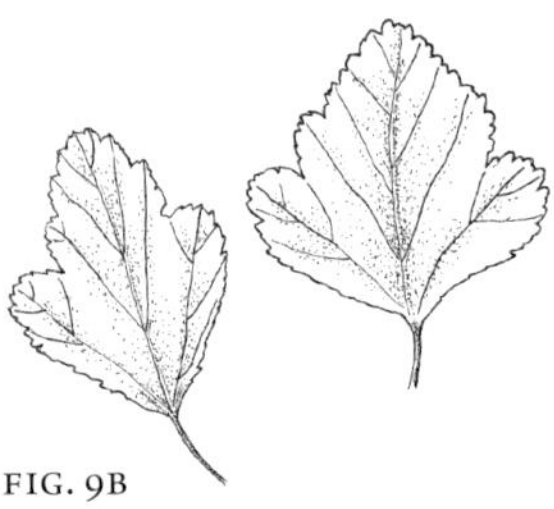

FIG. 9B

19. Most leaves wider than long (fig. 9a), in some species dotted with tiny yellow glands beneath (use magnifying glass); flowers and developing fruits in racemes at the nodes: currant, *Ribes* (see page 24 for key to species)
19. Most leaves slightly longer than wide (fig. 9b), not gland-dotted beneath; flowers and developing fruits in terminal corymbs: ninebark, *Physocarpus opulifolius*
20. Leaves toothed: 21
20. Leaves entire or wavy-margined: 36

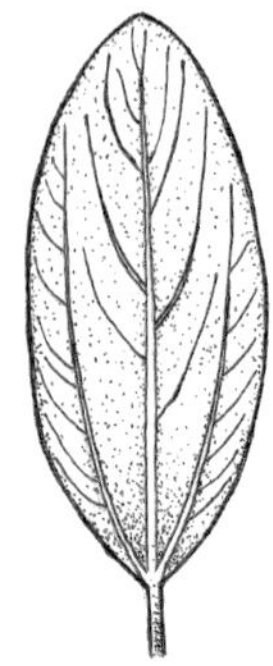

FIG. 10

21. Each leaf with 3 main veins originating from the point where the blade joins the petiole, with smaller veins branching from these (fig. 10); dwarf prairie shrub: New Jersey tea, *Ceanothus* (see page 19 for key to species)
21. Each leaf with one principal vein in middle, with smaller veins branching from it at regular intervals: 22
22. Side veins curving upward and following the margin (see fig. 13 in step 36): buckthorn, *Rhamnus* (see page 23 for key to species)
22. Veins not following the margin: 23

FIG. 11

23. Side veins running straight into the tips of the teeth (fig. 11b): 24

23. Side veins becoming indistinct near the margin or branching and forming a network near the margin (fig. 11a): 28
24. Leaves oblong to broadly elliptic, at least twice as long as wide, with a few large teeth on each side; terminal bud and several lateral buds clustered at twig tip: dwarf chinkapin oak, *Quercus prinoides*
24. Leaves not much longer than wide, with many small teeth; buds not clustered at twig tip: 25
25. Bud with 2 scales: speckled alder, *Alnus rugosa*
25. Bud with 3 or more overlapping scales: 26
26. Bud elongate, red or red-green; fruit berrylike: serviceberry, *Amelanchier* (see page 19 for key to species)
26. Bud not much longer than wide, brown or tan; fruit not berrylike: 27
27. Leaves very small, less than 4 cm long; shrub of fens and wet prairies: bog birch, *Betula pumila*
27. Leaves at least 6 cm long; shrub of woods and edges: hazelnut, *Corylus* (see page 21 for key to species)
28. Bud with 1 scale; flowers and fruits in catkins: willow, *Salix* (see page 31 for key to species)
28. Bud with more than 1 scale; flowers and fruits not in catkins: 29

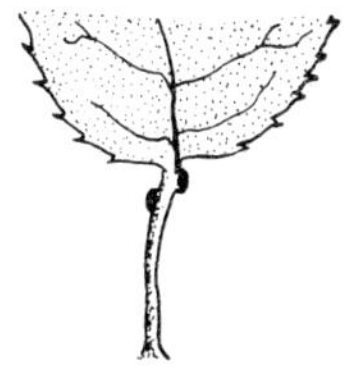

FIG. 12

29. Petioles with dotlike glands near their junctions with the leaf blades (fig. 12): cherry and plum, *Prunus* (see page 23 for key to species)
29. Petioles not glandular: 30
30. Leaves narrow, more than 3 times longer than wide: 31
30. Leaves 1 to 3 times longer than wide: 32
31. Leaves with long, tapered, entire bases; petioles 5 or more mm long: dwarf or sand cherry, *Prunus pumila*
31. Leaves toothed almost to the base, nearly sessile with petioles no more than 5 mm long: meadowsweet, *Spiraea alba*
32. Dwarf shrub of sandy habitats in extreme eastern Iowa, growing no more than knee-high: lowbush blueberry, *Vaccinium angustifolium*
32. Shrub much taller than knee-high: 33

33. Leaves bearing tiny elongated glands along the midvein on the upper surface (best seen with magnifying glass); buds strongly flattened on the twig side: aronia berry or chokeberry, *Aronia*
33. Leaves lacking these glands; buds roundish in cross section: 34
34. Bud elongate and either red or red and green: serviceberry, *Amelanchier* (see page 19 for key to species)
34. Bud not both elongate and red: 35
35. Each leaf scar with 3 bundle scars: cherry and plum, *Prunus* (see page 23 for key to species)
35. Each leaf scar with 1 bundle scar: winterberry, *Ilex verticillata*

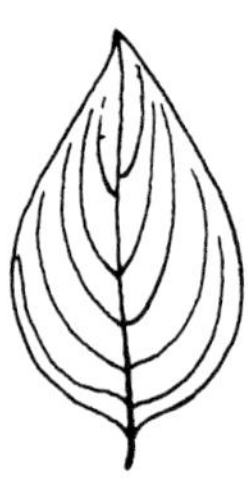

FIG. 13

36. Side veins curving upward and following the margin (fig. 13): 37
36. Side veins not strongly following the margin: 38
37. Bud naked; flowers and developing fruits in small bunches at the nodes: glossy buckthorn, *Rhamnus frangula*
37. Bud 2-scaled; flowers and developing fruits in terminal corymb-like cymes: pagoda or alternate-leaf dogwood, *Cornus alternifolia*
38. Side veins running straight to the edge of the leaf: witch-hazel, *Hamamelis virginiana*
38. Side veins becoming indistinct near the margin or branching and forming a network near the margin: 39
39. Bud enclosed by a single scale: willow, *Salix* (see page 31 for key to species)
39. Bud with more than 1 scale or hidden within the base of the petiole: 40
40. Dwarf shrub growing less than waist-high: 41
40. Medium-size to tall shrub: 43
41. Trailing shrub with evergreen leaves and red fruits: bearberry, *Arctostaphylos uva-ursi*
41. Upright shrub with deciduous leaves; ripe fruits blue or black: 42
42. Undersurface of leaf dotted with tiny yellow glands (use magnifying glass): black huckleberry, *Gaylussacia baccata*
42. Undersurface not dotted: blueberry, *Vaccinium* (see page 32 for key to species)
43. Leaf undersides and twigs coated with tiny silver scales (use magnifying glass): autumn olive, *Elaeagnus umbellata*
43. Leaves and twigs not scaly: leatherwood, *Dirca palustris*
44. Leaves compound: 45
44. Leaves simple: 46

45. Leaflets 3 in each leaf: bladdernut, *Staphylea trifolia*
45. Leaflets 5 or more in each leaf: elderberry, *Sambucus* (see page 32 for key to species)
46. Leaves palmately 3-lobed, with teeth along the edges of the lobes: 47
46. Leaves not lobed, or if lobed then the lobes entire: 50
47. Glands on upper part of petiole (see fig. 12 in step 29): highbush-cranberry, *Viburnum* (see page 33 for key to species)
47. No glands on petiole: 48

FIG. 14

48. Middle leaf lobe much elongated (fig. 14); cultivated shrub, sometimes escaping: Amur maple, *Acer ginnala*
48. Middle leaf lobe not elongated, about half the length of the entire leaf; native in far northeastern Iowa: 49
49. Bud with 2 scales that meet along the edge without overlapping: mountain maple, *Acer spicatum*
49. Bud with several overlapping scales: mapleleaf viburnum, *Viburnum acerifolium*
50. Margins of leaves toothed: 51
50. Margins of leaves entire: 54
51. Leaves subopposite; twigs often thorn-tipped: common buckthorn, *Rhamnus cathartica*
51. Leaves opposite; twigs not thorn-tipped: 52
52. Main veins running straight into the tips of the teeth (see fig. 11b in step 23): arrowwood, *Viburnum* (see page 33 for key to species)
52. Main veins ending and forming a network of smaller veins near the margin (see fig. 11a in step 23): 53
53. Bud 2-scaled; tall shrub of woods and edges: nannyberry and blackhaw, *Viburnum* (see page 33 for key to species)
53. Bud with several overlapping scales; dwarf shrub of shady slopes and ledges: bush honeysuckle, *Diervilla lonicera*
54. Leaf undersides coated with tiny scales that give them a silvery sheen (use magnifying glass to see scales); colonial, often thorny shrub of western Iowa: buffaloberry, *Shepherdia argentea*
54. Leaf undersides not scale-coated; shrub not thorny: 55

55. Twigs producing short leafy shoots in the leaf axils: shrubby St. John's–wort, *Hypericum prolificum*
55. Twigs not developing short leafy shoots: 56
56. Leaves in whorls of 3 at some nodes: buttonbush, *Cephalanthus occidentalis*
56. Leaves strictly opposite: 57
57. Side veins curving upward and following the margin (see fig. 13 in step 36); bud 2-scaled: dogwood, *Cornus* (see page 20 for key to species)
57. Side veins not strongly following the margin: 58

FIG. 15

58. Scales from last winter's buds persisting at the bases of the twigs (fig. 15): 59
58. Bud scales not persisting: privet, *Ligustrum*
59. Flowers and developing fruits in nearly sessile bunches at the nodes; low shrub forming colonies by suckering: wolfberry and coralberry, *Symphoricarpos* (see page 32 for key to species)
59. Flowers and developing fruits in stalked pairs from the leaf axils; tall shrub with its stems arising from a single crown: honeysuckle, *Lonicera*
60. Leaves alternate: 61
60. Leaves opposite: 67
61. Leaves compound: 62
61. Leaves simple: 63
62. Leaflets 3: poison ivy, *Toxicodendron* (see page 32 for key to species)
62. Leaflets 5: woodbine and Virginia creeper, *Parthenocissus* (see page 22 for key to species)
63. Leaves toothed: 64
63. Leaves entire: 65
64. Leaves lobed; vine climbing with tendrils: grape, *Vitis* and *Ampelopsis* (see page 34 for key to species)
64. Leaves not lobed; vine climbing by twining stems: bittersweet, *Celastrus* (see page 19 for key to species)
65. Stems prickly: greenbrier, *Smilax tamnoides* var. *hispida*
65. Stems not prickly: 66
66. Leaves palmately lobed and veined, as in a maple leaf: moonseed, *Menispermum canadense*
66. Leaves either unlobed or deeply lobed at base; veins pinnate: bittersweet nightshade, *Solanum dulcamara*
67. Leaves simple: wild honeysuckle, *Lonicera* (see page 22 for key to species)
67. Leaves compound: 68

68. Leaflets 3 to 7: clematis, *Clematis* (see page 20 for key to species)
68. Leaflets 9 or more: trumpet creeper, *Campsis radicans*

Key to Maples
(*Acer*)

1. Terminal leaf lobe elongated, about ⅔ to ¾ the length of the leaf (see fig. 14 in step 48 of main key); buds with 4 or more scales: Amur maple, *A. ginnala*
1. Terminal leaf lobe about half as long as the leaf or shorter; buds 2-scaled: mountain maple, *A. spicatum*

Key to Serviceberries
(*Amelanchier*)

1. Low shrub forming a colony by suckering: low serviceberry, *A. humilis* and related species
1. Tall shrub with stems arising from a single crown: roundleaf serviceberry, *A. sanguinea*

Key to Leadplant and Indigo Bush
(*Amorpha*)

1. Leaflets finely gray-hairy: leadplant, *A. canescens*
1. Leaflets green, either glabrous or sparsely hairy: 2
2. Leaflets 2.5 or more cm long; tall shrub of shores and wetlands: indigo bush, *A. fruticosa*
2. Leaflets 1 cm long or less; dwarf prairie shrub: dwarf indigo bush, *A. nana*

Key to New Jersey Tea and Redroot
(*Ceanothus*)

1. Clusters of flowers/fruits on long leafless stalks arising from nodes well below the branch tips; leaves ovate to elliptic: New Jersey tea, *C. americanus*
1. Clusters of flowers/fruits on short stalks at the ends of the branches; leaves narrowly elliptic: redroot or narrowleaf New Jersey tea, *C. herbaceus*

Key to Bittersweets
(*Celastrus*)

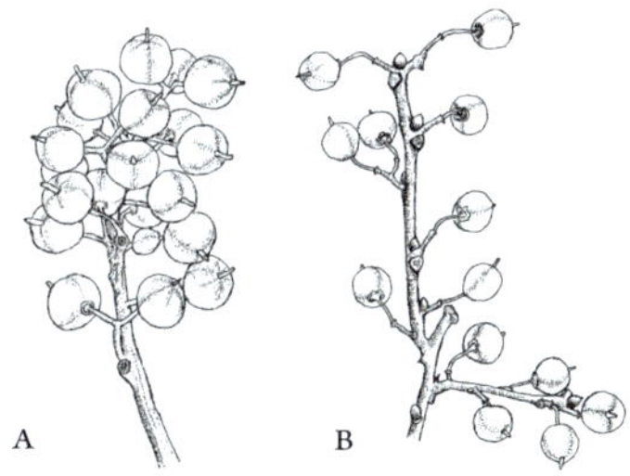

FIG. 16

1. Fruits in elongated, racemelike panicles from the tips of the branches (fig. 16a); leaves ovate to elliptic, about twice as long as wide: American bittersweet, *C. scandens*

1. Fruits in small clusters from the leaf axils (fig. 16b); leaves round or roundish, not much longer than wide: Oriental bittersweet, *C. orbiculatus*

Key to Clematis (*Clematis*)

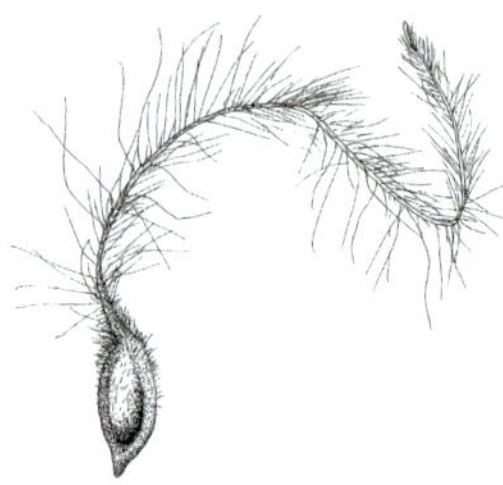

FIG. 17

1. Leaflets 3 to 7, the terminal one often replaced by a tendril; fruits lacking long feathery appendages: leather flower, *C. pitcheri*
1. Leaflets 3; fruits with long feathery tails (fig. 17), clustered in moplike heads: 2
2. Flowers small, white, blooming late in the growing season, arranged in large panicles: virgin's bower, *C. virginiana*
2. Flowers large, purplish, blooming early in the growing season, solitary on long stalks: purple clematis, *C. occidentalis*

Key to Dogwoods (*Cornus*)

Dogwoods are most easily identified in late summer and fall when ripe fruits and mature twigs are available. Identifications may not be accurate when made earlier in the season using foliage alone.

1. Leaves alternate: pagoda or alternate-leaf dogwood, *C. alternifolia*
1. Leaves opposite: 2
2. Dwarf plant with herbaceous stems and red fruits: bunchberry, *C. canadensis*
2. Large woody shrub; ripe fruits white or blue: 3
3. Fruits blue: 4
3. Fruits white: 5
4. Leaves nearly round; pith of 2-year-old and older branchlets white: roundleaf dogwood, *C. rugosa*
4. Leaves ovate to elliptic or narrower; pith of 2-year-old and older branchlets brown: silky dogwood, *C. obliqua*
5. Bark of branchlets and main stems greenish or bright red: red-osier dogwood, *C. stolonifera*
5. Bark of stems gray: 6

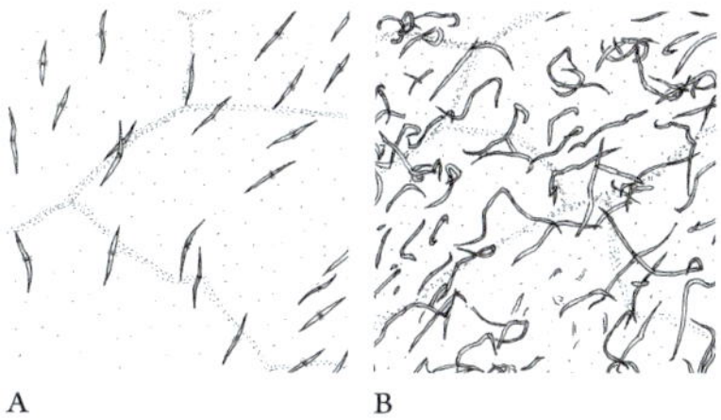

FIG. 18

6. Underside of leaves glabrous or with sparse short, straight hairs that lie flat on the surface and are not visible without magnification (fig. 18a); fruit clusters panicle-like, taller than wide: gray dogwood, *C. racemosa*
6. Underside of leaves with curly and/or erect hairs that are often visible without magnification (fig. 18b); fruit clusters about as wide as tall: roughleaf dogwood, *C. drummondii*

Key to Hazelnuts (*Corylus*)

1. Husk of fruit broad, coarsely incised along its edge; stalked glands often present on petioles and twigs: American hazelnut, *C. americana*
1. Husk of fruit narrowed into a long tube that extends well past the nut; no stalked glands on petioles and twigs: beaked hazelnut, *C. cornuta*

Key to Burning Bush and Wahoo (*Euonymus*)

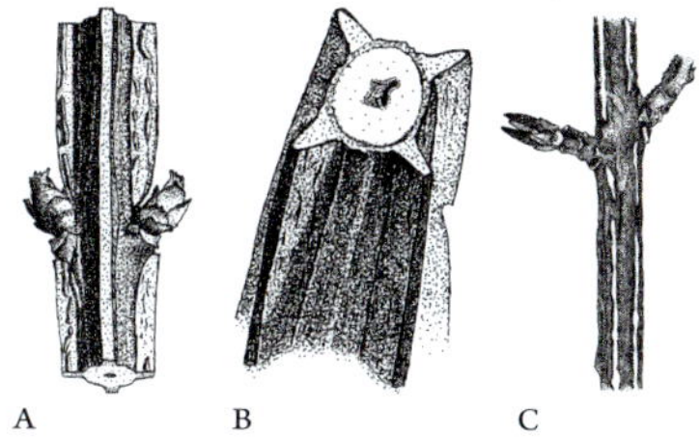

FIG. 19

1. Brown winglike projections running lengthwise down twigs (fig. 19a, b); flowers yellowish; pod (capsule) divided almost to its base, so its sections are nearly separate: burning bush, *E. alatus*
1. Twigs sometimes lined but not winged (fig. 19c); flowers purple; pod deeply lobed but not divided to its base: wahoo, *E. atropurpureus*

Key to Junipers (*Juniperus*)

1. Leaves in whorls of 3, needlelike, more than 5 mm long, pointing away from the twig: common juniper, *J. communis* var. *depressa*
1. Leaves opposite, at least some of them scalelike, appressed to the twig, and no more than 3 mm long: creeping juniper, *J. horizontalis*

Key to Honeysuckles (*Lonicera*)

1. Shrub: Eurasian honeysuckles (species not keyed)
1. Vine: 2
2. Flowers white tinged with purple; fruits black; opposing leaves of flowering/fruiting stems not joined at the base: Japanese honeysuckle, *L. japonica* (see page 90 for discussion)
2. Flowers yellow or reddish purple; fruits red; pair of leaves beneath each cluster of flowers/fruits fused into a disk encircling the twig: 3
3. Pair of disklike leaves nearly round, their upper surfaces partly to completely coated with a pale waxy material, giving them a blue-green color: grape honeysuckle, *L. reticulata*
3. Pair of disklike leaves obviously longer than wide, often with tapered ends, their upper surfaces green: wild honeysuckle, *L. dioica* var. *glaucescens*

Key to Woodbine and Virginia Creeper (*Parthenocissus*)

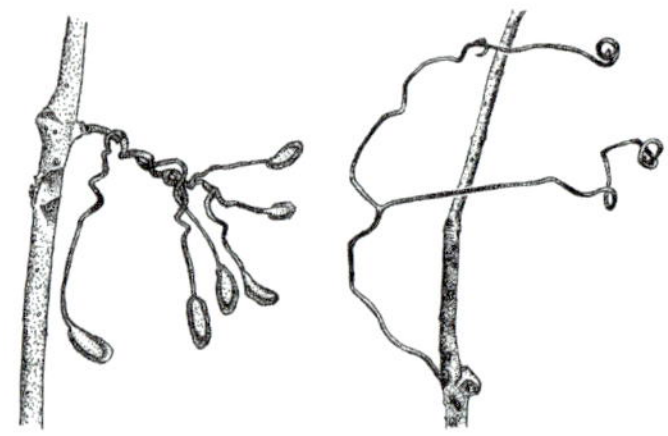

A B
FIG. 20

1. Tendril short, forked into several branches, each tipped by an adhesive disk (fig. 20a), or vine climbing with aerial roots instead of tendrils; petioles hairy: Virginia creeper, *P. quinquefolia*
1. Tendril elongated, forked into no more than 2 or 3 branches, the branch tips slender or sometimes swollen when growing in crevices of tree bark (fig. 20b); leaf petioles glabrous: woodbine, *P. vitacea*

Key to Cinquefoils (*Potentilla*)

1. Small woody shrub; most leaves divided into 5 to 7 leaflets and/or lobes: shrubby cinquefoil, *P. fruticosa*
1. Dwarf trailing plant, woody at the base only; each leaf with 3 leaflets: three-toothed cinquefoil, *P. tridentata*

Key to Cherries and Plums (*Prunus*)

The following key includes all *Prunus* native in Iowa, including those that are commonly trees.

1. Terminal bud absent, the twig tipped by a lateral bud or short stub; fruit 1.8 or more cm long, with a shallow groove running from one end to the other: plums, go to step 2
1. Terminal bud present; fruit 1.5 cm long or less, not grooved: cherries, go to step 5
2. Leaf teeth gland-tipped: 3
2. Leaf teeth not gland-tipped: 4
3. Leaves more than twice as long as wide, with fine teeth less than 1 mm long; shrub of extreme southeast Iowa: wild goose plum, *P. hortulana*
3. Leaves about 1.5 to 2 times longer than wide, with teeth more than 1 mm long; shrub of northeast or central Iowa: Canada plum, *P. nigra*
4. Shrub suckering to form thickets: American plum, *P. americana*
4. Shrub not suckering: big-tree plum, *P. mexicana*
5. Dwarf shrub of sandy or rocky places with narrow willowlike leaves: dwarf or sand cherry, *P. pumila*
5. Tall shrub with ovate, elliptic, or oval leaves: 6

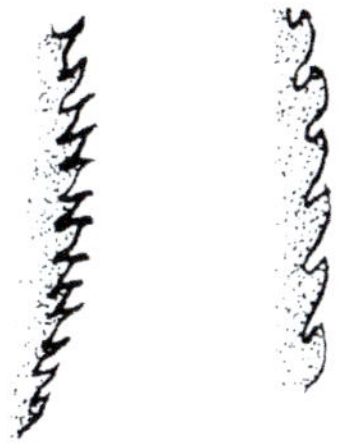

A B

FIG. 21

6. Leaves with sharp outward-pointing teeth (fig. 21a): choke cherry, *P. virginiana*
6. Leaves with fine inward-curving teeth (fig. 21b): 7
7. Flowers and fruits in racemes; ripe fruits black; tall tree: black cherry, *P. serotina* (not discussed in this book)
7. Flowers and fruits in small umbel-like clusters; ripe fruits bright red; shrub or small tree: pin cherry, *P. pensylvanica*

Key to Buckthorns (*Rhamnus*)

1. Leaves entire: glossy buckthorn, *R. frangula*
1. Leaves toothed: 2
2. Leaves subopposite; twigs often tipped by a short thorn: common buckthorn, *R. cathartica*
2. Leaves alternate; twigs not thorn-tipped: 3

3. Dwarf colonial shrub of algific slopes in northeast Iowa, not more than 1 meter tall; flower parts in 5s: alderleaf buckthorn, *R. alnifolia*
3. Upright shrub of upland woods and edges, southern ⅔ of state; flower parts in 4s: lanceleaf buckthorn, *R. lanceolata*

Key to Sumacs (*Rhus*)

1. Leaflets 3: fragrant sumac, *R. aromatica*
1. Leaflets 7 or more: 2
2. Leaflets entire; rachis (axis) of leaf winged: winged sumac, *R. copallina*
2. Leaflets toothed; rachis not winged: 3
3. Twigs densely hairy: staghorn sumac, *R. typhina*
3. Twigs glabrous: smooth sumac, *R. glabra*

Key to Currants and Gooseberries (*Ribes*)

1. Stems prickly and/or bristly: 2
1. Stems not prickly or bristly: 4
2. Ovary of flowers bearing stiff hairs that develop into prickles on the fruit: prickly gooseberry, *R. cynosbati*
2. Ovary and fruit smooth: 3
3. Stamens of flowers much longer than the lobes of the calyx; spines at twig nodes stout and sharp, up to 2 cm long; common and widespread shrub: Missouri gooseberry, *R. missouriense*
3. Stamens of flowers shorter than or about as long as the lobes of the calyx; spines at twig nodes less than 1 cm long or absent; moist ground in Van Buren County: swamp gooseberry, *R. hirtellum*
4. Flowers bright yellow, strongly clove-scented, blooming in early spring; undersides of leaves lacking yellow dots: clove or buffalo currant, *R. odoratum*
4. Flowers white or yellow-green, not clove-scented; undersides of leaves bearing tiny yellow dots: 5
5. Flowers yellow-green; leaves bearing tiny yellow dots on both surfaces; widely distributed shrub: wild black currant, *R. americanum*
5. Flowers white; leaves dotted on lower surface only; shrub of algific slopes in northeast Iowa: northern black currant, *R. hudsonianum*

Key to Roses (*Rosa*)

Identification of wild roses is complicated by variation within species and hybridization between them. The following key will identify typical plants only. The term "hypanthia" in steps 4 and 6 refers to the green urn-shaped structures immediately below the petals and sepals of the flower.

R. carolina and *R. arkansana* illustrate the difficulty you often encounter in identifying roses. Though classified in different sections of the genus, they have the same growth form and habitat and are thus easy to mistake for one another. Typical plants can be recognized by their foliage, but many plants are not typical, appearing intermediate between the two species. In such cases, it is perhaps best to admire these plants for their natural beauty and utility, and not try to name them.

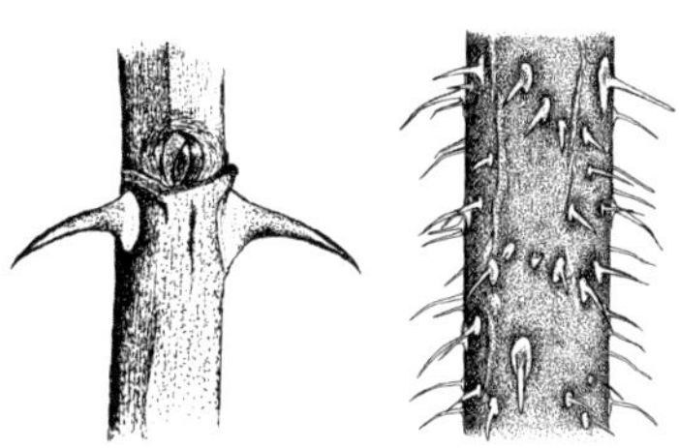

A B

FIG. 22

1. Tall shrubs with arching or climbing stems; prickles stout, often curved or hooked, either confined to the nodes or scattered along the stems (fig. 22a): 2
1. Low to medium-size shrubs with upright stems; prickles slender or absent, when present often abundant and crowded between the nodes, especially on the lower stems (fig. 22b): 5
2. Leaflets 3 or 5: prairie rose, *R. setigera*
2. Leaflets mostly 7 or 9: 3

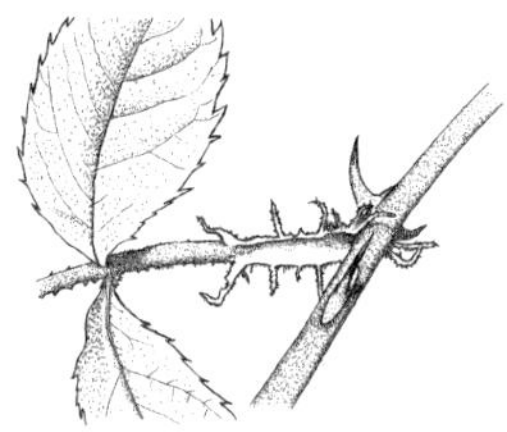

FIG. 23

3. Stipules deeply divided, comblike (fig. 23); weedy shrub of pastures, brushy areas, and similar habitats: multiflora rose, *R. multiflora*
3. Stipules not comb-like; uncommon native shrub: 4
4. Flower stalks (pedicels) and hypanthia bearing stalked glands; prickles curved; shrub of moist places, southwest Iowa: swamp rose, *R. palustris*
4. Flower stalks and hypanthia lacking stalked glands; prickles straight; shrub of dry habitats, northern and western Iowa: wild rose, *R. woodsii*
5. Flowers and fruits produced on stems that sprouted from the ground this year, as well as on lateral branches of older stems; dwarf prairie shrub: 6
5. Flowers and fruits produced only on lateral branches of stems that are 1 year old or older, not on this

year's stems; small to medium-size shrub, habitats various: 7

6. Flower stalks (pedicels) and hypanthia bearing stalked glands; leaves usually with 5 or 7 leaflets, essentially glabrous: pasture rose, *R. carolina* (see note above)
6. Flower stalks and hypanthia lacking stalked glands; leaves usually with 9 leaflets, the rachis and petiole finely hairy: sunshine or wild rose, *R. arkansana* (see note above)
7. Twigs of the current season lacking prickles or with only a few scattered ones; common and widespread shrub of open habitats: smooth wild rose, *R. blanda*
7. Twigs either densely prickly or with paired prickles at each node; uncommon shrub of northern and western Iowa: 8
8. Stems densely prickly; shrub of algific slopes in extreme northeast Iowa: prickly wild rose, *R. acicularis*
8. Prickles in pairs at the nodes and sometimes scattered between the nodes; shrub of dry habitats in northern and western Iowa: wild rose, *R. woodsii*

Key to Blackberries, Raspberries, and Related Plants (*Rubus*)

The following key was prepared by Mark Widrlechner based on his extensive studies of the genus *Rubus* in Iowa. We have modified it slightly to provide consistency in style with the other keys in the book.

The four subgenera of *Rubus* represented in Iowa's flora can be easily distinguished by the following adaptation of Fernald's (1950) key. Botanical terms used in this key and the species key are defined in the glossary at the end of this book and are generally based on definitions presented by Bailey (1941) and Fernald (1950).

1. Flowering stems herbaceous: subgenus *Cylactis*
1. Flowering stems woody: 2
2. Stems (canes) erect, 1 to 2 meters tall, not prickly or bristly; leaves simple, lobed: subgenus *Anoplobatus*
2. Canes prostrate to erect, 0.1 to 2.5 meters tall, armed with prickles and/or bristles; leaves compound: 3
3. Leaves of primocanes (first-year canes) whitish beneath; petals of flowers inconspicuous, generally less than 7 mm long; ripe fruits readily falling intact from the dry torus: subgenus *Idaeobatus*

3. Leaves of primocanes green to gray-green beneath (whitish only in precocious blackberry, *R. praecox*); petals showy, generally at least 7 mm long; ripe fruits not separating from the torus: subgenus *Rubus*

Subgenus *Anoplobatus*

Purple-flowering raspberry, *R. odoratus*, a showy shrub with large rose-pink flowers, is naturalized in Wapello County. It is native to the eastern United States and Canada.

Subgenus *Cylactis*

Iowa has 1 native species, dwarf raspberry, *R. pubescens*, which occurs on cool, moist sites in the northeastern part of the state.

Subgenus *Idaeobatus*

Iowa's 5 members of subgenus *Idaeobatus* can be distinguished with the following adaptation of Widrlechner and Rabeler's (1991) key.

1. Canes erect to arching, not rooting at the tips: 2
1. Canes arching to decumbent, often rooting at the tips: 3
2. Primocanes with stiff bristles and stalked glands: American red raspberry, *R. idaeus* var. *strigosus*
2. Primocanes lacking stiff bristles and stalked glands: cultivated red raspberry, *R. idaeus* var. *idaeus* (not discussed in this book)
3. Primocanes with stalked glands; ripe fruits purple: purple raspberry, *Rubus* ×*neglectus*
3. Primocanes lacking stalked glands; ripe fruits some other color: 4
4. Primocanes purple (rarely yellow-green) in winter, often glaucous; terminal leaflet of each leaf with an acuminate tip and a cordate to truncate base; ripe fruits purple-black (rarely amber): black raspberry, *R. occidentalis*
4. Primocanes reddish brown in winter, not glaucous; terminal leaflets with blunt tips and wedge-shaped bases; ripe fruits red: Asian red raspberry, *R. parvifolius*

Subgenus *Rubus*

Iowa's 27 members of subgenus *Rubus* can be distinguished with the following adaptation of Widrlechner's (1998) key.

1. Canes bearing stiff bristles and/or needlelike prickles of varying strength but lacking broad-based prickles (in some species, prickles are too weak to tear skin); terminal leaflet of primocane leaf elliptic to obovate, rarely ovate: 2
1. Canes bearing needlelike to broad-based prickles usually strong enough to tear skin; terminal leaflet of primocane leaf ovate to elliptic-rhombic, rarely obovate: 8

2. Canes prostrate, rooting at the tips, with stiff bristles and stalked glands (use magnifying glass); flowers 2 cm or less in diameter: section *Hispidi*, continue to step 3 for key to species
2. Canes erect to arching, not rooting at the tips, with needlelike prickles; flowers at least 2 cm in diameter: section *Setosi*, continue to step 4 for key to species
3. Primocane leaves persisting through winter until plants flower the next year; floricanes weak, rarely more than 2 mm in diameter, with most of the bristles broken off; flowers mostly 1 to 1.5 cm in diameter: bristly dewberry, *R. hispidus*
3. Primocane leaves deciduous in autumn; floricanes 2 to 4 mm in diameter, typically bristly; flowers mostly 1.5 to 2 cm in diameter: Fuller's bristly dewberry, *R. fulleri*
4. Leaves pilose beneath, soft to touch when expanded: 5
4. Leaves thinly pubescent beneath, not soft to touch when expanded: 6
5. Inflorescences bearing stalked glands: swamp bristleberry, *R. semisetosus*
5. Inflorescences lacking stalked glands: Missouri bristleberry, *R. missouricus*
6. Primocane leaves with stipules at least 2 cm long; inflorescence open and branched with prominent bracts: Big Horseshoe Lake bristleberry, *R. stipulatus*
6. Primocane leaves with stipules 2 cm long or less; inflorescence condensed and unbranched, often leafy, but bracts not prominent: 7
7. Primocane leaves mostly with 3 leaflets; prickles numbering 8 to 30 per cm of cane; flower pedicels less than 1.5 cm long: uniform bristleberry, *R. uniformis*
7. Primocane leaves mostly with 5 leaflets (early leaves may have 3); prickles usually numbering fewer than 8 per cm of cane; pedicels typically more than 1.5 cm long: Wisconsin bristleberry, *R. wisconsinensis*
8. Inflorescences racemelike, ascendate, or occasionally corymblike, not branched; plants usually flowering from May 15 to June 15: 9
8. Inflorescences corymblike or paniclelike, often branched; plants usually flowering from June through September: 26
9. Canes arching to prostrate, rooting at the tips: section *Procumbentes* (syn. section *Flagellares*), continue to step 10 for key to species
9. Canes erect to arching, not rooting at the tips: 20

10. Leaves pilose beneath, soft to touch when expanded: 11
10. Leaves thinly pubescent beneath, not soft to touch when expanded: 16
11. Inflorescences bearing stalked glands (use magnifying glass): bottomland dewberry, *R. leviculus*
11. Inflorescences lacking stalked glands: 12
12. Inflorescences racemelike; canes robust, frequently exceeding 4 mm in diameter, forming a large mounding tangle: mounding dewberry, *R. satis*
12. Inflorescences 1- to 10-flowered, not racemelike; canes whiplike, mostly 2.5 to 5 mm in diameter, low-arching to prostrate: 13
13. Inflorescences condensed in a terminal corymb: short-stalked dewberry, *R. curtipes*
13. Inflorescences 1-flowered or ascendate: 14
14. Terminal leaflet of primocane leaf with jagged-incised margins; inflorescences usually 1-flowered; calyx lobes with a prominent spatulate tip 1 to 3 mm long: garden dewberry, *R. aboriginum*
14. Terminal leaflet of primocane leaf with regular, serrate margins; inflorescences usually 2- to 8-flowered; calyx lobes lacking a prominent spatulate tip: 15
15. Terminal leaflet of primocane elliptic, rounded at the base: dry-slope dewberry, *R. meracus*
15. Terminal leaflet of primocane ovate, cordate at the base: Lucretia dewberry, *R. roribaccus*
16. Primocane leaves plicate along veins; inflorescence condensed into a terminal corymb or raceme: plait-leaved dewberry, *R. plicatifolius*
16. Primocane leaves not plicate; inflorescence 1-flowered, ascendate, or open-corymbose: 17
17. Primocane leaves with 3 leaflets; inflorescences 1-flowered, generally 5 to 8 cm long: Enslen's dewberry, *R. enslenii*
17. Primocane leaves with 3 and/or 5 leaflets; inflorescences 1- to 12-flowered, generally 5 to 20 cm long: 18
18. Primocane leaves with 3 leaflets; inflorescences 1- to 6-flowered; prickles 1 to 2 mm long: Steele's dewberry, *R. steelei*
18. Primocane leaves mostly with 5 leaflets; inflorescences 4- to 12-flowered; prickles at least 2 mm long: 19
19. Terminal primocane leaflet gradually tapered to an acuminate tip; primocanes with 1 to 3 prickles per cm: rapid-growing dewberry, *R. celer*
19. Terminal primocane leaflet shouldered, abruptly acuminate; primocanes with 3 to 5 prickles per cm: northern dewberry, *R. flagellaris*

20. Primocane tips, inflorescences, and (often) pedicels with stalked glands (use magnifying glass): section *Allegheniensis*, continue to step 21 for key to species
20. Plants lacking stalked glands: section *Arguti*, continue to step 23 for key to species
21. Inflorescences narrowly racemose, at least twice as long as wide; calyx lobes about 3 mm wide by 7 mm long or smaller: Allegheny blackberry, *R. allegheniensis*
21. Inflorescences corymbose or racemose, if racemose less than twice as long as wide and leafy; calyx lobes at least 3 mm wide by 7 mm long: 22
22. Primocane terminal leaflets wide-ovate, usually at least ¾ as wide as long: rose blackberry, *R. rosa*
22. Primocane terminal leaflets ovate to elliptic-oblong, usually about ⅔ as wide as long: old-field blackberry, *R. alumnus*
23. Prickles more or less needlelike (resembling section *Setosi*); primocanes with at least 5 prickles per cm of stem: cluster-flowered blackberry, *R. cauliflorus*
23. Prickles more or less broad-based (resembling section *Allegheniensis*); primocanes with 3 or fewer prickles per cm of stem: 24
24. Primocane terminal leaflets elliptic; floricanes (second-year flowering canes) erect to high-arching, usually at least 1 m tall; inflorescences narrowly racemose: ablate blackberry, *R. ablatus*
24. Primocane terminal leaflets ovate-elliptic to nearly orbicular; floricanes generally arching to low-arching, between 50 and 130 cm tall; inflorescences racemose and leafy to irregular: 25
25. Leaflets regularly serrate; inflorescences racemose, leafy to near the apex: Yankee blackberry, *R. frondosus*
25. Leaflets with jagged-incised margins; inflorescences generally leafy, corymbose, racemose, or irregular, often varying widely on a single floricane: recurved blackberry, *R. recurvans*
26. Primocanes glaucous (especially in winter), armed with small declined to hooked prickles 2 to 4 mm long, arching to prostrate, typically rooting at tips; leaves pubescent beneath but not whitened; stipules narrowly ovate to lanceolate; inflorescence axes with simple hairs (section *Caesii*). Iowa has one species: European dewberry, *R. caesius*.
26. Primocanes not glaucous, armed with large stout prickles 7 to 9 mm long, erect to arching, rarely rooting at tips; leaves tomentose beneath with dense gray-white

hairs; stipules linear to filiform; inflorescence axes with clustered stellate hairs (section *Rubus*). Iowa has one species: precocious blackberry, *R. praecox*.

Key to Willows

(*Salix*)

The following key will identify typical specimens of Iowa's shrubby willows, based on their mature leaves. Because of variation within species and hybridization between species, it is difficult to devise a usable key that will identify every individual you might find. Where there are doubts about the identity of a specimen, compare it to specimens in an herbarium or arboretum.

When flowers are present, readers may wish to use the keys in Swink and Wilhelm 1994 or Smith 2008, which although not designed for Iowa include the species native here.

1. Leaves entire or with a few shallow indentations along the margin, but not obviously toothed: 2
1. Leaves conspicuously toothed: 8
2. Leaves hairy beneath: 3
2. Leaves glabrous: 6
3. Lower leaf surfaces with a thick feltlike coating of white woolly hairs, strikingly different in color from the green upper surfaces: sage willow, *S. candida*
3. Lower leaf surfaces paler than the upper but not white-hairy as described above: 4
4. Leaves elliptic to obovate, less than 3 times longer than wide: Bebb's willow, *S. bebbiana*
4. Leaves lanceolate to oblanceolate, at least 3 times longer than wide: 5
5. Lower leaf surface with a thin, pale waxy coating (glaucous); tall shrub of moist prairies and wetlands: meadow willow, *S. petiolaris*
5. Lower surface light green to gray-green, not glaucous; dwarf prairie shrub: prairie willow, *S. humilis*
6. Leaf tips blunt or rounded; low shrub of fens: bog willow, *S. pedicellaris*
6. Leaf tips pointed; tall shrub of various wet habitats: 7
7. Leaves elliptic to obovate, not more than 4 times longer than wide: pussy willow, *S. discolor*
7. Leaves lanceolate, more than 4 times longer than wide: meadow willow, *S. petiolaris*
8. Leaves linear, at least 10 times longer than wide, with widely spaced teeth: sandbar willow, *S. interior*
8. Leaves lanceolate to ovate-lanceolate, with closely or widely spaced teeth: 9

9. Lower leaf surface covered with long, appressed, silky hairs: silky willow, *S. sericea*
9. Lower leaf surface glabrous or sparsely hairy: 10
10. Leaves elliptic or obovate: pussy willow, *S. discolor*
10. Leaves narrowly to broadly lanceolate: 11
11. Leaves broadly lanceolate, glossy above, with dotlike glands at the base of the blade: shining willow, *S. lucida*
11. Leaves lanceolate, lacking glands at the base of the blade: 12
12. Stipules prominent, persisting through summer: rigid or heart-leaved willow, *S. eriocephala*
12. Stipules absent: meadow willow, *S. petiolaris*

Key to Elderberries (*Sambucus*)

1. Pith of twigs white; fruit dark purple; inflorescence corymblike, wider than tall: common elderberry, *S. canadensis*
1. Pith of twigs brown; fruit red; inflorescence paniclelike, taller than wide: red elderberry, *S. pubens*

Key to Coralberry, Wolfberry, and Snowberry (*Symphoricarpos*)

1. Fruit red; twigs with solid pith: coralberry, *S. orbiculatus*
1. Fruit white; twigs hollow: 2
2. Petioles 4 or more mm long; flowers sessile; common shrub of the prairie-forest border: wolfberry, *S. occidentalis*
2. Petioles 3 mm long or less; flowers short-stalked; ledges and bluffs in extreme northeast Iowa: snowberry, *S. albus*

Key to Poison Ivies (*Toxicodendron*)

1. Plant a dwarf colonial shrub, its stems either not branched or with a few short, stublike branches; petioles hairy: western poison ivy, *T. rydbergii*
1. Plant a tall shrub or climbing vine with long horizontal branches; petioles glabrous or sparsely hairy: poison ivy, *T. radicans* subsp. *negundo*

Key to Blueberries (*Vaccinium*)

1. Leaf margins bearing tiny gland-tipped teeth: lowbush blueberry, *V. angustifolium*
1. Leaf margins entire and conspicuously hairy: velvetleaf blueberry, *V. myrtilloides*

Key to Viburnums
(*Viburnum*)

1. Leaves lobed: 2
1. Leaves not lobed: 4

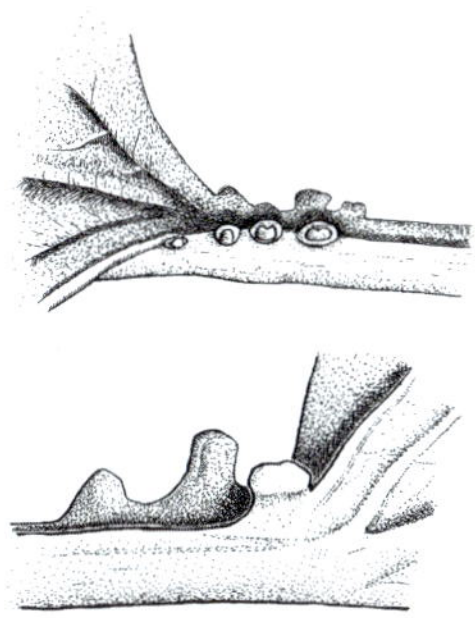

FIG. 24

2. Petioles bearing glands near their junction with the blades (fig. 24a, b); fruits red: 3
2. Petioles not glandular; fruits purple-black: mapleleaf viburnum, *V. acerifolium*
3. Glands on petiole oval or bean-shaped in outline with concave tips (fig. 24a): Eurasian highbush-cranberry, *V. opulus*
3. Glands on petiole club-shaped with flattish tips (fig. 24b): American highbush-cranberry, *V. trilobum*
4. Leaves very finely and inconspicuously toothed; buds naked: wayfaring tree, *V. lantana*
4. Leaves conspicuously toothed; buds each with 2 or more scales: 5
5. Veins of leaves or their main branches running into the tips of the teeth (see fig. 11b in step 23 of main key); buds with 2 pairs of scales: 6
5. Veins of leaves dividing and forming a network near the margin (see fig. 11a in step 23 of main key); buds with 1 pair of scales: 8
6. Style of flower pubescent; stipules usually absent; planted species, sometimes escaping: southern arrowwood, *V. dentatum*
6. Style of flowers glabrous; stipules usually present at the base of the petioles; native species: 7
7. Leaf blades 3 to 4 times longer than the petioles; bark of main stems exfoliating like that of a birch tree; southeast Iowa only: Kentucky viburnum, *V. molle*
7. Leaf blades 6 to 10 times longer than the petioles; bark not birchlike: downy arrowwood, *V. rafinesquianum*
8. Leaf tips blunt or pointed (acute); branchlets bearing short, stiff, nearly perpendicular twigs; southeast Iowa only: blackhaw, *V. prunifolium*
8. Leaf tips tapered to a slender point (acuminate); branchlets lacking short, stiff twigs; statewide distribution: nannyberry, *V. lentago*

Key to Grapes
(*Vitis* and *Ampelopsis*)

1. Lower surface of leaves green and glabrous, or if hairs are present these limited to the veins or vein axils: 2
1. Lower surface of leaves whitened and/or hairy between the veins: 4
2. Pith of twigs white; fruits pale blue or greenish blue: raccoon grape, *Ampelopsis cordata*
2. Pith of twigs brown; fruits dark purple, with or without a thin coating of white waxy material: 3
3. Leaves lobed; pith of twigs bearing cross walls (diaphragms) at each node, the walls less than 1 mm thick; fruits with a white waxy bloom: riverbank grape, *Vitis riparia*
3. Many if not all leaves unlobed; pith bearing cross walls at least 2 mm thick; fruits not bloomy: frost grape, *V. vulpina*
4. Leaves whitened beneath; hairs rusty in color: summer grape, *V. aestivalis*
4. Leaves green beneath; hairs gray: fox grape, *V. cinerea*

Key to Fruits of Shrubs and Vines

THE FOLLOWING KEY will identify the fruits of most wild shrubs and vines in Iowa. Conifers ("evergreens") and some very rare shrubs are excluded. The key is based primarily on characteristics of the fruits themselves but in some cases uses leaf, twig, and other features to make identification easier.

1. Fruit berrylike or plumlike, with a soft or juicy pulp surrounding the seeds: 2
1. Fruit a dry pod, nut, samara, or achene: 49
2. Vine: 3
2. Shrub: 11
3. Ripe fruit white or yellowish white: poison ivy, *Toxicodendron* (see page 32 for key to species). The fruit of raccoon grape, *Ampelopsis cordata,* is white in its early stages. *Ampelopsis* is a vigorous vine with grapelike leaves, native in southern Iowa.
3. Ripe fruit some other color: 4
4. Ripe fruit red, orange, or bright yellow: 5
4. Ripe fruit blue, purple, or black: 7
5. Fruit splitting open to reveal the fleshy red-orange seeds inside: bittersweet, *Celastrus* (see page 19 for key to species)
5. Fruit not splitting open: 6
6. Leaves and leaf scars opposite: wild honeysuckle, *Lonicera* (see page 22 for key to species)
6. Leaves and leaf scars alternate: bittersweet nightshade, *Solanum dulcamara*
7. Stems prickly: greenbrier, *Smilax tamnoides* var. *hispida*
7. Stems not prickly: 8
8. Climbing by means of twining stems; leaves entire: 9
8. Climbing by means of outgrowths of the stems (tendrils or aerial roots); leaves or leaflets toothed: 10

9. Leaves and leaf scars alternate: moonseed, *Menispermum canadense*
9. Leaves and leaf scars opposite: Japanese honeysuckle, *Lonicera japonica* (see page 90 for discussion)
10. Leaves simple: grape, *Vitis* and *Ampelopsis* (see page 34 for key to species)
10. Leaves palmately compound: woodbine and Virginia creeper, *Parthenocissus* (see page 22 for key to species)
11. Ripe fruit white or yellowish white: 12
11. Ripe fruit some other color: 14
12. Leaves compound with 3 leaflets; buds naked: poison ivy, *Toxicodendron* (see page 32 for key to species)
12. Leaves simple; buds with 2 or more scales: 13
13. Fruits in panicle- or corymblike cymes with red or reddish stems; medium to tall shrub: dogwood, *Cornus* (see page 20 for key to species)
13. Fruits in compact, nearly sessile bunches; dwarf shrub: wolfberry, *Symphoricarpos occidentalis*
14. Ripe fruit uniformly red or orange: 15
14. Ripe fruit partly to wholly green, blue, purple, or black: 32
15. Leaves and leaf scars alternate: 16
15. Leaves and leaf scars opposite: 27
16. Twigs armed with thorns, spines, prickles, or bristles: 17
16. Twigs without these structures: 22
17. With spines, prickles, or bristles at each node or between the nodes: 18
17. With short thorn-tipped twigs: 24
18. Fruit a raspberry or raspberrylike, composed of tiny round units packed tightly together: *Rubus* (see page 26 for key to species)
18. Fruit not a raspberry or raspberrylike: 19
19. Fruit containing tiny oil glands that impart a citrusy odor when fruit is crushed, eventually splitting open to reveal the single black seed inside; spines in pairs at each node: prickly-ash, *Zanthoxylum americanum*
19. Fruit not citrus-scented or splitting open; spines or prickles solitary or paired at nodes or attached to twig between the nodes: 20

FIG. 25

20. Tail-like remnants of the flower (sepals) persisting on the end of the fruit opposite its stem (fig. 25): rose, *Rosa* (see page 24 for key to species)

20. Sepals not persisting: 21
21. Leaves simple; twigs with one spine at each node, the spines often branched: Japanese barberry, *Berberis thunbergii*
21. Leaves compound; twigs with scattered or dense prickles between the nodes: rose, *Rosa* (see page 24 for key to species)

FIG. 26

22. Fruits red, hairy, arranged in compact upright panicles (fig. 26); leaves compound: sumac, *Rhus* (see page 24 for key to species)
22. Fruits not hairy, not arranged in compact panicles; leaves simple: 23
23. Fruit resembling a miniature apple, with the remnants of the flower (sepals) persisting on the end opposite the stem: serviceberry, *Amelanchier* (see page 19 for key to species)
23. Fruit not applelike: 24
24. Fruit more than 1 cm (usually 2 to 3 cm) long: plum, *Prunus* (see page 23 for key to species)
24. Fruit less than 1 cm long: 25
25. Leaves entire; twigs coated with minute brown and silver scale-like structures (best seen with magnifying glass): autumn olive, *Elaeagnus umbellata*
25. Leaves finely toothed; twigs lacking scales: 26
26. Fruit with a single large seed, each on a long stalk, grouped in umbel-like clusters: pin cherry, *Prunus pensylvanica*
26. Fruit with several seeds, each on a stalk shorter than the fruit, solitary or in small clusters: winterberry, *Ilex verticillata*
27. Fruit splitting open to reveal the orange or red seeds inside; twigs often lined or winged: *Euonymus* (see page 21 for key to species)
27. Fruit not splitting open: 28
28. Fruit in terminal panicle- or corymblike cymes; leaves or leaflets toothed: 29
28. Fruit in pairs or small clusters at the nodes; leaves entire: 30
29. Fruit 1-seeded in corymblike clusters, persisting through winter; leaves simple and lobed: highbush-cranberry, *Viburnum* (see page 33 for key to species)
29. Fruit with several seeds in paniclelike clusters, not persisting; leaves compound: red elderberry, *Sambucus pubens*

30. Lower leaf surfaces and twigs coated with tiny scalelike structures that give them a silvery sheen (individual scales best seen with magnifying glass); branchlets often thorny: buffaloberry, *Shepherdia argentea*
30. No tiny scales on leaves and twigs; shrubs not thorny: 31
31. Fruit in stalked pairs, 1 pair from each leaf axil: honeysuckle, *Lonicera*
31. Fruit bunched at the upper nodes: coralberry, *Symphoricarpos orbiculatus*
32. Leaves and leaf scars alternate: 33
32. Leaves and leaf scars opposite or subopposite: 45
33. Twigs spiny or prickly: 34
33. Twigs not spiny or prickly (may have short thorns at tips of twigs only): 35
34. Fruit a blackberry or blackberry-like, composed of tiny round units packed tightly together: *Rubus* (see page 26 for key to species)
34. Fruit not blackberrylike; leaves simple, lobed: gooseberry, *Ribes* (see page 24 for key to species)
35. All fruits with a single large stonelike seed: 36
35. Most or all of the fruits with 2 or more seeds: 39
36. Fruits in an elongated raceme: choke cherry, *Prunus virginiana*
36. Fruits in corymblike cymes or small bunches at the nodes: 37
37. Leaves toothed; shorter twigs sometimes thorn-tipped: plum and cherry, *Prunus* (see page 23 for key to species)
37. Leaves entire; twigs not thorny: 38
38. Fruit ripening to dark purple in late summer or fall, in corymblike clusters with bright red stems and stalks: pagoda or alternate-leaf dogwood, *Cornus alternifolia*
38. Fruit ripening to green or greenish in late spring or early summer, in bunches of 2 to 4 at the nodes: leatherwood, *Dirca palustris*
39. Fruit 3-lobed, eventually splitting into 3 parts and falling, leaving the tiny cup-shaped receptacle behind: New Jersey tea or redroot, *Ceanothus* (see page 19 for key to species)
39. Fruit round, not splitting: 40
40. Remnants of the flower visible at the top of the fruit (i.e., the end opposite the stem): 41
40. No flower remnants at the top of the fruit: buckthorn, *Rhamnus* (see page 23 for key to species)
41. Leaves lobed: currant, *Ribes* (see page 24 for key to species)
41. Leaves not lobed: 42
42. Dwarf shrub growing mostly less than waist-high; eastern Iowa: 43
42. Medium-size to tall shrub: 44
43. Undersurface of leaf dotted with tiny yellow glands (use magnifying glass): black huckleberry, *Gaylussacia baccata*

43. Undersurface of leaf not dotted: blueberry, *Vaccinium* (see page 32 for key to species)
44. Fruit in elongated racemes: serviceberry, *Amelanchier* (see page 19 for key to species)
44. Fruit in corymblike cymes: aronia berry or chokeberry, *Aronia*
45. Leaves compound; fruits very small (about 5 mm long), in large corymblike cymes often of 100 or more: common elderberry, *Sambucus canadensis*
45. Leaves simple; fruits larger and in smaller clusters than described above: 46
46. Leaves and leaf scars subopposite; twigs often thorn-tipped: common buckthorn, *Rhamnus cathartica*
46. Leaves and leaf scars opposite; twigs not thorn-tipped: 47
47. Remnants of the flower persisting at the base (stem end) of the fruit; fruits in panicles: privet, *Ligustrum*
47. Remnants of the flower persisting at the top of the fruit (i.e., the end opposite the stem); fruits in corymblike cymes: 48
48. Leaves toothed: viburnum, *Viburnum* (see page 33 for key to species)
48. Leaves entire: dogwood, *Cornus* (see page 20 for key to species)
49. Leaves or leaf scars alternate: 50
49. Leaves or leaf scars opposite: 61
50. Fruit a nut: 51
50. Fruit not a nut: 52
51. Nut an acorn (i.e., enclosed at its base in a scaly cup-shaped structure): dwarf chinkapin oak, *Quercus prinoides*
51. Nut partially to completely enclosed by a papery husk: hazelnut, *Corylus* see page 21 for key to species)
52. Fruit resembling a miniature pine cone; shrub of wet places in northern Iowa: 53
52. Fruit podlike or winged: 54
53. Bud with 2 scales that meet along the edge without overlapping: speckled alder, *Alnus rugosa*
53. Bud with several overlapping scales: bog birch, *Betula pumila*
54. Fruit a flat roundish samara, with the seed in the center: hoptree, *Ptelea trifoliata*
54. Fruit podlike (hollow with the seeds inside): 55
55. Pod ripening and opening by midsummer and immediately shedding its seeds, then falling; seeds with long cottony hairs: willow, *Salix* (see page 31 for key to species)
55. Pod ripening and opening in late summer or fall; seeds lacking long cottony hairs: 56
56. Pods in long racemes; leaves pinnately compound with 9 or more leaflets: leadplant and indigo bush, *Amorpha* (see page 19 for key to species)

56. Pods arranged otherwise; leaves simple or if compound then with 7 or fewer leaflets: 57
57. Pod thick-walled and woody, forcibly ejecting its shiny black seeds: witch-hazel, *Hamamelis virginiana*
57. Pod thin-walled and papery: 58

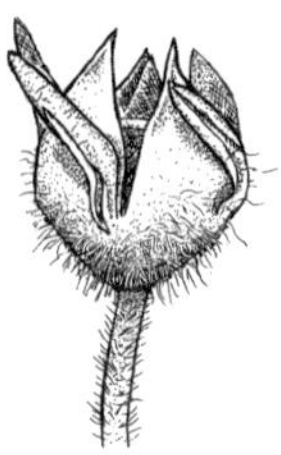

FIG. 27

58. Sepals of flower bending inward, covering the seeds (achenes) inside, forming a 5-sided structure resembling a pod (fig. 27): shrubby cinquefoil, *Potentilla fruticosa*
58. Small pods present in bunches of 2 to 6 at the ends of individual flower stalks: 59
59. Pods in 3s at the end of each flower stalk, falling in late summer or early fall, leaving the small cup-shaped receptacles behind: New Jersey tea or redroot, *Ceanothus* (see page 19 for key to species)
59. Pods in bunches of 2 to 6 at the end of each flower stalk, persisting into winter: 60

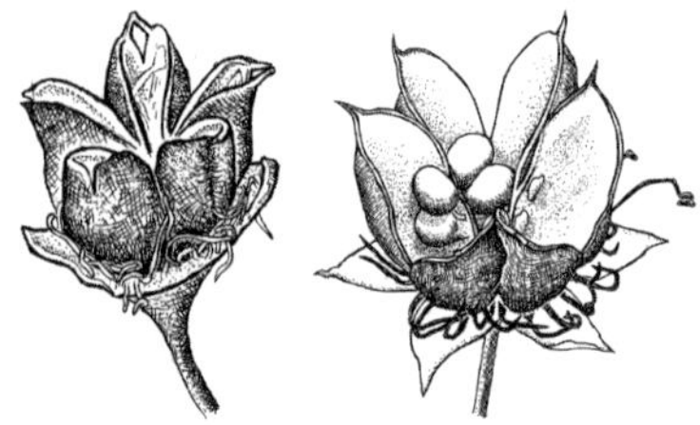

A B

FIG. 28

60. Pod 3 to 4 mm long, splitting open along its inside seam only (fig. 28a); fruiting clusters forming large panicles: meadowsweet, *Spiraea alba*
60. Pod 5 or more mm long, splitting open along both its inside and outside seams (fig. 28b); fruiting clusters in corymbs: ninebark, *Physocarpus opulifolius*
61. Vine: 62
61. Shrub: 63
62. Slender weak vine clambering over shrubs; fruits (achenes) no more than 0.5 cm long, sometimes with a long hairy tail: clematis, *Clematis* (see page 20 for key to species)
62. Strong vine climbing flat against trees and other surfaces using aerial roots; fruits thick and woody, cigar-shaped, about 15 cm long: trumpet creeper, *Campsis radicans*

63. Fruit a hard brown ball: buttonbush, *Cephalanthus occidentalis*
63. Fruit a pod or samara with thin papery walls: 64

FIG. 29

64. Fruit a key-shaped samara with the seed at one end (fig. 29): maple, *Acer* (see page 19 for key to species)
64. Fruit a hollow pod: 65

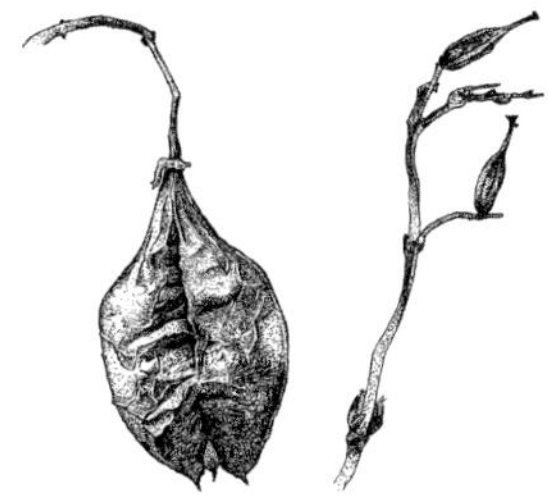

A B

FIG. 30

65. Fruit bladder-shaped, 3-lobed, 2 to 3 cm in diameter (fig. 30a); leaves compound with 3 leaflets: bladdernut, *Staphylea trifolia*
65. Fruit cylindrical, less than 0.5 cm in diameter (fig. 30b); leaves simple: 66
66. Leaves toothed; leaf scars each with 3 bundle scars: bush honeysuckle, *Diervilla lonicera*
66. Leaves entire; leaf scars each with 1 bundle scar: shrubby St. John's-wort, *Hypericum prolificum*

Native and Naturalized Shrubs and Vines

THE FOLLOWING PAGES identify shrubs and vines and discuss their natural history and uses. All species native in Iowa are included, along with frequently seen naturalized ones. Photographs and scans are provided for most species. Species are listed in alphabetical order by their botanical name.

Descriptions are brief, focusing on the information most useful for identification, and use a minimum of scientific terminology. Terms not used in everyday speech are defined in the glossary. Readers desiring a more complete description of a particular species are referred to the many excellent botanical references cited in the bibliography.

To identify an unknown shrub or vine, first flip through the pages to see if an image matches your specimen. If you do not find it there, try the key. Once you have made a tentative identification, be sure to confirm it by comparing your specimen to the written description of that species.

Lengths are given in metric units: centimeters (cm) and millimeters (mm). Whenever possible, we determined these by measuring specimens collected wild in Iowa. Leaf measurements indicate the size of healthy, mature foliage and should not be regarded as the absolute minimum or maximum sizes for a species' leaves. Vigorous sucker shoots can have leaves that are larger than normal, while plants in poor condition or in difficult habitats can have unusually small leaves.

Distribution information is based on published reports, a review of specimens in the Ada Hayden Herbarium at Iowa State University and the Iowa Lakeside Laboratory herbarium, and field work by the authors. When a species is known from only a few counties, each county is listed; otherwise its range is described generally. While we believe this information to be reasonably complete, species may occur in places not known to us and thus not reported in this book.

Acer, Maple

Our familiar maples are all large trees, but many of the world's 124 species are very modest in size. Two shrubby species can be found as wild plants in Iowa.

Acer ginnala Maxim., Amur Maple

DISTINGUISHING CHARACTERISTICS Large shrub or small tree. Leaves simple, opposite; blades 3-lobed with the middle (end) lobe much elongated, 3 to 8 cm long, the margins coarsely toothed. Flowers greenish white, regular, unisexual, 5-parted, about 0.5 cm long, in panicles at the ends of the branches, blooming in late spring or early summer. Fruit a key-shaped samara with the seed at the narrower end, each attached to another samara forming a V-shaped pair; samaras about 2.5 cm long, often red at first, then turning brown, persisting through winter.

DISTRIBUTION IN IOWA Escaped from cultivation locally.

Amur maple is a tough, hardy species from northeastern Asia, planted in Iowa for landscaping and conservation. As with many of our native maples, its fall color can be quite striking, bright red when it's at its best. Its fruits, which are often produced prolifically, are also red at first, then turn brown and persist through the winter. Unfortunately, these sometimes disperse to wild areas, creating new trees there. Because of this invasive potential, Amur maple should be closely monitored in Iowa (Farrar 2001; Smith 2008).

Acer spicatum Lam., Mountain Maple

DISTINGUISHING CHARACTERISTICS Large shrub or small multiple-stemmed tree. Leaves simple, opposite; blades 3-lobed with the middle (end) lobe about half the length of the leaf, 6 to 12 cm long, the margins coarsely toothed. Flowers very small, yellow-green, regular, unisexual, 5-parted, in narrow upright panicles at the tips of the branches. Fruit a key-shaped samara with the seed at the narrower end, each attached to another samara forming a V-shaped pair; samaras about 2 cm long, ripening in autumn.

DISTRIBUTION IN IOWA Native in Allamakee, Clayton, Dubuque, and Winneshiek counties.

Mountain maple is a common sight in the North Woods of our Great Lakes states, but in Iowa it is very rare. Like many other northern plants, it was probably more common here immediately following glaciation, when Iowa's climate was colder than it is today. When the climate later warmed, mountain maple could survive only in very cool habitats in the northeastern corner of the state.

Mountain maple has a twin in northeastern Asia, *A. ukurunduense*. If you were to visit the forests where it grows, you would be struck by how closely the trees and shrubs there resemble those of our own North Woods. The woods in both areas are remnants of a great forest that once encircled the Northern Hemisphere and that was later fragmented by geologic and climate change. Once separated, the plants in each area adapted to local conditions and became different species, though retaining similar foliage, flowers, and fruit.

Mountain maple has striking orange fall color and would be a nice landscape plant if it were easier to grow. Unfortunately, it does not seem to like our hot summers and often heavy soils. Plants grown from native Iowa seed might do better than those from farther north, but this is not ensured considering the special habitats in which they grow.

Alnus, Alder

The alders are a genus of about thirty trees and shrubs, characteristic of northern and mountainous regions. They are easily recognized at all times of the year by their flowering, fruiting, or overwintering catkins. One species grows wild in Iowa.

Alnus rugosa (Du Roi) Sprengel, Speckled Alder

SYNONYM *Alnus incana* (L.) Moench subsp. *rugosa* (Du Roi) Clausen

DISTINGUISHING CHARACTERISTICS Tall shrub; next year's catkins present on twigs during autumn and winter. Leaves simple, alternate; blades elliptic, 5 to 11 cm long, the margins with both large and small teeth, the veins running straight into the tips of the larger teeth. Flowers in catkins at the tips of the branches before the leaves in spring, the staminate and the pistillate on the same plant; staminate long and drooping; pistillate short, red, and conelike. Fruit conelike, 1 to 2 cm long, with tiny winged nutlets, persisting in winter.

DISTRIBUTION IN IOWA Native in Allamakee, Black Hawk, Buchanan, Chickasaw, Clayton, Fayette, Howard, Mitchell, and Winneshiek counties.

This tall shrubby alder is common in the Great Lakes region of the northeastern U.S. and adjacent Canada. In Iowa it is rather rare, confined to a few northeastern counties. As in other parts of its range, it is most often found near streams and in other low moist places, sometimes forming large thickets. It is so similar to the European gray alder, *Alnus incana*, that some botanists consider it to be a variety of that species.

Though too large for landscaping, speckled alder can be used for conservation purposes in wet areas. Goldfinches eat its seeds, while beaver and deer feed on its woody parts and foliage. An interesting predatory caterpillar, the larvae of the harvester butterfly, eats the woolly aphids often found on this species.

Amelanchier, Serviceberry

Serviceberries are among the first woody plants to bloom every year, standing out in the otherwise bare landscape of early spring. Their fruits ripen early, too, leading to another common name, Juneberry. Red or purple in color and about the size of a pea, they are much appreciated by songbirds and chipmunks. Later, in autumn, the foliage is often colorful as well.

As their virtues have become better known, serviceberries have become increasingly popular as ornamentals, especially those that grow to be small trees. Our native shrubby species are useful, too, for both naturalistic landscaping and wildlife habitat. The dwarf types spread outward via suckers but not quickly or aggressively so.

Though distinctive as a genus, serviceberries are not always easy to identify. The shrubby types are particularly vexing, with botanists disagreeing on how to organize them into species. Pending further study, we are treating Iowa's shrubby serviceberries as two species that differ mostly in growth form.

Amelanchier humilis Wieg., Low Serviceberry

DISTINGUISHING CHARACTERISTICS Medium-size to tall shrub, forming colonies by suckering. Leaves simple, alternate; blades variously shaped but typically broadly oval to nearly round, 3 to 7 cm long, the margins bearing

Leaves of *A. humilis*.

This image is representative of all shrubby serviceberries.

large teeth on at least the upper half, the main veins or their forks running into the tips of the teeth. Flowers white, regular, perfect, 5-parted, the petals 0.5 to 1 cm long, in racemes at the ends of leafy shoots, blooming before the leaves are full grown in early spring. Fruit a berrylike pome about 1 cm in diameter, changing from green to red to nearly black as it ripens in early to midsummer, usually quickly removed by animals.

DISTRIBUTION IN IOWA Native in the northern part of the state.

Low serviceberry is a medium-size to large shrub, spreading via suckers to form colonies. Subtle variations in leaves and other features have led some botanists to separate it into several species, including *A. alnifolia* Nutt., *A. spicata* (Lam.) K. Koch, and *A. stolonifera* Wieg. It grows in a variety of sunny to partly sunny places including bluffs, ridges, wood edges, and prairies.

Amelanchier sanguinea (Pursh) DC., Roundleaf Serviceberry (not illustrated)

DISTINGUISHING CHARACTERISTICS Tall multiple-stemmed shrub with the stems arising from 1 crown (i.e., not colonial). Otherwise similar to *A. humilis*.

DISTRIBUTION IN IOWA Native in north and east central Iowa.

Roundleaf serviceberry is a tall shrub of varied habitats including woods, prairies, edges, and algific slopes. In contrast to low serviceberry, its stems are clumped from a single crown. Despite its common name, its leaves are not especially round; in fact, those of low serviceberry are often much rounder.

Amorpha

Amorpha is a small genus found only in North America, with three species in Iowa. It resembles other legumes in leaf and fruit, but its tiny purplish flowers are unique, containing a single petal that wraps around the stamens like a sleeve. The flowers appear in summer at a time when few other shrubs are blooming, in dense showy clusters that attract bees and other pollinators.

Amorpha canescens Pursh, Leadplant

DISTINGUISHING CHARACTERISTICS Small to medium-size shrub with gray-green to light gray foliage. Leaves pinnately compound, alternate; leaflets 16 to about 30, oblong to ovate-lanceolate, 1 to 1.5 cm long, entire, finely gray-hairy. Flowers and fruits similar to *A. fruticosa* except flowers blooming in midsummer, the racemes in bunches of 5 or more at the branch tips; fruit about 4 mm long.

DISTRIBUTION IN IOWA Native statewide.

Leadplant is a characteristic species of Iowa prairies, especially on dry hills and sandy sites. Though usually dwarf in size, it can grow up to shoulder-high. Its grayish foliage stands out among the prairie grasses among which it grows, helping you recognize it even when it is not in bloom.

Leadplant is an excellent choice for sunny naturalistic gardens, tolerating drought and requiring little maintenance. Good companion plants are low-growing prairie grasses such as side-oats grama and prairie dropseed and the shorter prairie wildflowers such as butterfly milkweed. Its growth form is quite irregular, so to keep it compact and attractive, it is best to prune it every year in early spring.

Amorpha fruticosa L., Indigo Bush

DISTINGUISHING CHARACTERISTICS Large shrub. Leaves pinnately compound, alternate; leaflets 9 to 21, oblong to elliptic, 1.5 to 5 cm long, entire. Flowers perfect, with a single purple petal about 0.5 cm long wrapped around the orange or yellow stamens, in dense upright racemes at the tips of the branches, the racemes solitary or in clusters of 2 to 4, blooming in early summer. Fruit a 1-seeded pod (legume) 5 to 9 mm long, ripening in late summer or autumn and persisting into winter.

DISTRIBUTION IN IOWA Native statewide.

Indigo bush is a tall shrub bordering lakes, streams, and wetlands throughout much of Iowa. When in bloom it looks very similar to its better-known relative the leadplant, except for its much larger size and greener foliage.

If you check indigo bush in winter, you might notice a spindle-shaped swelling, or gall, at the ends of some main stems. This is home for the caterpillar of the cat willow moth, which will emerge as an adult insect in spring. The caterpillar is parasitized by at least four species of small wasps, and its vacated galls provide homes for still other insects, including a bee that nests in the galls and is itself parasitized by at least two other insects (Brandhorst 1962). This one shrub, then, directly or indirectly supports eight species of animals, not including the pollinators that visit its flowers and the caterpillars that feed on its foliage.

Though not much planted, indigo bush could be used for naturalistic landscaping and conservation plantings in wet areas. If untended it becomes rather leggy, so plants used for landscaping need regular renewal pruning or rejuvenation to maintain their best appearance.

Amorpha nana Nutt., Dwarf Indigo Bush (not illustrated)

DISTINGUISHING CHARACTERISTICS Small shrub. Leaves pinnately compound, alternate; leaflets 9 to 21, oblong, mostly 7 to 12 mm long, entire, dotted with small glands beneath. Flowers and fruits similar to *A. fruticosa* except racemes all solitary at branch tips, fruits about 5 mm long.

DISTRIBUTION IN IOWA Native in north Iowa.

This miniature version of the indigo bush grows in low moist prairies. It is uncommon and considered a threatened species in Iowa. Though not much planted, it could be tried in naturalistic gardens.

Ampelopsis

These Asian and North American vines are related to grapes and can have very similar leaves. Some are grown as ornamentals for their attractive turquoise, light blue, or even whitish berries, which have a porcelainlike appearance. One species is native in Iowa.

Ampelopsis cordata Michx., Raccoon Grape

DISTINGUISHING CHARACTERISTICS Vine climbing with tendrils; pith white. Leaves simple, alternate; blades heart-shaped, 6 to 12 cm long, coarsely toothed, nearly glabrous. Flowers greenish, regular, 5-parted, about 4 mm long, functionally unisexual with rudimentary stamens in the pistillate flowers and vice versa, in small panicles that have repeatedly forking branches, the panicles opposite the leaves. Fruit a bluish porcelainlike berry 7 to 10 mm long.

DISTRIBUTION IN IOWA Reported from Fremont, Lee, Polk, and Pottawattamie counties. Native.

This rare vine resembles wild grape, except for its much paler blue or greenish blue fruits. It grows on bluffs and in low woods in a few southern Iowa counties.

Arctostaphylos

This mostly North American genus is best known in California, where several species called manzanitas grow to be tall shrubs or small trees and are an important part of the chaparral vegetation. Iowa's single species is much different in growth form.

Arctostaphylos uva-ursi (L.) Sprengel, Bearberry (not illustrated)

DISTINGUISHING CHARACTERISTICS Dwarf shrub with stems sprawling on the ground. Leaves simple, alternate, evergreen; blades oval to obovate, 1 to 1.5 cm long, entire. Flowers white, regular, perfect, with 5 united petals, about 0.5 cm long, resembling a tiny bottle or urn, in short racemes at the ends of the branches, blooming in spring. Fruit a red berry about 1 cm in diameter with mealy flesh, ripening in late summer or early autumn.

DISTRIBUTION IN IOWA Native in Fayette and Winneshiek counties.

Bearberry is a trailing evergreen shrub that grows in northern latitudes around the globe. It barely ranges into northeast Iowa; because of its rarity, it is listed as an endangered species here.

Our wild bearberries are limited to rocky wooded bluffs, but the species is quite adaptable to cultivation, and with its attractive leaves and bright red berries it can be used as a groundcover. A sunny site and well-drained soil are best.

Aronia

A generation ago, few people had heard of this small genus of North American shrubs. Today it is receiving much attention because its berrylike fruits are reputed to be very healthful. The fruit, technically a pome like an apple or a pear, is now being grown commercially in Iowa. One species is native here.

Aronia melanocarpa (Michx.) Ell., Aronia Berry or Black Chokeberry

SYNONYM *Photinia melanocarpa* (Michx.) Robertson & Phipps

DISTINGUISHING CHARACTERISTICS Medium-size to large colonial shrub. Leaves simple, alternate; blades oval, 2.5 to 3.5 cm long, with small incurved teeth along their margins, bearing glands along the midvein on their upper surface. Flowers white, regular, perfect, 5-parted, the petals about 0.5 cm long, in corymblike cymes at the ends of the branches and on short side shoots, blooming in spring. Fruit a blackish berrylike pome 6 to 8 mm in diameter, maturing in autumn.

DISTRIBUTION IN IOWA Native on sandstone ledges in Winneshiek County, planted elsewhere.

It is ironic that the black chokeberry, now so widely grown in its cultivar forms, is as a native plant endangered in Iowa. Like so many other northern species, it just reaches the northeast corner of our state.

In addition to having useful fruits, chokeberry has attractive small flowers and often striking autumn color. Wild plants can vary considerably in height, with the dwarf types being the most desirable for landscaping. A sunny site is best. Plants are fairly adaptable as to soil.

Berberis, Barberry

The barberries are a large genus of prickly shrubs, unusual among woody plants in that they are indigenous on five continents (North and South America, Europe, Asia, and Africa). Some are banned in commerce because they serve as the alternate host of wheat rust disease. None is native in Iowa, but two Eurasian species have escaped from cultivation, especially the following.

Berberis thunbergii DC., Japanese Barberry

DISTINGUISHING CHARACTERISTICS Small to medium-size shrub with spiny twigs. Leaves simple, alternate or in bunches at the ends of short spur shoots; blades obovate, 1 to 3 cm long, tapered to a very narrow base, with blunt or rounded tips, the margins entire. Flowers yellow, regular, perfect, 6-parted, about 8 mm across, solitary or in small fascicles, blooming in spring. Fruit a bright red ellipsoid berry about 1 cm long, ripening in autumn and persisting on the branches in winter.

DISTRIBUTION IN IOWA A common escape from cultivation.

Japanese barberry was introduced for landscaping because it is easy to grow and modest in size, has colorful berries and autumn leaves, and in some cultivars has variegated or purple foliage. Unfortunately, it is now invading natural areas in Iowa, spread by birds that feed on its fruits. Farrar (2001) lists it as one of Iowa's "dirty dozen" invasive woody species.

Betula, Birch

Birches are familiar sights in Iowa, having been planted almost everywhere. Three trees and the following shrubby species are native here.

Betula pumila L., Bog Birch

DISTINGUISHING CHARACTERISTICS Medium-size to large shrub. Leaves simple, alternate; blades broadly oval to nearly round, 2 to 4 cm long, toothed, the lower surface dotted with numerous tiny glands (seen with magnifying glass). Flowers in small upright catkins on short spur shoots as the leaves begin to develop in spring, the staminate and the pistillate on the same plant. Fruit cylindric, conelike, 1 to 2 cm long, with tiny winged nutlets.

DISTRIBUTION IN IOWA Native in the northeast in Allamakee, Black Hawk, Bremer, Chickasaw, Clayton, Howard, and Mitchell counties.

On casual inspection you might not guess this is a birch, with its small roundish leaves and shrubby habit. It ranges far to the north and east of Iowa, being common as close to us as Minnesota (Smith 2008). Here it is uncommon, so to see it you must visit the fens and moist prairies where it grows. It is listed as a threatened species in Iowa.

Though not highly ornamental, bog birch is potentially useful for conservation plantings and naturalistic landscaping. For the landowner who would like to experiment, it would be worth trying in low, wet, sunny places. Someone could make a real contribution by identifying and propagating plants that are compact, have healthy foliage, and color well in autumn. Then more Iowans might plant and enjoy this interesting native species.

Campsis

Repeating a common pattern, this is a genus of only two species, one in eastern North America and one in eastern Asia. (See the explanation under *Acer spicatum*.) It belongs to a mostly tropical family, the Bignoniaceae, known for its large showy flowers. Iowans who winter in warmer climates may be familiar with some of its relatives, including the jacaranda, trumpet trees, and African tulip tree.

Campsis radicans (L.) Seem. ex Bureau, Trumpet Creeper

DISTINGUISHING CHARACTERISTICS Large vine climbing with aerial rootlets. Leaves pinnately compound, opposite; leaflets 9 to 15, oval to elliptic or ovate, tapered to slender tips, 4 to 9 cm long, with a few large teeth along each margin. Flowers perfect, with 5 orange petals forming a trumpet-shaped corolla 6 to 9 cm long, in tight clusters at the tips of leafy shoots, blooming in midsummer. Fruit a beanlike capsule 10 to 15 cm long, ridged along 2 sides and tapered at both ends, turning brown when ripe in autumn, containing numerous large winged seeds.

DISTRIBUTION IN IOWA Escaped from cultivation locally.

This vigorous, high-climbing vine is native to the southeastern U.S. as far north as Pennsylvania and Missouri. In Iowa it is planted for its large orange, trumpet-shaped flowers. Like poison ivy, it attaches to surfaces using roots that grow out of the stem, rather than by twining or with tendrils. Its distinctive seed pods resemble cigars.

Trumpet creeper sometimes escapes to wild places via its windblown seeds. Once established it can spread aggressively via suckers, so it should be removed when found in natural areas.

Ceanothus

Like *Arctostaphylos*, this genus of shrubs and small trees is most diverse in the Pacific Coast region, where it is an important constituent of the chaparral. Iowa's two species are dwarf shrubs. When in bloom, all are much appreciated by butterflies and other native insects.

Ceanothus americanus L., New Jersey Tea

DISTINGUISHING CHARACTERISTICS

Small shrub. Leaves simple, alternate; blades ovate to elliptic, mostly 4 to 7 cm long, finely and rather obscurely toothed, with 3 main veins originating from a common point at the base of the blade. Flowers very small, white, regular, perfect, 5-parted, the petals about 2 mm long, in compact panicles on long leafless stalks, the stalks emerging from leaf axils well below the tips of the branches, usually blooming in late June or July. Fruit small, drupelike, 3-lobed, nearly black, when dispersed leaving behind a saucer-shaped receptacle about 3 mm in diameter.

DISTRIBUTION IN IOWA Native throughout most of the state.

This and the following species resemble one another closely, except in the arrangement of their flowers and fruits and sometimes in the shape of their leaves. New Jersey tea is more widely distributed in Iowa, inhabiting prairies and other open habitats such as old fields, fencerows, wood edges, and grassy clearings. Its name comes from the use of its leaves as a tea substitute during the American Revolution.

Though not much planted, New Jersey tea is an attractive shrub worth trying in sunny gardens, either in combination with low-growing prairie plants or grouped with other dwarf shrubs such as spireas and roses. In author van der Linden's observation, the species is somewhat finicky in cultivation, in some cases surviving for years with little attention and in other cases thriving for a while before dying back unexpectedly. The plants bloom on new wood, so they can be treated as perennials if desired and pruned back severely in early spring (Morton Arboretum staff 1990).

Ceanothus herbaceus Raf., Redroot or Narrowleaf New Jersey Tea

DISTINGUISHING CHARACTERISTICS Similar to *C. americanus* except leaves narrowly elliptic and often smaller; inflorescences umbel-like, on short stalks from the ends of the branches, usually blooming earlier.

DISTRIBUTION IN IOWA Native in west, central, south central, and extreme northeast Iowa.

Redroot is a characteristic plant of dry upland prairies, for example, on the ridges and slopes of Iowa's Loess Hills and on sandstone bluffs in northeast Iowa. As suggested by its second common name, its leaves are usually narrower than those of New Jersey tea. It is a handsome plant that could be tried in gardens. A well-drained soil is best.

Celastrus, Bittersweet

The bittersweets are a genus of some thirty species, mostly climbing vines, much beloved for their attractive fall fruits. Two species grow wild in Iowa, one of which is an exotic invasive plant.

Celastrus orbiculatus Thunb., Oriental Bittersweet

DISTINGUISHING CHARACTERISTICS Similar to *C. scandens* except leaf blades broadly oval to round, flowers and fruits solitary or in clusters of 2 or 3 attached to the sides of this year's shoots.

DISTRIBUTION IN IOWA Naturalized locally.

Oriental bittersweet is an aggressive vine that has invaded natural areas in some parts of Iowa, killing or damaging trees and crowding out native vegetation. Infestations begin when its fruits are eaten and dispersed by birds or when people discard decorative items containing the fruits. In 2013 the legislature banned the sale and distribution of the plants and its seeds in Iowa. To help prevent further spread of the species, plants used for ornamental purposes should be destroyed and replaced with the American bittersweet, which is not invasive.

Celastrus scandens L., American Bittersweet

DISTINGUISHING CHARACTERISTICS Vine climbing by means of twining stems. Leaves simple, alternate; blades oval, elliptic, or obovate, 3 to 8 cm long, with small incurved teeth along the margin. Flowers greenish white, regular, 5-parted, about 0.5 cm across, unisexual with the staminate and the pistillate on separate plants, in panicles at the ends of leafy shoots, blooming in late spring or early summer. Fruit a ball-shaped orange or yellow capsule about 1 cm in diameter, splitting open along 3 seams to reveal the red fleshy seeds (arils) inside, ripening in autumn and often persisting after the leaves have fallen.

DISTRIBUTION IN IOWA Native throughout the state.

Iowa's autumn landscape is enhanced wherever this plant grows, its colorful fruits contrasting vividly with the fading grasses and turning foliage nearby. Though often called berries, they are technically small capsules or pods. The seeds inside are each covered with a fleshy coat, or aril, even more brightly colored than the capsules themselves. When the capsules eventually dry and split open, the arils attract birds that disperse the seeds to new places.

Though sometimes overcollected by its admirers, bittersweet is still fairly common in Iowa. It thrives wherever there are plentiful sunlight and a support upon which it can grow, including fences, trees at the edge of the woods, and prairie shrubs. Its tiny flowers are usually unisexual, with male and female on different plants. Both sexes are needed to produce the fruits, a good thing to remember when cultivating this species.

Cephalanthus

This is a small genus in the Rubiaceae, a large and mostly tropical family with only a few species native in Iowa. The following shrub is our only woody member of the family.

Cephalanthus occidentalis L., Buttonbush

DISTINGUISHING CHARACTERISTICS
Large shrub. Leaves simple, opposite or in whorls of 3; blades elliptic to oblong-elliptic or sometimes oval or ovate, 7 to 16 cm long, entire. Flowers white, regular, perfect, the 4 petals united along much of their length into a narrow tube, tightly packed in ball-shaped heads about 4 cm in diameter, the heads on long stalks from the tips of the branches and upper leaf axils, blooming in midsummer. Fruit ball-shaped, 1.5 to 2 cm in diameter, composed of numerous cone-shaped nutlets 6 to 8 mm long, turning from green or red to brown when ripe in autumn, persisting in winter.

DISTRIBUTION IN IOWA Native in eastern, southern, and central Iowa and in a few localities in the north.

Buttonbush is one of the most widely distributed shrubs in the United States, occurring in both the east and the west including the desert southwest. This large and distinctive shrub is also a very handsome one, with glossy foliage and showy white flowers. It almost always grows in or near water. Though

multiple-stemmed, it often produces individual stems that grow 15 to 20 feet tall, resembling small trees. The flowers occur in globe-shaped clusters about the size of a Ping-Pong ball and bloom in midsummer, an unusual time for shrubs. The seeds that follow are an important food for herbivorous waterfowl.

Buttonbush is one of the many fine native plants that has been neglected in landscaping. While it is too big for urban gardens, it is a good choice for rural places where plenty of space is available, and if necessary it can be maintained at less than full size by renewal pruning. A moist site is best. Buttonbush is more compact and attractive in full sun but does tolerate part-day shade.

Clematis

This large and broadly distributed genus is well known for its species that are vines, less so for those that grow as subshrubs or perennials (e.g., the blue-flowered clematis, *C. heracleifolia* DC., from China, a useful garden plant). Their showy flowers are diverse in size, color, arrangement, and time of bloom, and many cultivars have been developed for garden use.

Three species of *Clematis* are native in Iowa. Their stems are rather slender and weak compared to other vines, and they are easily overlooked except when in flower or fruit.

Clematis occidentalis (Hornem.) DC., Purple Clematis (not illustrated)

SYNONYM *C. verticillaris* DC.

DISTINGUISHING CHARACTERISTICS Vine climbing with twining petioles. Leaves compound, opposite; leaflets 3, ovate, 2.5 to 5.5 cm long, with a few shallow lobes or large teeth. Flowers blue or purple, regular, perfect, 4-parted, 3 to 5 cm long, nodding, solitary at the end of long stalks from the leaf axils, blooming in spring. Fruit similar to *C. virginiana*.

DISTRIBUTION IN IOWA Native in Allamakee, Clayton, Dubuque, and Winneshiek counties.

This species barely ranges into the northeastern corner of Iowa, where it inhabits cool steep, rocky slopes, including the algific slopes that harbor so many northern plants.

Clematis pitcheri T. & G., Leather Flower (not illustrated)

DISTINGUISHING CHARACTERISTICS Vine climbing with twining leaf tips. Leaves pinnately compound, opposite, often tipped by a tendril; leaflets 3 to 9, with 1 or 2 lobes or not lobed, when not lobed then oval, ovate, or elliptic in shape, 4 to 9 cm long, entire, the veins forming a prominent network underneath. Flowers purple, urn-shaped, perfect, 2 to 2.5 cm long, with 4 thick leathery sepals resembling petals, solitary on long stalks, blooming in early to midsummer. Fruit an achene with a short tail, not plumy as in other native species.

DISTRIBUTION IN IOWA Native in south and central Iowa.

The unusual purplish urn-shaped flowers of this species have a thick leather-like texture. The vines can be found in a variety of sunny to partly sunny habitats including thickets, clearings, fencerows, roadsides, and open sandy places.

Clematis virginiana L., Virgin's Bower

DISTINGUISHING CHARACTERISTICS Vine climbing with twining petioles. Leaves compound, opposite; leaflets 3, ovate or shallowly lobed, 4 to 8 cm long, coarsely toothed. Flowers white, regular, 4-parted, the sepals petal-like and 4 to 10 mm long, unisexual with the staminate and the pistillate on sepa-

rate plants, in showy panicles from the axils of the leaves, blooming in mid to late summer. Fruit an achene with a long, curly, plumelike tail, the seed portion about 4 mm long, aggregated in moplike heads, ripening in autumn.

DISTRIBUTION IN IOWA Native throughout the state.

Virgin's bower is the most vigorous and widely distributed of our native clematis. Its small white flowers bloom profusely in mid to late summer, with the male and female blossoms on separate plants. The fruits that follow are interesting, too, bearing long feathery tails and clustered in small heads resembling mops.

This species is easy to grow and suitable for naturalistic landscaping in sunny to partly sunny locations. It can be planted on a trellis or allowed to clamber over shrubs, as it often does in nature.

Cornus, Dogwood

Dogwoods are among the most common shrubs in Iowa, growing almost everywhere from wet to dry soils and open prairies to woodlands. They also have many uses from landscaping to windbreaks to conservation of water and soil. Many wild animals use them for food. Grouse, turkeys, bluebirds, cardinals, catbirds, robins, waxwings, finches, rabbits, chipmunks, and squirrels eat their fruits, while rabbits and deer browse their winter twigs. It would be hard to overemphasize their importance here.

Dogwoods are common outside Iowa, too, growing in temperate areas around the Northern Hemisphere. Some are easily recognized by their brightly colored stems or distinctive growth forms, while others are nondescript and not so easy to identify. There are about forty species altogether, of which seven are native here.

Cornus alternifolia L. f., Pagoda Dogwood or Alternate-leaf Dogwood

DISTINGUISHING CHARACTERISTICS Shrub or sometimes a small tree. Leaves simple, alternate; blades oval to ovate (often broadly so), tapered to a slender tip, 5 to 12 cm long, entire, the veins curving and following the margin and numbering 5 or 6 on each side. Flowers similar to *C. drummondii* except blooming in late spring. Fruit a dark purple drupe, ripening in late summer to early autumn.

DISTRIBUTION IN IOWA Native in the northeastern half of the state.

This is one of our most distinctive and attractive shrubs and the only dogwood with alternate leaves. Its buds form a cluster at the tip of each twig, and as they grow they produce branches in layers like the stories of a pagoda. Often one stem becomes dominant over the others and, growing much taller, turns the shrub into a small tree.

Pagoda dogwood usually grows on moist wooded slopes in Iowa, but you can find it in a variety of forested sites and occasionally sunny ones. It is one of our best native shrubs for landscaping, with handsome foliage, attractive flowers in late spring, dark purple fruits on bright red stalks, and yellow to purple autumn leaves. Give it a moist, partly shaded site with plenty of room to grow, and it will make a beautiful specimen in your garden.

Cornus canadensis L., Bunchberry

DISTINGUISHING CHARACTERISTICS Dwarf colonial shrub with only the underground stems woody, resembling a perennial herb. Leaves similar to those of other dogwoods, opposite, the pairs so close together that the leaves appear whorled near the ends of the stems. Flowers individually very small, greenish, crowded in a small head at the tip of the stem, each head subtended by 4 white petal-like bracts 1 to 2 cm long, the whole resembling an individual flower. Fruit a red drupe in bunches at the stem tips.

DISTRIBUTION IN IOWA Native in Allamakee, Clayton, Delaware, and Winneshiek counties.

This attractive little dogwood is essentially herbaceous, with only its underground stems woody. Though common in the North Woods, in Iowa it is restricted to algific slopes in a few of our northeastern counties. It is listed as a threatened species here.

Cornus drummondii C. A. Meyer, Roughleaf Dogwood

DISTINGUISHING CHARACTERISTICS Large colonial shrub, sometimes treelike. Leaves simple, opposite; blades ovate to elliptic, 4 to 12 cm long, entire, the veins curving and following the margin and numbering 3 to 5 on each side, the hairs on the lower surface dense, erect, and curly, often visible to the naked eye in good light when the leaf is folded in half and viewed along the fold. Flowers white, regular, perfect, 4-parted, about 1 cm across, in corymb-like cymes at the ends of leafy shoots, blooming in early summer. Fruit a white drupe, ripening in late summer to early autumn.

DISTRIBUTION IN IOWA Native in south, west, and central Iowa and in a few northern counties.

This is a southeastern dogwood that reaches the north edge of its range in Iowa. It is the common dogwood of the Loess Hills, abundant along the prairie-forest border and from there invading the prairie. Elsewhere in Iowa, it grows in a variety of open sites such as clearings and wood edges.

Another upland dogwood, *C. racemosa*, resembles this one and occupies the same kinds of habitats. Shrubs having characteristics intermediate between the two species are not hard to find and are presumably hybrids between them.

Cornus obliqua Raf., Silky Dogwood

SYNONYM *C. amomum* P. Miller subsp. *obliqua* (Raf.) J. S. Wilson

DISTINGUISHING CHARACTERISTICS Large shrub; twigs hairy; pith of 2-year-old and older twigs brown. Leaves simple, opposite; blades elliptic, oval or ovate (often narrowly so), tapered to a slender tip, 4 to 10 cm long, entire, the veins curving and following the margin and numbering 4 or 5 on each side, the lower surface more or less hairy, the hairs appressed and/or erect. Flowers similar to *C. drummondii*. Fruit a blue drupe about 7 mm in diameter, ripening in late summer to early autumn.

DISTRIBUTION IN IOWA Native across most of the state.

This species has foliage similar to *C. drummondii* and *C. racemosa* but differs in its blue fruits and tendency to grow in low wet places. It is often considered a variety of *C. amomum*, an eastern species that also has blue fruits but has much broader leaves.

Silky dogwood is a handsome shrub that is well suited to conservation plantings and naturalistic landscaping. It eventually grows quite large, a point to consider before planting.

Cornus racemosa Lam., Gray Dogwood

SYNONYM *Cornus foemina* P. Miller subsp. *racemosa* (Lam.) J. S. Wilson

DISTINGUISHING CHARACTERISTICS Medium-size to moderately large colonial shrub. Leaves simple, opposite; blades ovate to elliptic, 4 to 11 cm long, entire, the veins curving and following the margin and numbering 3 or 4 (sometimes 5) on each side, hairs on the lower surface short, straight, and appressed, often sparse, not easily visible to the naked eye. Flowers similar to *C. drummondii* except inflorescence paniclelike, often blooming a little earlier. Fruit a white drupe about 7 mm in diameter on a bright red stalk, ripening in late summer or early autumn. Plants intermediate between *C. racemosa* and *C. drummondii* are often seen in the field and presumably represent hybrids between them.

DISTRIBUTION IN IOWA Native across most of the state.

This is the common dogwood of northern Iowa uplands, though it can be found elsewhere in the state as well. It is a smaller and more refined plant than *C. drummondii*, useful for conservation plantings and naturalistic landscaping. Its attractive white fruits are supported on tall, bright red stems, which contrast nicely with its foliage as the latter changes from green to purple in fall.

When planting this species, keep two things in mind. First, it suckers outward to form colonies, which can become much wider than the shrub is tall. It is thus best to plant it in an area where it can be controlled by mowing or where its advancing stems won't be a problem. Second, be careful of your source. If other dogwoods are nearby, seeds collected from gray dogwoods won't necessarily produce plants resembling their parents. The resulting seedlings may be hybrids.

Cornus rugosa Lam., Roundleaf Dogwood

DISTINGUISHING CHARACTERISTICS Medium-size to large shrub; twigs green flecked with purple with white pith. Leaves simple, opposite; blades oval to nearly round, 5 to 14 cm long, entire, the veins curving and following the margin and usually numbering 7 or 8 on each side, the hairs on the lower surface erect and curly. Flowers similar to *C. drummondii*, blooming in late spring or early summer. Fruit a light blue drupe, ripening in late summer or early autumn.

DISTRIBUTION IN IOWA Native in northeast Iowa and locally west of there as far as the Des Moines River valley.

This may be our least common dogwood, but with its green and purple stems and large roundish leaves, it is one that is not hard to recognize. It usually grows on moist slopes in rugged wooded terrain.

Cornus stolonifera Michx., Red-osier Dogwood

SYNONYM *C. sericea* L.

DISTINGUISHING CHARACTERISTICS Large shrub with bright red stems from autumn through early spring; pith of twigs white. Leaves simple, opposite; blades oval to elliptic, 5 to 12 cm long, entire, the veins curving and following the margin and numbering 5 or 6 on each side, the hairs on the lower surface small and appressed. Flowers white, regular, perfect, 4-parted, about 8 mm wide, in umbel-like cymes at the ends of leafy shoots, blooming sporadically from late spring through summer. Fruit a white drupe 6 to 7 mm in diameter, ripening in summer or early autumn.

DISTRIBUTION IN IOWA Native locally in the northern half of the state and frequently planted.

This is one of the easiest dogwoods to identify, especially in winter when its bright red stems can hardly go unnoticed. Native plants grow in wetlands, seeps, and low areas, but the species has been so widely planted that it is not always easy to tell which plants are native and which are not. It is an excellent choice for both landscaping and conservation plantings.

Corylus, Hazelnut

This is a small but widespread genus related to the birches, found in northern and temperate areas of Europe, Asia, and North America. Its fruits, called hazelnuts or filberts, are grown commercially in some parts of the world. Small mammals appreciate the nuts, too, while browsing animals eat the twigs, catkins, and foliage. Two species are native to Iowa.

Corylus americana Walter, American Hazelnut

DISTINGUISHING CHARACTERISTICS Large colonial shrub; twigs and petioles bearing gland-tipped hairs; next year's catkins present on twigs during autumn and winter. Leaves simple, alternate; blades oval, elliptic, or ovate, 4 to 13 cm long, the margins with both large and small teeth, the veins running straight into the tips of the larger teeth. Flowers very small, apetalous, appearing on last year's twigs before the leaves develop in early spring, the pistillate concealed by the scales of the winter buds except for their red stigmas, the staminate in catkins. Fruit a nut 1 to 1.5 cm long, nearly enclosed in a papery husk that is toothed along the margin and about as long as wide.

DISTRIBUTION IN IOWA Native throughout the state.

Hazelnut may be one of our most underappreciated shrubs, useful for both landscaping and conservation and notable for its edible nuts, handsome foliage, and attractive autumn color. It was once a characteristic plant of the prairie-forest border, but much of that habitat is now gone, so you are most likely to see it in woods and clearings and along fencerows and the edges of woods.

If you decide to plant a hazelnut — and we recommend it — be aware that it spreads by suckering and can grow quite tall. Plants are usually more compact in full sun, where they don't have to reach for light, and their yellow, orange, and purple fall color develops better there, too. Be prepared to compete with squirrels and chipmunks for the nuts!

Corylus cornuta Marsh., Beaked Hazelnut

DISTINGUISHING CHARACTERISTICS Similar to *C. americana* except twigs and petioles lacking glandular hairs; husk of nut elongated into a long narrow beak.

DISTRIBUTION IN IOWA Native in the northeast corner of the state.

This is the boreal counterpart of American hazelnut, more common up north than it is in Iowa. Like other northern plants, it is restricted to cool wooded slopes in our northeastern counties. Though only subtly different from American hazelnut in its leaves, twigs, and buds, it is quite distinct in fruit.

Diervilla

This is a small genus restricted to eastern North America. It is closely related to the honeysuckles (*Lonicera*) but differs in having toothed rather than entire leaves. One species is native in Iowa.

Diervilla lonicera P. Miller, Bush Honeysuckle

DISTINGUISHING CHARACTERISTICS Small colonial shrub. Leaves simple, opposite; blades ovate-lanceolate to elliptic, the larger ones 7 to 13 cm long (often shorter near the base of the twig), tapered to a slender tip, toothed, the veins dividing and forming a network near the margin. Flowers pale yellow, turning orange, slightly irregular, perfect, 5-parted, the petals united into a tube at their base, about 1.5 cm long, in small clusters at the tips of the branches, blooming in early to midsummer. Fruit a brown bottle-shaped capsule about 1 cm long with 5 prongs (sepals) at the tip, ripening in late summer or early autumn and persisting in winter.

DISTRIBUTION IN IOWA Native in the northeast and in scattered localities in southeast, central, and northwest Iowa.

Don't judge this species by its common name, for it is a very nice shrub, not at all like the invasive honeysuckles that are such a nuisance in Iowa. It is native on bluffs and wooded slopes in some of our most scenic places, often in association with other northern species that find refuge there.

Though limited in its Iowa distribution, native bush honeysuckle adapts well to cultivation here, thriving in full sun or part-day shade. It suckers to form small colonies, making it useful for covering banks or filling the front of a shrub border. In nature it is quite dwarf, but plants sold in nurseries tend to grow considerably larger, reaching waist-high or more. Its attractive foliage turns yellow and purple in autumn.

Dirca

This is a genus of three species, each native in a different part of North America. One is widely distributed in the northeast United States and adjacent Canada, ranging into parts of Iowa.

Dirca palustris L., Leatherwood

DISTINGUISHING CHARACTERISTICS Medium-size to large shrub with unusually flexible branchlets, commonly single-stemmed and somewhat tree-like in form; buds hidden within the bases of the petioles. Leaves simple, alternate; blades oval, mostly 4 to 10 cm long, entire. Flowers light yellow, regular, perfect, tube-shaped with 4 small lobes at the end, 0.5 to 1 cm long, in small fascicles before the leaves appear in early spring. Fruit an ellipsoid green drupe about 1 cm long, ripening early in the growing season, not persisting.

DISTRIBUTION IN IOWA
Native in northeast, east central, and central Iowa, also reported from Decatur County.

This handsome shrub reaches the western edge of its range in Iowa, growing here and there on moist wooded slopes and in ravines. You will probably have to go to the wild to see it, as it is seldom planted and does not always thrive when cultivated.

Though shrubby in size, leatherwood often has a single stem branched just above the ground, suggesting an old oak tree plucked from its savanna home, shrunk greatly in size, and dropped in the woods. Its tough leathery bark lends a unique flexibility to its twigs, whose wood lacks the stiffness of most other shrubs. Its small yellow flowers appear in early spring before its leaves.

Elaeagnus

Despite the word "olive" in their common names, members of this genus are unrelated to the edible olive. They are instead part of the very distinctive oleaster family, or Elaeagnaceae, whose species have tiny scales on their leaves and twigs. Many Iowans are familiar with the Russian olive, *E. angustifolia*, a small Eurasian tree that is grown here as an ornamental and used for highway and conservation plantings. The following shrubby species can also be found in Iowa.

Elaeagnus umbellata Thunb., Autumn Olive

DISTINGUISHING CHARACTERISTICS Large shrub, often spiny, with minute brown and silver scales coating the twigs and branchlets. Leaves simple, alternate; blades elliptic to narrowly elliptic, 5 to 6 cm long, entire, coated with minute silvery scales beneath. Flowers yellowish white, fragrant, regular, apetalous, with 4 petal-like sepals that are united into a tube at their base and minutely scaly on the outside, about 1 cm long, perfect or unisexual, in small fascicles from the leaf axils in late spring. Fruit a drupe, subglobose to ovoid in shape, 6 to 8 mm long, covered with brown and silvery scales at first, then red when fully ripe later in the growing season.

DISTRIBUTION IN IOWA Naturalized, especially southward.

This east Asian shrub was introduced to Iowa for landscaping and wildlife plantings but unfortunately has adapted too well, spreading to roadsides, old fields, wood edges, stream corridors, and other uncultivated areas. It has been ranked as one of Iowa's "dirty dozen" invasive species (Farrar 2001).

Euonymus

This is a large genus found in North America, Eurasia, and Australia, closely related to bittersweet (*Celastrus*) and producing similar fruit. One species is native to Iowa, while others have been introduced for landscaping. The exotic species should be planted with discretion as they can escape to natural areas and may become invasive (Farrar 2001; Swink & Wilhelm 1994; Widrlechner 2001).

Euonymus alatus (Thunb.) Sieb., Burning Bush

DISTINGUISHING CHARACTERISTICS Large shrub, often somewhat treelike in form, usually bearing 4 corky wings running lengthwise along each branchlet. Leaves simple, opposite; blades elliptic, tapered to both the base and the tip, mostly 4 to 5 cm long, finely toothed, their veins dividing and forming a network near the margin. Flowers and fruits similar to *E. atropurpureus* except flowers greenish in short-stalked cymes, capsules smaller.

DISTRIBUTION IN IOWA A common escape from cultivation.

Burning bush was introduced from northeast Asia for its bright red fall foliage and has become popular for landscaping. Unfortunately, birds are attracted to its tiny red fruits and are dispersing it to Iowa woodlands. Farrar (2001) lists it as one of Iowa's "dirty dozen" problematic invasive woody plants.

Euonymus atropurpureus Jacq., Wahoo

DISTINGUISHING CHARACTERISTICS Large colonial shrub or small tree. Leaves simple, opposite; blades elliptic to oval, 4 to 13 cm long, finely toothed, their veins dividing and forming a network near the margin. Flowers purple, regular, perfect, 4-parted, about 0.5 cm across, in small, long-stalked cymes from the axils of the leaves, blooming in early summer. Fruit a pinkish lobed capsule 1 to 2 cm wide, splitting open in autumn to reveal the orange-red fleshy seeds (arils) inside, then fading to purple, often persisting after the leaves have fallen.

DISTRIBUTION IN IOWA Native throughout the state.

People who appreciate the introduced burning bush may not realize there is a native species along roadsides and fencerows and in clearings and other open habitats across the state. It, too, has striking fall foliage, and it offers attractive fruits as well. Its small purple flowers are an unusual color for a shrub, another reason to seek it out.

Wahoo can be used for naturalistic landscaping and conservation plantings in a variety of soil types and exposures. You can either train it as a small tree or allow it to sucker and form thickets. Fall color is best where it receives ample sun.

Gaylussacia, Huckleberry

The huckleberries number about fifty species, all in the Western Hemisphere. They are members of the heath family, related to blueberries, cranberries, azaleas, and rhododendrons. One species is native to Iowa.

Gaylussacia baccata (Wang.) K. Koch, Black Huckleberry

DISTINGUISHING CHARACTERISTICS Dwarf colonial shrub with slender brown twigs. Leaves simple, alternate; blades oval to elliptic, 2 to 5 cm long, entire, their lower surface dotted with tiny yellow glands (seen with magnifying glass). Flowers reddish, urn-shaped, perfect, 5-parted, about 0.5 cm long, in short racemes on twigs of the previous year, blooming in spring. Fruit a blackish berry with about 10 hard seeds, 6 to 8 mm in diameter, ripening in late summer.

DISTRIBUTION IN IOWA Native in Allamakee, Cedar, Clinton, Linn, and Muscatine counties.

This dwarf shrub inhabits sandy woods in a few of our eastern counties, where it forms small colonies via underground stems (rhizomes). It is easily mistaken for its close relatives the lowbush blueberries, with which it often grows. It is considered a threatened species in Iowa.

Hamamelis, Witch-Hazel

The witch-hazels are a small genus indigenous to east and central North America and east Asia. They are unrelated to the shrubs called hazel or hazelnut, which belong to the genus *Corylus* of the birch family.

Witch-hazels are noteworthy for their small, fragrant, bright yellow flowers, which bloom during the coolest part of the growing season, at either its beginning or its end. Their peculiar strap-shaped petals shrivel during spells of freezing weather, then reextend when the weather warms. The flowers give rise to small woody pods whose shiny black seeds are forcibly ejected when ripe.

Hamamelis virginiana L., Witch-Hazel

DISTINGUISHING CHARACTERISTICS Large shrub. Leaves simple, alternate; blades oval to nearly round, more or less asymmetric at the base, usually 5 to 12 cm long, their margins wavy or with large blunt teeth, their veins running straight to the margin or into the teeth. Flowers yellow and spiderlike with slender strap-shaped petals 1 to 2 cm long, regular, perfect, 4-parted, not stalked, in small bunches on the twigs, blooming in autumn. Fruit a woody capsule 1 to 1.5 cm long, green during the summer and then brown, forcibly ejecting the shiny black seeds in autumn.

DISTRIBUTION IN IOWA Native in northeast and east central Iowa as far south as Muscatine County, planted elsewhere.

Witch-hazel is a characteristic shrub of the eastern deciduous forest, inhabiting the woodland understory from Maine south to Florida and west to just beyond the Mississippi River. In Iowa it is limited to a few of our easternmost counties.

A good place to see it is Pikes Peak State Park, along a nice stairstep trail near the overlook.

Despite its small natural range in Iowa, witch-hazel can be cultivated throughout the state. If you have room in your garden for a tall shrub, witch-hazel is an excellent choice. It is our only shrub that blooms in autumn, often as its leaves are turning yellow. Some individuals flower consistently after the leaves have dropped, and these are the best for landscaping, as their blossoms are easier to see.

Hudsonia

The three species in this genus are dwarf evergreen shrubs of open sandy places in Canada and the east and north U.S. One species barely reaches Iowa.

Hudsonia tomentosa Nutt., Beach Heath (not illustrated)

DISTINGUISHING CHARACTERISTICS Dwarf shrub with its stems sprawling on the ground. Leaves simple, alternate, evergreen; blades scalelike and usually appressed to the twig, about 2 mm long, entire. Flowers yellow, regular, perfect, 5-parted, 6 to 10 mm across, solitary at the ends of short leafy side branches, blooming in early summer. Fruit an egg-shaped capsule about 3 mm long, hidden by the hairy, persistent sepals of the flower.

DISTRIBUTION IN IOWA Native in Jackson County.

This unusual little shrub is rare in Iowa and listed as an endangered species here. Its main range is to our east, including the Great Lakes region, where it grows on dunes, beaches, and sandy plains. It is not commonly cultivated.

Hyperium, St. John's–wort

This is a large genus of mostly herbaceous plants, common in temperate areas of the Northern Hemisphere. Most species have yellow flowers with a conspicuous brush of yellow stamens. Their common name refers to the fact that European species are often in bloom on St. John's Day, June 24. One of the shrubby species is native in Iowa.

Hypericum prolificum L., Shrubby St. John's–wort

DISTINGUISHING CHARACTERISTICS Medium-size shrub; twigs often bearing short leafy shoots in the leaf axils. Leaves simple, opposite; blades narrowly oblong, 4 to 7 cm long, entire, their surfaces dotted with numerous tiny translucent glands (seen with magnifying glass). Flowers yellow, regular, perfect, 5-parted, with numerous stamens in a tight bunch around the pistil, about 2 cm across, in small cymes at the ends of the branches, blooming in summer. Fruit an ellipsoid brown capsule about 1 cm long with a slender beak at the end, ripening in autumn.

DISTRIBUTION IN IOWA
Native in southeast Iowa, north to Clinton County and west to Story County.

Though not much cultivated, this is an attractive summer-blooming shrub, modest in size with peeling brown bark. It can be found in a variety of habitats including bluffs, slopes, clearings, thickets, and pastures, in soils either moist or dry. When not in flower, it can be recognized by its narrow leaves and the tufted shoots that grow from their axils.

Ilex, Holly

We admire hollies for their evergreen leaves and bright red fruits, perhaps not realizing that some are deciduous, including the lone species native in Iowa. There are about three hundred species overall, in both temperate and tropical areas of the world. Plants are either male or female, and it is necessary to plant both if you want fruits in your garden.

Ilex verticillata (L.) Gray, Winterberry

DISTINGUISHING CHARACTERISTICS Large shrub. Leaves simple, alternate; blades oval to elliptic or sometimes obovate, 4 to 9 cm long, finely toothed, their veins dividing and forming a network near the margin. Flowers very small, whitish, regular, 4- to 8-parted, the petals about 2 mm long, polygamous or with staminate and pistillate flowers on separate plants, solitary or in small clusters from the leaf axils, with stalks shorter than the petioles, blooming in early summer. Fruit a bright red berry about 6 mm in diameter, ripening in autumn and persisting on the branches into winter.

DISTRIBUTION IN IOWA Native in Allamakee, Bremer, Chickasaw, Howard, Linn, and Mitchell counties.

Though common elsewhere, winterberry is rare and considered an endangered species in Iowa. To see it you will have to go to the northeast part of the state, searching along streams and in openings in upland woods. Fall is perhaps the best time to find it, as its berries make it more visible then.

In soils with low pH, winterberry is a very nice plant for landscaping. The dwarf cultivars are best for smaller gardens, as the wild type can grow quite tall.

Juniperus, Juniper

The junipers are an important genus of evergreen conifers, with at least one species indigenous to most parts of the Northern Hemisphere. They are remarkably diverse in habit, ranging from groundcovers to upright shrubs to medium-size trees.

The distinctive cones of junipers are small, fleshy, and berrylike, adapted for dispersal by animals. Many songbirds relish them, including the cedar waxwing, purple finch, robin, bluebird, catbird, hermit thrush, and yellow-rumped warbler. Junipers are dioecious, so the cones are found only on female plants.

Three junipers are native to Iowa. Our most common species is a tree, the eastern redcedar, *J. virginiana* L., which grows in sunny places throughout the state. Two shrubby species are discussed below.

Juniperus communis L. var. *depressa* Pursh, Common Juniper

DISTINGUISHING CHARACTERISTICS Low shrub with spreading branches. Leaves simple, evergreen, needlelike, in whorls of 3, 1 to 1.5 cm long, sharp-pointed, entire, their upper surface concave with a long white band. Reproductive parts in small unisexual cones that "flower" in spring, the male and the female on separate plants; male cones yellowish, falling soon after shedding their pollen; female cones green at first, later berrylike and nearly black, 6 to 8 mm in diameter, usually bearing 3 seeds.

DISTRIBUTION IN IOWA
Native in the northeast corner of the state and in Hardin County.

Common juniper has perhaps the broadest range of any woody plant, growing around the world in northern latitudes. It has differentiated over time into several distinct varieties, including the low, spreading type native to Iowa. Though sometimes used for landscaping, it is in general a less attractive plant than some of the other junipers.

In Iowa common juniper grows on elevated, well-drained sites such as hill prairies, bluffs, rocky slopes, and ledges. Like several northern plants, it is found mainly in the northeast corner of the state, with an outlying population along the Iowa River in Hardin County. The latter is thought to be a relict of a much colder postglacial climate, when northern plants were more widespread in Iowa than they are today. They persisted along the Iowa River after disappearing elsewhere, because the bluffs and steep slopes there provide a microclimate favorable to their growth.

Juniperus horizontalis Moench, Creeping Juniper

DISTINGUISHING CHARACTERISTICS Dwarf shrub, its stems trailing on the ground. Leaves simple, opposite, evergreen, entire, of two types: (1) scalelike, appressed to the twig, 1 to 2 mm long, and (2) needlelike, angled away from the twig, 2 to 6 mm long. Reproductive parts similar to *J. communis* var. *depressa* except mature cones light blue in color, 1- to 4-seeded.

DISTRIBUTION IN IOWA Native in Allamakee, Floyd, and Mitchell counties, planted elsewhere.

This low, trailing shrub inhabits dry hill prairies and bluffs in northeast Iowa. Though common elsewhere, it is rare enough here to be included on our state's list of threatened species. It ranges from New England west to Montana and north to Alaska and Hudson Bay.

Creeping juniper is a nice groundcover in sunny well-drained places. A great many cultivars have been developed for landscaping.

Ligustrum, Privet

The privets are a genus of Eurasian shrubs with attractive small leaves and blackish berries. Several species are cultivated in North America, especially in hedges, and from there they are spreading to woods and other natural areas. Two of these have been reported from Iowa: European privet, *L. vulgare* L., from Europe and west Asia, and border privet, *L. obtusifolium* Sieb. & Zucc., from Japan (Farrar 2001). Because they are potentially invasive, any wild privet should be removed when discovered.

Their distinguishing characteristics are as follows. Large shrubs. Leaves simple, opposite; blades variously shaped depending upon species, usually narrowly elliptic to oblong, 3 to 6 cm long, entire. Flowers small, white, regular, perfect, 4-parted, the petals united at their base into a slender tube, in panicles at the ends of the branches, blooming in early summer, often rather strongly scented. Fruit a dark purple or blackish berry, 6 to 8 mm long, ripening in autumn.

This image is representative of the privets.

Lonicera, Honeysuckle

This large and diverse genus is widely distributed in the Northern Hemisphere. Several species are native to the Upper Midwest, including two in Iowa. Others were introduced from Europe and Asia, and it is these that have invaded our woods and other natural areas, giving the whole genus a bad name.

The invasive honeysuckles include several large shrubs and one vine, Japanese honeysuckle, *L. japonica* Thunb. In Eurasia their ranges are largely separate from one another, but when we brought them together in America we gave them the opportunity to hybridize with one another, which they have freely done. Their hybrid offspring grow in natural areas, too, possessing characteristics intermediate between those of their parents. This makes identification of wild honeysuckles especially difficult.

All honeysuckles produce small brightly colored flowers in spring. Their fruits are colorful, too, and often borne prodigiously. Birds feed eagerly on these, spreading them to new locations.

A complete treatment of all the honeysuckles you might find in Iowa is beyond the scope of this book. The following discussion includes our two native species and two common exotics. For more information on other exotic and hybrid honeysuckles, see Swink and Wilhelm 1994 and Smith 2008.

Lonicera dioica L. var. *glaucescens* (Rydb.) Butters, Wild Honeysuckle

DISTINGUISHING CHARACTERISTICS Vine climbing with twining stems. Leaves simple, opposite, entire, of two types: (1) ordinary foliage leaves that are oblong to elliptic and 4 to 9 cm long and (2) a pair of leaves fused into a disk beneath each cluster of flowers or fruits, the disks longer than wide and tapered at each end. Flowers red or purple-red, irregular, perfect, 5-parted, their petals united into a long tube for most of their length, about 2 cm long (3 cm including the stamens), in whorls at the ends of leafy shoots in spring to early summer. Fruit a globose to ovoid red berry about 1 cm long, ripening in summer.

DISTRIBUTION IN IOWA Native throughout most of the state.

With so many weedy honeysuckles growing wild in Iowa, it is a treat to encounter one of our two native species. Both are handsome vines with bright red berries. If you examine the tips of their flowering and fruiting stems, you will find that each pair of leaves is fused into a disk encircling the shoot. The small colorful flowers (and later the fruits) appear directly above each disk.

This species is widely distributed in Iowa but not common everywhere. Look for it in wooded habitats such as bluffs, slopes, and banks above lakes. Its flowers are usually red or reddish, sometimes yellow.

Lonicera maackii (Rupr.) Herder, Amur Honeysuckle

DISTINGUISHING CHARACTERISTICS Large shrub. Leaves simple, opposite; blades oval to elliptic, tapered to a slender tip, 3 to 8 cm long, entire. Flowers white, perfect, irregular, the petals united into a tube at their base, about 2 cm long, in pairs from the axils of the leaves, with each pair on a stalk shorter than the petiole of the leaf, blooming in late spring or early summer. Fruit a red berry.

DISTRIBUTION IN IOWA Naturalized throughout the state.

This common shrub was not listed in Eilers and Roosa's Iowa flora in 1994, showing how quickly an invasive species can spread. It is certainly not a species you might overlook; its distinctive flowers bloom after other honeysuckles, and it sometimes flowers a second time late in the growing season.

Amur honeysuckle is named for the Amur River, which forms the border between Siberia and Manchuria. The surrounding region is home to a number of woody plants that thrive when grown in the Midwest. More than one of those has escaped from cultivation, so plants bearing the name Amur (or its Latin equivalent, *amurensis*) should be regarded cautiously by horticulturists and conservationists.

Lonicera reticulata Raf., Grape Honeysuckle

SYNONYM *L. prolifera* (Kirchner) Rehder

DISTINGUISHING CHARACTERISTICS Similar to *L. dioica* var. *glaucescens* except both types of leaves nearly round, not tapered to distinct ends, upper surface of disk leaves often coated with a white waxy material (glaucous); flowers light yellow.

DISTRIBUTION IN IOWA Native in the eastern half of the state and the southern Loess Hills.

This vine is a true midwesterner, native from west of the Appalachians to Iowa, Missouri, and Kansas. In Iowa it can be found in a variety of wooded habitats.

With its attractive blue-green leaves, grape honeysuckle is well worth growing in a sunny to partly sunny garden. It can either be trained on a trellis or planted without support, in which case it will form a large mound. Its flowers are yellow.

Lonicera tatarica L., Tatarian Honeysuckle

DISTINGUISHING CHARACTERISTICS Large shrub. Leaves simple, opposite; blades variably shaped, oval to ovate or narrower, 2.5 to 6 cm long, entire. Flowers commonly pink or red, irregular, perfect, 5-parted, their petals united into a short tube at their base, about 1 cm long, in pairs from the leaf axils in spring, each pair on a stalk longer than the petioles. Fruit a red or orange berry 6 to 10 mm in diameter.

DISTRIBUTION IN IOWA Naturalized throughout the state.

Tatarian honeysuckle has been cultivated for more than 250 years, and during this time many cultivars have been selected. If you encounter a honeysuckle with red or pink flowers, it is probably this species or its hybrid offspring. It is indigenous to Russia and central Asia.

Menispermum

This is a genus with one species in eastern North America, one species in eastern Asia, and none anywhere else. (See the explanation under *Acer spicatum*.) Both species are twining vines whose grapelike fruits contain kidney- or crescent-shaped seeds. The male and the female flowers occur on separate plants, so only some bear fruit. Once established, plants also spread by suckering.

Menispermum canadense L., Moonseed

DISTINGUISHING CHARACTERISTICS Vine climbing by means of twining stems, also forming colonies using underground stems. Leaves simple, alternate; blades palmately lobed and veined, 5 to 18 cm long and about as wide, deeply notched at base, entire. Flowers whitish, very small, regular, with 6 to 9 petals, unisexual with the staminate and the pistillate on different plants, in panicles from the leaf axils, blooming in early summer. Fruit a drupe about 8 mm in diameter, resembling a small grape.

DISTRIBUTION IN IOWA
Native throughout the state.

This species is common in Iowa woodlands, where it is easily recognized by its peculiar leaves and bright green stems. Its fruits resemble bunches of wild grapes but should not be mistaken for them, as they are poisonous (Kingsbury 1965).

Moonseed is an interesting and attractive vine, though rarely cultivated. Where it appears spontaneously and is not a threat to children, it is worth retaining in the landscape.

Parthenocissus

This is a small genus of woody vines found in North America, eastern Asia, and the Himalayas. It is closely related to the grapes, producing similar fruits and climbing with tendrils as grapes do. Perhaps the best-known species is the Boston ivy, *P. tricuspidata* (Sieb. & Zucc.) Planch., which so famously adorns the walls of America's college campuses and the outfield wall at Wrigley Field, though it is not native to North America. Two other species grow wild in Iowa.

Parthenocissus quinquefolia (L.) Planch., Virginia Creeper

DISTINGUISHING CHARACTERISTICS Vine climbing with tendrils or root-like structures or sprawling on the ground; tendrils short, dividing into several branches that are tipped with adhesive disks. Leaves, flowers, and fruits similar to *P. vitacea* except petioles hairy, panicles usually taller than wide, fruits a little smaller.

DISTRIBUTION IN IOWA Native throughout the state.

This and the following species are nearly identical, and you could be forgiven for assuming they are one and the same. They are perhaps most easily distinguished by the way they climb, although there are differences in foliage and fruit as well as subtle distinctions in habitat and distribution.

Virginia creeper is an eastern and southern species, reaching the northwest edge of its range in Iowa. If you find a *Parthenocissus* deep in the woods, climbing flat against trees using aerial roots, it is most certainly this one. It climbs using tendrils, too, especially as a young vine, but these are shorter and more highly branched than those of *P. vitacea* and have adhesive disks on their tips.

Both species are standouts in early autumn, livening the landscape with their bright red or wine-colored leaves. They are also valued by wildlife, their berries providing food for thrushes, chickadees, bluebirds, catbirds, flickers, robins, brown thrashers, vireos, and other birds.

Parthenocissus vitacea (Knerr) Hitchc., Woodbine

DISTINGUISHING CHARACTERISTICS Vine climbing with tendrils or growing on the ground; tendrils long, forking once or twice, with slender or slightly swollen tips. Leaves palmately compound, alternate, with long glabrous petioles; leaflets 5, oval to broadly oval, up to 15 cm long, with conspicuous large teeth along the margins. Flowers greenish, regular, perfect, 5-parted, about 7 mm long, with swept-back petals, in broad umbel-like panicles at the ends of short leafy shoots, blooming in early summer. Fruit a dark purple berry about 8 mm in diameter, ripening in late summer to early autumn, often with bright red stems.

DISTRIBUTION IN IOWA Native throughout the state.

This species is more western and northern than *P. quinquefolia*, although in Iowa their ranges overlap considerably. Woodbine is a habitat generalist, growing along edges and fencerows and in other sunny areas in addition to the forest understory, often trailing on the ground and forming large colonies. When climbing, it uses its long tendrils to either twine around branches or probe deep into tree bark.

Though too aggressive for a small garden, woodbine is a good groundcover for large landscapes, in either shade or part sun. Seeds collected and sown in the fall will germinate the following spring. Established plants resist drought and require minimal maintenance, mainly the removal of tree and shrub seedlings that volunteer into their colonies.

Physocarpus, Ninebark

This is a small genus indigenous to North America and northeast Asia, closely related to *Spiraea*. One species is native in Iowa.

Physocarpus opulifolius (L.) Maxim., Ninebark

DISTINGUISHING CHARACTERISTICS Medium-size to large shrub. Leaves simple, alternate; blades shallowly lobed or on vigorous shoots more deeply lobed and maplelike, the lowest pair of lobes the most prominent, 2.5 to 9 cm long, toothed. Flowers white, regular, perfect, 5-parted, the petals roundish and 4 to 5 mm long, in corymbs at the ends of leafy shoots in late spring or early summer. Fruit a brown follicle about 0.5 cm long, arranged in a compact sessile cluster of 3 to 5 fruits at the end of each branch of the corymb, each cluster resembling a small capsule; follicles each splitting open along 2 seams, persisting on the twigs in winter.

DISTRIBUTION IN IOWA Native in east, central, and south central Iowa, planted there and elsewhere.

This handsome shrub is easily recognized by its peeling bark, white flowers, and small papery pods, which persist on its branches in winter. It inhabits a remarkable range of habitats in Iowa, from dry bluffs and ledges to riverbanks and seeps, usually as a secondary rather than a dominant species. In moist fertile soils it can grow quite large, but as is so often the case in nature, drier sites have a dwarfing effect.

As you might expect with such an adaptable species, ninebark is very easy to grow. It is a good choice for conservation plantings and large landscapes in sunny to partly sunny sites. It tends to become untidy with time, so regular pruning (renewal and heading back) is advised. Mildew sometimes causes dieback of shoots. Cultivars with purple or yellow foliage are available for gardens.

Potentilla, Cinquefoil

The cinquefoils are a large group of primarily herbaceous plants, most with yellow flowers. There is considerable variation among the species, and some botanists prefer to recognize this by classifying them into several genera.

As their common name suggests, many cinquefoils have compound leaves with five leaflets. The woody species are dwarf or trailing shrubs, including the following two that are native in Iowa.

Potentilla fruticosa L., Shrubby Cinquefoil

SYNONYMS *Dasiphora fruticosa* (L.) Rydb., *Pentaphylloides fruticosa* (L.) Schwarz

DISTINGUISHING CHARACTERISTICS Small shrub. Leaves compound, alternate, with 5 to 7 divisions that are narrowly elliptic to oblong, 1 to 1.5 cm long, and entire; stipules forming a partial sheath around the twig. Flowers yellow (white or pink in some cultivars), regular, perfect, 5-parted, the petals roundish and about 1 cm long, solitary or in small clusters at the tips of leafy shoots, blooming in summer. Fruit an achene, enclosed with other achenes by the upright persisting sepals and bracts of the flower, which form a brown capsulelike structure about 0.5 cm long.

DISTRIBUTION IN IOWA Native in Allamakee, Floyd, Jackson, Jones, Linn, and Winneshiek counties, planted throughout the state.

Shrubby cinquefoil is often planted in Iowa gardens, so you might not expect it to be a threatened species here. However, as a native plant it is very rare, growing on bluffs and ledges in a few of our eastern counties.

Outside of Iowa shrubby cinquefoil has a broad range, both in North America and Eurasia. In some places, it grows primarily in wetlands and moist swales. As you might expect in such a widely distributed species, natural selection has produced a number of regional variations that are sometimes recognized with their own names.

Because it is so useful for landscaping, shrubby cinquefoil has also been subject to much artificial selection. The many cultivars offer a range of flower color: white, pale yellow, bright yellow, and pink. Plants sold in nurseries are not necessarily of midwestern provenance; in fact, most probably originated in other regions.

Cultivars do best in a sunny well-drained site. Plants are more compact and attractive when headed-back severely every year in late winter or early spring. Renewal pruning should be done at the same time.

Potentilla tridentata Aiton, Three-toothed Cinquefoil (not illustrated)

SYNONYM *Sibbaldiopsis tridentata* (Aiton) Rydb.

DISTINGUISHING CHARACTERISTICS Miniature trailing shrub, woody at the base only. Leaves compound, alternate, evergreen; leaflets 3 in number, 1 to 2 cm long, entire except for 3 teeth at the tip. Flowers white, regular, perfect, 5-parted, the petals about 0.5 cm long, in small cymes on leafy shoots, blooming in early summer. Fruit similar to *P. fruticosa*.

DISTRIBUTION IN IOWA Native in Allamakee and Winneshiek counties.

Few people would call this small trailing plant a shrub, but it has partly woody stems and is thus worth mentioning in a book like this. It is an endangered species in Iowa, inhabiting sandstone ledges in our northeast corner. Though not commonly cultivated, it is an attractive plant with three-parted evergreen leaves and small white flowers and could be tried in rock gardens.

Prunus

This is a large genus of trees and shrubs that is valued for both its beautiful flowers and its edible fruits. Important commercial species include the peaches, plums, cherries, and almond. Most regions of the Northern Hemisphere have at least one species, and there are even a few in South America.

Iowa's flora includes the black cherry, *P. serotina* Ehrh., which grows to be a large tree, and the species discussed below. Most of our native species are intermediate between trees and shrubs in both in size and habit, showing that nature does not always fit neatly into the categories we use to classify the diversity around us.

Prunus americana Marsh., American Plum

DISTINGUISHING CHARACTERISTICS Large shrub or small tree, suckering to form thickets. Leaves simple, alternate; blades elliptic to oval, tapered to slender tips, 5 to 9 cm long, sharply toothed, the veins dividing and forming a network near the margin; petioles sometimes bearing 1 or 2 glands; stipules long, slender, often persisting into summer. Flowers white, fragrant, regular, perfect, 5-parted, the petals about 1 cm long, in fascicles of 2 to 3 from overwintering buds, blooming just before the leaves expand in spring. Fruit a red or purple drupe usually 2 to 3 cm long, ripening in early autumn.

DISTRIBUTION IN IOWA Native throughout the state.

This is the most common of the four plums that grow wild in Iowa, forming colonies along wood edges and fencerows and in similar habitats almost everywhere. During most of the year it seems to disappear into the vegetation around it, but it really stands out in spring when its fragrant white flowers appear.

Once you know where the plants grow, be sure to visit them in fall and taste their fruits, which though smaller than cultivated varieties are clearly recognizable as plums. There is considerable variation in flavor among these, and it is interesting to compare fruits from different plants.

Where soils drain well, wild plum is a good choice for conservation plantings and naturalistic landscaping. Its dense and often thorny branches provide excellent cover for birds and other animals, though its fruits are of far less value to wildlife than its close relatives the cherries.

Prunus hortulana L. H. Bailey, Wild Goose Plum (not illustrated)

DISTINGUISHING CHARACTERISTICS Small tree. Leaves simple, alternate; blades elliptic-lanceolate, tapered to slender tips, 6 to 9 cm long, with fine gland-tipped teeth, the veins dividing and forming a network near the margin; petioles usually bearing 1 or more glands. Flowers white, regular, perfect, 5-parted, the petals 5 to 7 mm long, in fascicles of 2 to 4 from overwintering buds, blooming when the leaves are partly expanded in spring. Fruit a red drupe 2 to 3 cm long.

DISTRIBUTION IN IOWA Native in Appanoose, Des Moines, Johnson, Lee, and Van Buren counties.

This rare but distinctive plum grows in low moist woods and open areas in a few of our southeastern counties. It is sometimes cultivated for its fruit.

Prunus mexicana S. Wats., Big-tree Plum (not illustrated)

DISTINGUISHING CHARACTERISTICS Small tree, similar to *P. americana* except not thicket-forming.

DISTRIBUTION IN IOWA Reported from scattered localities around the state.

This southern species is very similar to American plum, but it does not sucker to form thickets. It has been found growing wild in a few Iowa counties, but it is not known if it is actually native here.

Prunus nigra Aiton, Canada Plum

DISTINGUISHING CHARACTERISTICS Similar to *P. americana* except leaf blades 6 to 11 cm long, relatively broad (1.6 to 2 times longer than wide) with gland-tipped teeth.

DISTRIBUTION IN IOWA Native in Allamakee, Boone, Clayton, Hamilton, and Winneshiek counties.

This is a northern species that is rare in Iowa, growing on cool wooded slopes in the northeast corner of the state and also reported from two central counties. It is included on our state list of endangered species.

Prunus pensylvanica L. f., Pin Cherry

DISTINGUISHING CHARACTERISTICS Large colonial shrub or small tree with smooth red-brown bark marked with short horizontal lines (lenticels). Leaves simple, alternate; blades ovate to elliptic, often narrowly so, tapered to a slender tip, 4 to 8 cm long, finely toothed with incurved and gland-tipped teeth, their veins dividing and forming a network near the margin; petioles bearing small glands near their junction with the blades. Flowers white, regular, perfect, 5-parted, the petals about 5 mm long, in small fascicles from overwintering buds, blooming as the leaves are expanding in spring. Fruit a bright red drupe about 6 mm in diameter, ripening in summer.

DISTRIBUTION IN IOWA Native in northeast and north central Iowa as far south as Boone, Johnson, Marshall, Scott, and Story counties.

This is another species that ranges into Iowa from the Great Lakes states, although it is distributed farther to the south and west than other northern plants. It is what naturalists call a pioneer species, colonizing places where trees have been removed or active management withheld. Like many other pioneers, it

often forms patches by suckering. Look for it on bluffs, along the edges of woods and along fencerows, and even on prairies, especially where the soil is sandy.

The flowers and fruits of pin cherry occur in small bunches on the stems and in this respect are more similar to plums and commercial cherries than other wild cherries. Bright red when ripe, the fruits are relished by many kinds of birds and mammals.

Though not commonly planted, pin cherry is an attractive small tree that could be used for naturalistic landscaping and conservation. A well-drained site is best.

Prunus pumila L., Dwarf Cherry or Sand Cherry (not illustrated)

DISTINGUISHING CHARACTERISTICS Small upright or sprawling shrub. Leaves simple, alternate; blades narrowly elliptic to narrowly obovate, 3.5 to 5.5 cm long, finely toothed, their veins dividing and forming a network near the margin. Flowers white, regular, perfect, 5-parted, the petals about 0.5 cm long, solitary or in small fascicles from overwintering buds, blooming as the leaves are expanding in spring. Fruit a dark purple or blackish drupe 8 to 15 mm in diameter, ripening in summer.

DISTRIBUTION IN IOWA Reported from Allamakee, Buchanan, Delaware, Louisa, Lyon, Muscatine, and Winneshiek counties. Native.

This is the least common of Iowa's native cherries, growing in sandy places, on hill prairies, and on rock outcrops in a few of our northern and eastern counties. As its name suggests, it is a small shrub no more than a few feet high.

Dwarf cherry can be divided into four varieties that differ in their leaves and habits of growth. Joseph Rohrer, who has studied this species in the Midwest, considers Iowa's plants to be *P. pumila* var. *besseyi*, although he has seen specimens from the northeast corner of the state whose leaves resemble *P. pumila* var. *pumila* (personal communication). For more information, see Rohrer (2000).

Prunus virginiana L., Choke Cherry

DISTINGUISHING CHARACTERISTICS Large shrub or small tree, often forming thickets. Leaves simple, alternate; blades oval to elliptic or obovate, 4 to 15 cm long, finely and sharply toothed, the veins dividing and forming a network near the margin; petioles usually bearing a pair of small glands near their junction with the blade. Flowers white, regular, perfect, 5-parted, the petals 2 to 4 mm long, in racemes at the ends of short leafy shoots in spring. Fruit a drupe 8 to 9 mm in diameter, changing from light purple to nearly black as it ripens in mid to late summer.

DISTRIBUTION IN IOWA Native throughout the state.

It would be hard to find a forest in Iowa where the choke cherry doesn't grow, and it is often one of the most common woody plants in the understory. It is also among our most valuable native plants for wildlife, its fruits providing food for many songbirds, game birds, and small mammals.

Adaptable and easy to grow, choke cherry can be used for conservation plantings and naturalistic landscaping. Unfortunately, it is sometimes afflicted by the unsightly galls of the black knot fungus, which cause dieback of stems, and a slow decline caused by a phytoplasma. Premature autumn color, often quite brilliant and repeated year after year, is one of the main symptoms of the latter. Neither condition can be treated, and removal of infected plants is the best means of slowing their spread. If you do decide to plant choke cherries, be sure to give them plenty of room, as they sucker to form small colonies.

Ptelea, Hoptree

The hoptrees are widely distributed in North America but not found elsewhere in the world. Botanists do not entirely agree on how to classify the diversity in the genus, so descriptions of species and their ranges vary from one book to another.

Ptelea trifoliata L., Hoptree

DISTINGUISHING CHARACTERISTICS Large shrub. Leaves compound, alternate; leaflets 3, oval to elliptic, not stalked, with inconspicuous small teeth along the margin, the terminal one 5 to 11 cm long. Flowers greenish white, regular, unisexual (or the pistillate with nonfunctional stamens), 4- or 5-parted, the petals about 0.5 cm long, in paniclelike cymes at the tips of the branches, blooming in spring. Fruit a roundish samara with the seed in the center, 1.5 to 2.5 cm long, ripening in summer and often persisting in winter.

DISTRIBUTION IN IOWA Native from Lee County north to Muscatine County and west to Van Buren and Washington counties; in Boone, Hamilton, and Story counties; and in Fremont and Page counties.

This interesting shrub is a member of the citrus family, though its dry elmlike fruits are nothing like the oranges and lemons we buy in the grocery store. When its fruits are absent, it can easily be mistaken for poison ivy, bearing very similar three-parted leaves (though its middle leaflet is not stalked).

Hoptree and its varieties are broadly distributed across the southern and central U.S., from the southern Great Lakes to Florida and the Gulf Coast, then west to Utah and Arizona. In Iowa its range is very spotty. It is most common in the southeastern part of the state, where it occurs in a variety of woodsy or open sites, from bluffs and ridges to sand mounds and streamside thickets. Smaller populations occur in central and extreme southwest Iowa.

As a larval host plant for the giant swallowtail butterfly, hoptree is worth including in landscapes designed for wildlife. It grows too tall and gangly for gardens, however, and is a favorite plant of the potato leafhopper, which can leave it unsightly by the middle of the summer.

Quercus, Oak

"The oak" is our state tree and needs little introduction to Iowans. We generally think of oaks as large and majestic, but a few species are shrubby, including the one described below.

Quercus prinoides Willd., Dwarf Chinkapin Oak (not illustrated)

DISTINGUISHING CHARACTERISTICS Large shrub or small tree. Leaves simple, alternate; blades narrowly elliptic to narrowly obovate, 5 to 15 cm long, with 3 to 8 large teeth on each side. Flowers very small, apetalous, unisexual, the staminate and the pistillate on the same plant, appearing with the leaves in spring; the staminate in long drooping catkins; the pistillate red, cup-shaped, in small clusters in the leaf axils. Fruit a small acorn, the cap covering the lower third to half of the nut.

DISTRIBUTION IN IOWA Native in south central and southwest Iowa.

One can argue that this is a dwarf type of chinkapin oak, *Q. muhlenbergii* Engelm., and not a separate species, but it is nevertheless an interesting and unusual plant: multiple-stemmed, modest in size, and bearing acorns when still very small. Look for it in the dry woods of southern Iowa, or try planting it in your garden, as it is not hard to grow.

Rhamnus, Buckthorn

This genus has gained a bad reputation because some introduced species have become invasive, including the common buckthorn from Europe. Worldwide there are about a hundred species, and not all are weedy. Two are native in Iowa.

Rhamnus alnifolia L'Hér., Alderleaf Buckthorn

DISTINGUISHING CHARACTERISTICS Small colonial shrub. Leaves simple, alternate; blades elliptic to oval, mostly 6 to 9 cm long, toothed, with 5 or more major veins on each side, the tips of the veins curving and following the margin. Flowers tiny, yellow-green, regular, 5-parted, apetalous, with functional stamens and pistils in separate flowers on different plants, solitary or in small fascicles from the axils of the leaves in late spring. Fruit a blackish berry 6 to 8 mm in diameter.

DISTRIBUTION IN IOWA Native in Allamakee, Clayton, Delaware, Dubuque, Fayette, Howard, Jackson, and Winneshiek counties.

This handsome buckthorn is a natural dwarf, growing up to about waist-high and spreading by suckers to form small colonies. In Iowa it is limited to algific slopes in the northeast corner of the state. While more difficult to cultivate than other buckthorns, it sometimes succeeds when planted in cool, moist, shady locations and offers an interesting challenge to those who like to grow native plants.

Rhamnus cathartica L., Common Buckthorn

DISTINGUISHING CHARACTERISTICS Large shrub or small tree; twigs often tipped by a short thorn. Leaves simple, subopposite, remaining green until late autumn; blades variably shaped, from elliptic or ovate to nearly round, 3 to 8 cm long, toothed, with 2 to 4 major veins on each side, the tips of the veins curving and following the margin. Flowers green, regular, 4-parted, 4 to 5 mm long, unisexual with the staminate and the pistillate on separate plants, in fascicles at the base of leafy shoots in late spring. Fruit a blackish berry 5 to 8 mm in diameter, ripening in autumn and often persisting into winter.

DISTRIBUTION IN IOWA Naturalized throughout the state.

If we could go back in time and change decisions made by others, we would certainly block the importation of this species into North America. An innocuous plant in its native Europe, it has unfortunately become a terrible weed here, completely overrunning the understory of many natural woodlands. It is often single-stemmed and can grow to be a substantial small tree, shading the forest floor and eliminating most of the native plants there.

Buckthorns are dioecious, meaning the flowers are either male or female and found on different plants. Thus, only some of the plants bear the blackish berries that are a hallmark of the species. These and the buckthorn's long-persisting green leaves make it easy to identify in late fall, after native species have lost their foliage. That is also a good time to control it, by cutting its stems near the ground and then treating the stumps with herbicide. When controlling a large infestation, it is wise to remove the fruiting plants first, so birds do not eat the berries and spread the species further.

Other cultivated buckthorns sometimes escape in Iowa, including glossy buckthorn, *R. frangula* L. (see top right), and Dahurian buckthorn, *R. davurica* Pallas. These are potentially invasive and as a precaution should be removed when seen.

Rhamnus frangula L., Glossy Buckthorn (not illustrated)

SYNONYM *Frangula alnus* P. Miller

DISTINGUISHING CHARACTERISTICS Large shrub with naked buds. Leaves simple, alternate; blades oval to obovate, 3 to 7 cm long, glossy, entire, with 6 to 9 major veins on each side, the tips of the veins curving and following the margin. Flowers small, greenish, regular, perfect, 5-parted, in small fascicles from the leaf axils, blooming in late spring or early summer. Fruit a berry about 1 cm in diameter, turning from red to purple-black as it ripens later in the growing season.

DISTRIBUTION IN IOWA An occasional escape from cultivation.

As if Iowa did not have enough invasive species, this is a potential threat to our wetlands. It is a nuisance in states to our east and should be watched for here. It is indigenous to Europe and west Asia.

Rhamnus lanceolata Pursh, Lanceleaf Buckthorn

DISTINGUISHING CHARACTERISTICS Medium-size shrub. Leaves simple, alternate; blades elliptic to oblong, 4 to 8 cm long, very finely toothed, with 5 or more rather indistinct veins on each side. Flowers 4-parted with petals 0.5 to 1 mm long, otherwise similar to *R. alnifolia*. Fruit a blackish berry.

DISTRIBUTION IN IOWA Native in southern and extreme eastern Iowa and in the Loess Hills north to Woodbury County.

This is the only native buckthorn throughout most of its Iowa range, growing in a variety of habitats including woods, wood edges, streambanks, prairies, and other open places. In northeast Iowa its range overlaps slightly with *R. alnifolia*, a dwarf shrub with a very specialized habitat. Like the latter, it is rarely cultivated.

Rhus, Sumac

This is a large genus in a mostly tropical family, the Anacardiaceae, which also includes the pistachio, cashew, and mango. *Rhus* has two main divisions, which in this book are treated as separate genera. *Rhus* proper includes the sumacs with red fruits. The white-fruited species with skin-irritating oils are listed under the genus *Toxicodendron*.

Sumacs are much admired in autumn for their bright red and purple-red leaves. Their fruits are attractive as well, usually remaining on the branches through winter. While not a favorite food of most wild animals, they are eaten by many game birds and songbirds when preferred foods are scarce. Deer and rabbits browse the vegetative parts of the plants.

Sumacs are polygamo-dioecious, meaning that individual plants may have perfect or unisexual flowers or both, but usually their flowers are either all male or all female. As a result, some plants never bear fruits.

The following four species are native in Iowa.

Rhus aromatica Aiton, Fragrant Sumac

DISTINGUISHING CHARACTERISTICS Small to medium-size shrub; twig tips bearing upright, catkinlike flower buds for next year. Leaves compound, alternate; leaflets 3, not stalked, the terminal broadly ovate to diamond-shaped and 3 to 9 cm long, the other 2 usually smaller, margins coarsely toothed. Flowers small, pale yellow, regular, 5-parted, mostly unisexual with the staminate and the pistillate on separate plants, in small compact clusters at the

tips of the twigs, blooming before or as the leaves emerge in spring. Fruit a red hairy drupe about 0.5 cm in diameter, forming irregular clumps at the tips of last year's twigs, ripening in summer and persisting after the leaves have fallen.

DISTRIBUTION IN IOWA Native in the southeast and in scattered locations in the central and eastern parts of the state.

When not in fruit, this handsome shrub is more likely to be mistaken for poison ivy than a sumac, bearing similar three-parted leaves. As its common and botanical names suggest, it emits a distinctive aroma when disturbed. It is common in the southeastern part of Iowa and occasionally seen elsewhere, inhabiting woods, edges, rocky bluffs, and open areas.

Sumac species differ considerably in size and this is one of the shortest, making it useful for landscaping. Like other sumacs, it spreads by suckers to form colonies. A cultivar named Gro-low has declining stems and is often planted as a groundcover.

Rhus copallina L., Winged Sumac (not illustrated)

DISTINGUISHING CHARACTERISTICS Similar to *R. glabra* except leaflets entire, rachis winged.

DISTRIBUTION IN IOWA Native in the southeast corner of the state.

This distinctive sumac is also Iowa's rarest. John Pearson of the Iowa Department of Natural Resources found a patch in Henry County in 2013, the first time it had been recorded in the state since the 1940s. It should be looked for elsewhere in southeast Iowa along roadsides, along the edges of woods, and in rocky glades.

Rhus glabra L., Smooth Sumac

DISTINGUISHING CHARACTERISTICS Medium-size to large colonial shrub, the individual stems treelike in form; shoots and twigs glabrous. Leaves pinnately compound, alternate; leaflets 13 to 19, ovate-lanceolate to oblong-lanceolate, tapered to a slender tip, 6 to 10 cm long, toothed, essentially glabrous. Flowers yellowish green, regular, 5-parted, about 0.5 cm across, mostly unisexual with the staminate and the pistillate on separate plants, in large upright panicles at the tips of the branches, blooming in early summer. Fruit a red drupe about 4 mm in diameter, very finely hairy (hairs less than 0.5 mm long), in large, compact, upright clusters, ripening in late summer to early autumn and persisting through winter.

DISTRIBUTION IN IOWA Native throughout the state.

This is our most common sumac and a characteristic plant of the prairie-forest border. Once established it spreads aggressively by suckers, forming large clones with the founding stem in the center and progressively shorter ones toward the edge. It is typically one of the first woody plants to color in fall, enlivening our roadsides, fencerows, and wood edges with its red- and purple-toned leaves.

Because it is easy to grow and valuable to wildlife, smooth sumac is useful for large landscapes and conservation plantings. Considering its tendency to spread, however, it should not be planted in gardens or near prairie restorations.

Rhus typhina L., Staghorn Sumac

SYNONYM *R. hirta* (L.) Sudworth

DISTINGUISHING CHARACTERISTICS Large colonial shrub or small tree; shoots and twigs hairy. Leaves pinnately compound, alternate; leaflets 15 to 27, oblong-lanceolate, tapered to a slender tip, 4 to 12 cm long, toothed; rachis and petioles hairy. Flowers and fruits similar to *R. glabra* except fruits conspicuously hairy, with hairs more than 0.5 mm long.

DISTRIBUTION IN IOWA Native in northeast and central Iowa, also reported from Emmet and Palo Alto counties in the northwest.

Few plants are more aptly named than the staghorn sumac. One look at its stems will convince you: stout, sparsely branched, and coated with soft velvety hairs, they really do resemble the antlers of a deer.

Staghorn is the tallest of our native sumacs, often becoming a small tree. Iowa is at the west edge of its range, which includes all the northeast U.S. and adjacent Canada. It is most common in the northeast corner of the state, forming colonies along the edges of woods.

Where its suckering can be contained by mowing or is not an issue, staghorn sumac is an interesting addition to landscapes. A form with dissected foliage is available in the nursery trade.

Ribes

This is a large genus of low to medium-size shrubs with maplelike leaves, common in cold and temperate regions of both the Western and the Eastern hemispheres. For practical purposes the species can be divided into two groups, one with spiny stems called gooseberry, the other unarmed and called currant. Both produce edible berries. While the fruits are not especially popular in the United States, the shrubs are often cultivated for them elsewhere. Wild birds and mammals appreciate them, too.

Most native and some cultivated *Ribes* serve as the alternate host of the white pine blister rust, a serious disease of the eastern white pine and related western pines. The disease was accidentally introduced from Europe in the early 1900s, and for many decades after, attempts were made to control it by eradicating gooseberries and currants. These efforts were eventually abandoned when they proved to be ineffective (Maloy 2001; Smith 2008).

Iowa has three native gooseberries and three native currants. One species grows in almost every woodland in the state, while some others are very rare.

Ribes americanum P. Miller, Wild Black Currant

DISTINGUISHING CHARACTERISTICS
Small to medium-size shrub. Leaves simple, alternate on ordinary long shoots, clustered and apparently whorled at the tips of spur shoots; blades resembling small maple leaves with 3 or 5 palmate lobes and veins, 2 to 9 cm long, sharply toothed, dotted on both surfaces with tiny yellow glands (seen with magnifying glass). Flowers light yellow-green, perfect, 5-parted, about 1 cm long, in drooping racemes at the ends of leafy spur shoots in spring. Fruit a berry 6 to 9 mm in diameter, turning from green to dark red to blackish as it ripens during the summer.

DISTRIBUTION IN IOWA Native in the northern two-thirds of the state.

This is our most common currant, inhabiting a variety of usually moist habitats including lakeshores, marsh edges, seeps, ditches, fens, wet prairies, and low woods. Though not especially ornamental, it is an interesting native shrub, offering small yellowish flowers in spring and berries for the birds in summer.

Ribes cynosbati L., Prickly Gooseberry

DISTINGUISHING CHARACTERISTICS Similar to *R. missouriense* except ovaries of flowers bristly, becoming prickly on the fruit.

DISTRIBUTION IN IOWA Native in the northeast half of the state.

If it were not for its odd prickly fruits, this species would be easily mistaken for the more abundant Missouri gooseberry. It grows in a variety of wooded habitats in eastern, central, and northern Iowa.

Ribes hirtellum Michx., Swamp Gooseberry (not illustrated)

DISTINGUISHING CHARACTERISTICS Similar to *R. missouriense* except spines absent or not well developed, prickles sparse; stamens of flowers neither elongated nor closely enclosing the style.

DISTRIBUTION IN IOWA Native in Van Buren County.

This gooseberry is rare in Iowa, limited to moist woods and fens in one southeastern county. Its principal range is to the north, east, and west of Iowa.

Ribes hudsonianum Richards., Northern Black Currant (not illustrated)

DISTINGUISHING CHARACTERISTICS Similar to *R. americanum* except flowers white, in upright racemes; leaf blades with glands on lower surface only.

DISTRIBUTION IN IOWA Native in Allamakee, Clayton, Delaware, and Dubuque counties.

Included on our state list of threatened species, northern black currant grows on algific slopes in a few of our northeast counties. Its main range is far to the north, and our plants are thought to be remnants of a once more widespread population that grew here at the end of the ice age, surviving in their special habitat only because the microclimate there is so much cooler than it is elsewhere in Iowa.

Ribes missouriense Nutt., Missouri Gooseberry

DISTINGUISHING CHARACTERISTICS Small to medium-size shrub; lower parts of stems often prickly; twigs armed with 1 to 3 sharp spines at each node. Leaves simple, alternate on ordinary long shoots, clustered and apparently whorled at the tips of spur shoots; blades palmately lobed and veined, 2 to 6 cm long and similar in width, coarsely toothed. Flowers greenish white, regular, perfect, 5-parted, about 1.5 cm long, the stamens elongated and closely enclosing the style; in small drooping clusters at the ends of leafy spur shoots in spring. Fruit a berry about 1 cm in diameter, at first green with narrow white stripes, turning nearly black when ripe later in the summer.

DISTRIBUTION IN IOWA Native throughout the state.

Missouri gooseberry is an opportunistic shrub inhabiting a variety of shady environments including mature forests, unmanaged savannas, and pastured woods (since livestock avoid it). At times it can become too abundant, reminding us of an invasive species.

Ribes odoratum Wendl., Clove Currant or Buffalo Currant (not illustrated)

DISTINGUISHING CHARACTERISTICS Medium-size colonial shrub. Leaves simple, alternate; blades palmately lobed and veined, 2 to 4 cm long, entire on their lower half, entire or coarsely toothed on the upper. Flowers yellow, regular, perfect, 5-parted, the sepals united into a slender tube for most of their length, strongly clove-scented, in nodding racemes when the leaves are partly grown in spring. Fruit a blackish (or sometimes yellow) berry 8 to 10 mm in diameter.

DISTRIBUTION IN IOWA Native in the Loess Hills (Novacek et al. 1985) and in south central Iowa (Eilers and Roosa 1994).

This western currant is rare as a native plant in Iowa, although you might see it in a garden or as an escape from cultivation. It is perhaps the nicest of our native currants for landscaping, producing bright yellow clove-scented flowers in early spring.

Rosa, Rose

Almost everyone recognizes a rose when they see one, especially in a garden. Many people know the wild roses, too, if for no other reason than that they're Iowa's state flower. If you take a drive in June along any country road in the state, you will likely see their showy pink flowers along the way.

When we compare our wild roses to the cultivated ones, it is hard to imagine they are even related. Garden roses are the result of careful hybridization, selected for the size, color, and fragrance of their blossoms and for flowers with extra petals. The source of this variation is the world's hundred-plus species of roses, which are amazingly diverse in their size, habit, foliage, and floral characteristics. You could easily fill a garden with just the species hardy in Iowa.

Seven of those species are native here. They range in size from dwarf prairie shrubs to a tall, almost vinelike species that can ramble up into trees. Most favor dry or well-drained places, but one is found only in wetlands and another on cold-air slopes. Even their "thorns" differ: some species produce stout curved ones resembling cat's claws, while others have slender needlelike prickles.

All the species are useful to wildlife, providing pollen for bees, fruits for birds, and even foliage for browsers (despite their prickles!). Their bright red berrylike fruits, or hips as they are often called, are also valued by people for their abundant vitamin C.

If you want to grow wild roses in your garden, try propagating them by seed. You will need to be patient, though, as the seeds will not germinate until the second spring after you sow them. Once they have established, your plants will resist drought and thrive with little attention, requiring only an annual pruning in early spring and the removal of any stray suckers that appear.

In the following descriptions, these characteristics common to all roses are not listed: leaves alternate and pinnately compound, with the stipules attached as a wing along the petiole; flowers regular, perfect, 5-parted, blooming in early summer; fruit a red berrylike hip ripening in late summer or autumn and often persisting through winter.

Rosa acicularis Lindl., Prickly Wild Rose (not illustrated)

DISTINGUISHING CHARACTERISTICS Small to medium-size colonial shrub; stems and twigs densely prickly; prickles slender and needlelike. Leaflets 5 to 7, oval to elliptic, toothed, 2.5 to 5 cm long. Margins of stipules entire, bearing stalked glands. Flowers pink, the petals 2 to 3 cm long, usually solitary, located on side branches of overwintering stems. Hips globose to ellipsoid, 1 to 2 cm long, with the sepals persisting on the end opposite the stem.

DISTRIBUTION IN IOWA Native in Allamakee, Clayton, Delaware, Dubuque, Fayette, Jackson, and Winneshiek counties.

This hardy rose grows all around the Northern Hemisphere, but it is so rare in Iowa that it is considered an endangered species here. It is another one of the many plants that grow only on algific slopes in the northeast corner of the state. If you visit northern Minnesota, you are more likely to see it there than in Iowa.

Rosa arkansana Porter, Sunshine Rose or Wild Rose

SYNONYM *R. suffulta* Greene

DISTINGUISHING CHARACTERISTICS Dwarf colonial shrub with prickly stems and twigs; prickles slender and needlelike. Leaflets 7 to 11 (usually 9), elliptic or obovate, toothed, the larger ones 3 to 5 cm long. Margins of stipules entire or with shallow gland-tipped teeth. Flowers pink, the petals 2 to 2.5 cm long, in leafy clusters, the clusters located on stems that sprouted from the ground this year or on side branches of overwintering stems. Hips globose to subglobose in shape, 1 to 1.5 cm long, with the sepals persisting on the end opposite the stem.

DISTRIBUTION IN IOWA Native in west, central, north, and parts of eastern Iowa.

If we had to choose a particular rose to be our state flower, it would probably be this one, as it is a characteristic plant of Iowa prairies, especially westward. Though much of its original habitat is now gone, it continues to thrive in what remains of the prairie and has found new places to grow along grassy roadsides and in pastures.

Sunshine rose is a true dwarf, dying back at least partway to the ground every winter and producing flowers at the ends of new canes as well as on the old ones. It shares this method of growth with the pasture rose, for which it is sometimes mistaken. Some Iowa plants are intermediate between the two and may represent hybrids between them (see Gleason 1952).

Because of its small size, sunshine rose is a good choice for native plant gardens. Suitable companion plants are leadplant, smaller grasses such as side-oats grama, and low-growing prairie wildflowers.

Rosa blanda Aiton, Smooth Wild Rose

DISTINGUISHING CHARACTERISTICS Small to medium-size colonial shrub; shoots and twigs of the current year not prickly or with a few scattered prickles; lower stems often densely prickly; prickles slender and needlelike. Leaflets mostly 7 or 9, elliptic, toothed, the larger ones 3 to 6 cm long. Stipules entire or with shallow gland-tipped teeth. Flowers pink, the petals about 2.5 cm long, in small clusters at the ends of leafy side branches of overwintering stems. Hips similar to *R. arkansana*.

DISTRIBUTION IN IOWA Native statewide.

As its common and botanical names suggest, this rose is largely devoid of prickles, though only on the newest growth. It resembles the sunshine rose in foliage and fruit but grows taller, producing its flowers and fruits only on side branches of the main stems. An adaptable species, it thrives in a variety of open habitats including prairies, roadsides, fencerows, clearings, wood edges, beaches, and railroad rights-of-way.

Smooth wild rose is useful for naturalistic landscaping and conservation plantings, for example, to cover banks or in the front of a shrub border. Its reddish stems and persistent red fruits add a touch of color in winter and early spring, especially when highlighted by the sun. Plants spread by suckering but not aggressively so, forming small colonies. A sunny site is best.

Rosa carolina L., Pasture Rose (not illustrated)

DISTINGUISHING CHARACTERISTICS Small colonial shrub. Similar to *R. arkansana* except leaflets usually 5 or 7; flowers often solitary, their stalks (pedicels) and urn-shaped bases (hypanthia) bearing stalked glands; sepals mostly deciduous in fruit.

DISTRIBUTION IN IOWA Native in east, south, and central Iowa.

Iowans from the eastern part of the state would probably select this species as our state flower, as it is common there and a very attractive dwarf shrub. Its habitats include prairie remnants, roadsides, open woods, and sandy areas. In central Iowa it overlaps in distribution with the sunshine rose, with which it apparently hybridizes.

Rosa multiflora Thunb. ex Murray, Multiflora Rose

DISTINGUISHING CHARACTERISTICS Large shrub of fountainlike habit with stout, broad-based, often curved prickles. Leaflets 5 to 9, oval to elliptic or obovate, toothed, the larger ones 3.5 to 5 cm long. Stipules divided nearly to their base into slender segments, resembling combs. Flowers white, the petals about 1 cm long, in panicles at the ends of leafy shoots. Hips globose to subglobose, 6 to 9 mm long, the sepals deciduous.

DISTRIBUTION IN IOWA Naturalized, especially eastward and southward.

This aggressive shrub was introduced to Iowa to benefit wildlife and instead has become a nuisance, invading pastures and other open areas and being difficult to remove because of its wicked spines. It is easily distinguished from our native roses by its small white flowers and, when these are absent, by the peculiar comblike appendages (stipules) on the bases of its leafstalks. It is native to Korea and Japan.

Rosa palustris Marsh., Swamp Rose (not illustrated)

DISTINGUISHING CHARACTERISTICS Medium-size to large shrub with stout, curved, broad-based prickles. Leaflets 5 to 9 (usually 7), elliptic, finely toothed, 2 to 6 cm long. Stipules very narrow. Flowers pink, in clusters, their stalks (pedicels) and urn-shaped bases (hypanthia) bearing stalked glands. Hips globose to ellipsoid, about 8 mm long, the sepals deciduous.

DISTRIBUTION IN IOWA Native in Taylor County (Eilers and Roosa 1994; Iowa DNR 2014).

Though common farther east, this rose barely makes its way into Iowa. As its names suggest, it favors wet habitats.

Rosa setigera Michx., Prairie Rose

DISTINGUISHING CHARACTERISTICS Large shrub with long arching or climbing stems; prickles stout, broad-based, often curved. Leaflets mostly 3 or 5, elliptic to oval or ovate, toothed, 3.5 to 8 cm long. Stipules very narrow. Flowers pink fading to white, the petals 2 to 3 cm long, the stalks (pedicels) and urn-shaped bases (hypanthia) bearing stalked glands, in small clusters. Hips globose, about 1 cm in diameter, the sepals deciduous.

DISTRIBUTION IN IOWA Native locally in southern and central Iowa.

The common name of this rose is a bit misleading, because it is not the familiar wild rose of Iowa prairies, though it sometimes grows on prairies. You are more likely to see it in open woods or along the edges of woods, wherever some light is available. It is a much larger shrub than our other native roses, and when nearby trees or shrubs are available for support, its long canes may clamber on them in almost vinelike fashion.

Rosa woodsii Lindl., Wild Rose (not illustrated)

SYNONYM *R. fendleri* Crépin

DISTINGUISHING CHARACTERISTICS Small to medium-size colonial shrub; prickles straight, broad-based, in pairs at the nodes, smaller and scattered between the nodes. Leaflets 5 to 9 (usually 7), elliptic to oval or obovate, toothed, 1 to 3 cm long. Stipules with gland-tipped teeth or marginal glands. Flowers pink, the petals 1.5 to 2.5 cm long, in small clusters at the ends of side branches of overwintering stems. Hips similar to *R. arkansana.*

DISTRIBUTION IN IOWA Native in the Loess Hills (Novacek et al. 1985) and in northern Iowa (Eilers and Roosa 1994).

This is a western rose that reaches the edge of its range in Iowa. The extent of its distribution here is not precisely known, as it is easy to mistake it for more common species, especially *R. blanda,* and may hybridize with them (see Smith 2008).

Rubus

The plants in this genus share a unique habit of growth, producing long canes that survive two years only, though the plants themselves may live considerably longer, continually renewing themselves by resprouting from their crowns and by suckering. The canes flower and fruit in their second year only. Individual plants have both first- and second-year canes at the same time.

The genus has hundreds of species that differ greatly in habit, foliage, and fruit. This diversity is reflected in the many common names that are applied to *Rubus*: bramble, blackberry, raspberry, dewberry, bristle-berry, cloudberry, thimbleberry. The genus is not just large but is also complex taxonomically, so identification of species can be challenging.

As a group, the species of *Rubus* are very useful to wildlife for both the cover they provide and their edible fruits. A great many birds are partial to the succulent fruits: catbirds, robins, bluebirds, thrushes, cardinals, grosbeaks, blue jays, orioles, tanagers, thrashers, waxwings, titmice, and vireos among others. Raccoons, skunks, opossums, and squirrels appreciate them, too, and rabbits and deer often browse the stems in winter.

We prepared the following annotated list of Iowa *Rubus* based on information kindly provided by Mark Widrlechner, who has studied the genus extensively in Iowa and nearby states. Any errors are, of course, our responsibility.

For information about the distinguishing characteristics of the species listed, consult the key (see page 26).

Rubus ablatus L. H. Bailey, Ablate Blackberry (not illustrated)

DISTRIBUTION IN IOWA Native in the south and parts of east and central Iowa; also collected in Emmet County. Where it is native, this species commonly encroaches upon prairies.

Rubus aboriginum Rydb., Garden Dewberry (not illustrated)

DISTRIBUTION IN IOWA Native in the south, known from Page, Taylor, and Washington counties.

Rubus allegheniensis Porter, Allegheny Blackberry

DISTRIBUTION IN IOWA Native in all but the northwest corner.

This is the most widely distributed blackberry in Iowa, growing in woods and edges across most of the state.

Rubus alumnus L. H. Bailey, Old-field Blackberry (not illustrated)

DISTRIBUTION IN IOWA Known from Dubuque, Mahaska, Muscatine, and Scott counties. Native.

Rubus caesius L., European Dewberry (not illustrated)

DISTRIBUTION IN IOWA Escaped from cultivation in Hamilton and Story counties and possibly elsewhere.

This dewberry's natural range extends from Europe east to the Altai Mountains of central Asia.

Rubus cauliflorus L. H. Bailey, Cluster-flowered Blackberry (not illustrated)

DISTRIBUTION IN IOWA Known from Linn and Mahaska counties. Native but rare in sandy soils.

Rubus celer L. H. Bailey, Rapid-growing Dewberry (not illustrated)

DISTRIBUTION IN IOWA Native in Scott County at the northwest edge of its range.

Rubus curtipes L. H. Bailey, Short-stalked Dewberry (not illustrated)

DISTRIBUTION IN IOWA Native in extreme south Iowa, collected in Ringgold and Wayne counties.

Rubus enslenii Tratt., Enslen's Dewberry (not illustrated)

DISTRIBUTION IN IOWA Known from Decatur, Des Moines, Lee, Muscatine, and Van Buren counties in south Iowa. Native.

Rubus flagellaris Willd., Northern Dewberry

DISTRIBUTION IN IOWA Native in Scott County and possibly elsewhere in the east.

Rubus frondosus Bigelow, Yankee Blackberry (not illustrated)

DISTRIBUTION IN IOWA Native in the south, east, and central parts of the state.

Rubus fulleri L. H. Bailey, Fuller's Bristly Dewberry (not illustrated)

DISTRIBUTION IN IOWA Known from Black Hawk and Linn counties. Native.

Rubus hispidus L., Bristly Dewberry (not illustrated)

DISTRIBUTION IN IOWA Clinton County. Native, at the extreme west edge of its range.

Rubus idaeus L. var. *strigosus* (Michx.) Maxim., American Red Raspberry

DISTRIBUTION IN IOWA Native in northeast and north central Iowa as far west as Emmet County.

The American red raspberry grows worldwide in northern latitudes, though the plants in Europe and Asia are slightly different from ours and are classified as variety *idaeus*. In Iowa, variety *strigosus* is confined to the northern half of the state, where it often grows in moist or sandy woods. In addition to the color of its fruits, it differs from the more common black raspberry in having bristles instead of prickles and in its canes not arching all the way to the ground.

Rubus leviculus L. H. Bailey, Bottomland Dewberry (not illustrated)

DISTRIBUTION IN IOWA Native in the southeast, known from historical collections from Henry, Jefferson, Wapello, and Washington counties.

Rubus meracus L. H. Bailey, Dry-slope Dewberry (not illustrated)

DISTRIBUTION IN IOWA Native in the south, known from Decatur, Jasper, Jefferson, Lucas, Monroe, Muscatine, Polk, and Wapello counties.

Rubus missouricus L. H. Bailey, Missouri Bristleberry (not illustrated)

DISTRIBUTION IN IOWA Native in the south and extreme east, known from Clarke, Clinton, Decatur, Henry, Mahaska, Ringgold, Scott, Taylor, and Wayne counties.

Rubus ×*neglectus* Peck, Purple Raspberry (not illustrated)

DISTRIBUTION IN IOWA Known from Allamakee, Bremer, Franklin, Hamilton, Marshall, and Winneshiek counties.

This hybrid between the black and the red raspberries has been found in the wild in several counties in northeast and central Iowa, typically where the two parental species grow in proximity.

Rubus occidentalis L., Black Raspberry

DISTRIBUTION IN IOWA Native throughout.

Black raspberry grows almost everywhere in Iowa that is not cultivated or regularly mowed, especially where there is ample light. Old fields, open woods, clearings, and edges are a few of its favored habitats. It is easily identified by its long arching prickly canes, which touch the ground and root at their tips, and which in winter stand out with their purplish bark more or less coated with white wax.

Rubus odoratus L., Purple-flowering Raspberry (not illustrated)

DISTRIBUTION IN IOWA Introduced from eastern North America and naturalized in Wapello County.

Rubus parvifolius L., Asian Red Raspberry (not illustrated)

DISTRIBUTION IN IOWA Escaped from cultivation in scattered localities around the state. Introduced from China and Japan.

This species is becoming a serious invader of prairies and savannas.

Rubus plicatifolius Blanchard, Plait-leaved Dewberry (not illustrated)

DISTRIBUTION IN IOWA Native in south central and extreme eastern Iowa, known from Cedar, Clinton, Dubuque, Jasper, Jones, Lucas, Muscatine, Scott, and Wayne counties.

Rubus praecox Bertol., Precocious Blackberry (not illustrated)

DISTRIBUTION IN IOWA No populations currently known but formerly growing as an escape from cultivation in Story County.

Rubus pubescens Raf., Dwarf Raspberry (not illustrated)

DISTRIBUTION IN IOWA Native in northeast and east central Iowa.

The flowering stems of this species are herbaceous, arising from the crown of the plant and from trailing stems. It grows in cool, moist habitats in Iowa.

Rubus recurvans L. H. Bailey, Recurved Blackberry (not illustrated)

DISTRIBUTION IN IOWA Mitchell County at the southwest edge of its natural range.

Rubus roribaccus (L. H. Bailey) Rydb., Lucretia Dewberry (not illustrated)

DISTRIBUTION IN IOWA Native in south central, southeast, and east central Iowa.

Rubus rosa L. H. Bailey, Rose Blackberry (not illustrated)

DISTRIBUTION IN IOWA Native in eastern Iowa, also collected in Pottawattamie County.

Rubus satis L. H. Bailey, Mounding Dewberry (not illustrated)

DISTRIBUTION IN IOWA Allamakee and Polk counties. Native.

Rubus semisetosus Blanchard, Swamp Bristleberry (not illustrated)

DISTRIBUTION IN IOWA Known from Bremer County. Native.

Rubus steelei L. H. Bailey, Steele's Dewberry (not illustrated)

DISTRIBUTION IN IOWA Native in the eastern part of the state, known from Allamakee, Appanoose, Bremer, Clinton, Jones, Marion, and Wapello counties.

Rubus stipulatus L. H. Bailey, Big Horseshoe Lake Bristleberry (not illustrated)

DISTRIBUTION IN IOWA Formerly native in Scott County, probably extirpated.

Rubus uniformis L. H. Bailey, Uniform Bristleberry (not illustrated)

DISTRIBUTION IN IOWA Mitchell County at the south edge of its native range.

Rubus wisconsinensis L. H. Bailey, Wisconsin Bristleberry (not illustrated)

DISTRIBUTION IN IOWA Known from Mitchell, Hamilton, Hardin, and Winneshiek counties. Native.

Salix, Willow

The willows are among Iowa's most familiar woody plants, found wherever the land is low and wet and sometimes in other habitats, too. Twelve species are native here, including two that are medium-size trees. Some of the shrubby species are very rare, restricted to special habitats in the northern part of the state.

Some willows are easily identified by their very distinctive leaves, but others are perhaps best distinguished by their flowers, which unfortunately are present for only a brief time, the male and female on separate plants. The flowers are individually very small, greenish or yellow in color, and arranged in elongated clusters called catkins. In some species the catkins appear in late spring or summer at the ends of leafy shoots, while in others they develop directly from overwintering buds, either before the leaves appear or as the leaves are just expanding. In their earliest stage, as they are just emerging from the buds, catkins are the pussies so popular as spring decorations.

Willows are useful for conservation plantings in wet areas, and a few are desirable for naturalistic landscaping. Among their many benefits, they provide shelter and nesting cover for birds, browse for deer and other animals, and food for native insects, including the caterpillars of several butterflies. Early-blooming species such as the pussy willow and prairie willow are an important source of pollen for bees.

Characteristics that willows have in common are not included in the following descriptions. All have alternate, simple leaves. Their flowers are small, apetalous, and unisexual, each consisting of a single pistil or 2 to 7 stamens with a small scalelike bract at its base. The flowers are arranged in catkins, with the staminate and the pistillate catkins on different plants. The small greenish, bottle-shaped capsules, which closely resemble the pistils from which they develop, release their tiny cottony seeds during the late spring or summer.

Salix bebbiana Sarg., Bebb's Willow (not illustrated)

DISTINGUISHING CHARACTERISTICS Large shrub. Leaf blades elliptic to ovate, 4 to 9 cm long, entire or with a few short and widely spaced teeth, light green or grayish green and hairy underneath. Catkins appearing as the leaves are developing or shortly before, with a straw-colored bract at the base of each flower (*S. discolor* and *S. eriocephala* have brown or blackish bracts).

DISTRIBUTION IN IOWA Native in northeast and north central Iowa.

This northern willow is uncommon in Iowa, inhabiting low prairies, fens, and cool, moist slopes in some of our northern and central counties. It is one of our most handsome willows and, though rarely planted, has potential for conservation plantings and naturalistic landscaping. It usually grows as a large multi-stemmed shrub but can be trained as a small tree.

Bebb's willow blooms early, either just before its leaves appear or as they are beginning to grow. Like other willows, its male flowers are quite attractive with their bright yellow stamens. The grayish green female flowers are beautiful, too, but in a subtle way, adding an interesting color to their surroundings during the brief time they're in bloom.

Salix candida Flueggé, Sage Willow (not illustrated)

DISTINGUISHING CHARACTERISTICS Small to medium-size shrub. Leaf blades narrowly elliptic to linear, 3 to 10 cm long, entire, conspicuously white-woolly beneath. Catkins appearing as the leaves are developing or just before.

DISTRIBUTION IN IOWA Native in the northeast part of the state west to Hancock County and south to Johnson County, also reported from Emmet County.

If you encounter this rare willow in a fen or wet prairie, you will have no doubt as to identity, as its leaves are quite striking: long, narrow, without teeth, and coated with white feltlike hairs below. It is a shorter shrub than most other willows, growing only a few feet tall. Its main range is far to the north of Iowa, in Canada and the Great Lakes region.

Salix discolor Muhl., Pussy Willow

DISTINGUISHING CHARACTERISTICS Large shrub. Leaf blades oval to oblong, sometimes widest above the middle, acute, glabrous, 3 to 9 cm long, usually with widely spaced teeth along the margins, their lower surface thinly coated with a pale waxy material (glaucous). Stipules very small (about 1 mm long), sometimes larger on vigorous shoots. Catkins appearing before the leaves.

DISTRIBUTION IN IOWA Native throughout most of the northern three-fourths of the state.

This willow is well known for the soft furry pussies on its spring branches, but it is not the only willow that produces them. The pussy willows grown in gardens or sold by florists are often another species, for example, the goat willow, *S. caprea* L., or gray willow, *S. cinerea* L., both introduced from Eurasia.

Pussy willow grows in a variety of wet sites including marshes, low prairies, lakeshores, stream banks, and ditches. Its adaptability and attractive catkins make it suitable for conservation plantings and naturalistic landscaping in moist, open sites. Regular renewal pruning keeps it from growing too large and creates the vigorous new growth that produces the largest buds and catkins.

Salix eriocephala Michx., Rigid Willow or Heart-leaved Willow

SYNONYMS *S. rigida* Muhl., *S. cordata* Muhl.

DISTINGUISHING CHARACTERISTICS Large shrub. Leaf blades lanceolate, tapered to a slender tip, 4 to 12.5 cm long, closely and finely toothed, their lower surface thinly coated with a pale waxy material (glaucous). Stipules leafy, conspicuous, up to about 1.5 cm long, persisting on shoots during summer. Catkins appearing as the leaves are developing or shortly before.

DISTRIBUTION IN IOWA Native throughout the state.

It would be helpful if this common willow had a name that was truly descriptive; it is not especially rigid, nor are its leaves heart-shaped. It is in fact a variable and rather nondescript shrub easily confused with other willows, its persistent stipules being perhaps its most consistent and reliable feature. Habitats include streambanks, shores of lakes and ponds, ditches, and other wet places.

Salix humilis Marsh., Prairie Willow

DISTINGUISHING CHARACTERISTICS Small to medium-size shrub. Leaf blades broadly oblanceolate or narrowly oblong, 3 to 8.5 cm long, densely hairy beneath, their margins usually entire but sometimes wavy or with widely spaced teeth. Stipules small, mostly 2 to 5 mm long, sometimes absent. Catkins small, appearing before the leaves.

DISTRIBUTION IN IOWA Native throughout the state.

This attractive shrub could be mistaken for a miniature pussy willow, especially early in the season when its catkins appear. As its name suggests, it is most commonly seen on prairie remnants, though not necessarily on moist ones. You can also find it on dunes, loess bluffs, and other upland sites, often where the woods and prairie come together. Like other prairie plants, it is adapted to fire and will resprout vigorously after being burned (Smith 2008).

Though not much planted, prairie willow is an excellent choice for naturalistic landscaping, for example, on the sunny edge of a shrub border or in a garden of dwarf shrubs and perennials. The plants are not much more than waist-high but can eventually grow quite wide, so be sure to give them plenty of space.

Salix interior Rowlee, Sandbar Willow

SYNONYM *S. exigua* Nutt. subsp. *interior* (Rowlee) Cronq.

DISTINGUISHING CHARACTERISTICS Tall colonial shrub or small tree. Leaf blades linear, 4 to 12 cm long, nearly sessile, green on both surfaces, with widely spaced teeth along their margins. Catkins appearing on leafy shoots in late spring or early summer.

DISTRIBUTION IN IOWA Native throughout the state.

This is probably our most common willow and, with its exceptionally narrow leaves and distinctive method of growth, one of the easiest to identify. As suggested by its name, sandbars in rivers are a common habitat. Look for it also along streambanks and the shores of lakes and ponds and in wetlands, low prairies, marshes, and ditches, almost anywhere there is plenty of sun and ample moisture.

Most of our willows produce multiple stems from a single crown, but sandbar willow suckers outward to form colonies. As it grows taller, its stems become polelike with foliage mostly near the end. The thickets are especially noticeable in winter, when the reddish brown twigs are not obscured by the leaves. The species is useful for both erosion control and wildlife habitat along streams.

Salix lucida Muhl., Shining Willow

DISTINGUISHING CHARACTERISTICS Large shrub. Leaf blades narrowly elliptic to broadly lanceolate, tapered to a long slender tip, 8 to 13 cm long, finely toothed, green and glabrous underneath. Catkins appearing as the leaves are developing, on short leafy shoots.

DISTRIBUTION IN IOWA Native in the north as far west as Buena Vista, Clay, and Dickinson counties, also reported from Guthrie County.

This tall northern willow grows in wet habitats in the north part of Iowa. It is easily recognized by its leaves, which are broadly lance-shaped, with glossy upper surfaces, and have long tail-like tips. Because of its scarcity, it is included on our state list of threatened species.

Salix pedicellaris Pursh, Bog Willow (not illustrated)

DISTINGUISHING CHARACTERISTICS Small shrub. Leaf blades narrowly elliptic to oblong, 2.5 to 7 cm long, entire, often blunt-tipped, light green and glabrous underneath. Catkins small, appearing as the leaves are developing.

DISTRIBUTION IN IOWA Native in northeast and north central Iowa, also reported from Emmet County.

This species, listed as threatened by the state, grows in northern Iowa fens. It is a low shrub with distinctive small, broad leaves that are rounded or blunt at the tips.

Salix petiolaris J. E. Smith, Meadow Willow

DISTINGUISHING CHARACTERISTICS Large shrub. Leaf blades lanceolate to linear-lanceolate (4 to 7 times longer than wide), 4 to 10 cm long, usually toothed but not closely so, the lower surface thinly coated with a pale waxy material (glaucous). Catkins appearing as the leaves are developing or just before.

DISTRIBUTION IN IOWA
Native in eastern and north central Iowa.

This tall, narrow-leaved willow is common in the northern part of the state, less so elsewhere in its Iowa range. Habitats include low prairies, fens, marsh edges, and wet depressions.

Salix sericea Marsh., Silky Willow (not illustrated)

DISTINGUISHING CHARACTERISTICS Large shrub. Leaf blades lanceolate, 6 to 10 cm long, closely toothed, their lower surface covered with straight appressed hairs pointing in one direction. Catkins appearing before the leaves.

DISTRIBUTION IN IOWA Native locally in eastern Iowa.

This rare willow is named for the silky hairs on the undersides of its leaves. It grows in low, wet places in a few eastern Iowa counties.

Sambucus, Elderberry

The elderberries comprise a small genus that is widely distributed in both the Eastern and the Western hemispheres. Most species are shrubs, a few herbs or small trees. Their stout, pithy, and rather brittle stems are a characteristic feature. Many small birds eat their berries, including the rose-breasted grosbeak, bluebird, robin, catbird, brown thrasher, veery, red-bellied woodpecker, and wood thrush.

Two elderberries are native in Iowa. Each has a Eurasian counterpart resembling it so closely that the "twins" are often listed as subspecies of a single species. When they are viewed this way, the botanical name of the Eurasian species is used because it was published earlier and thus has priority under the rules of nomenclature.

Sambucus canadensis L., Common Elderberry

SYNONYM *S. nigra* L. subsp. *canadensis* (L.) R. Bolli

DISTINGUISHING CHARACTERISTICS Medium-size to large shrub. Leaves pinnately compound, opposite; leaflets 5 to 9 (mostly 7), elliptic to ovate-lanceolate or lanceolate, tapered to a slender tip, 4 to 11 cm long, toothed. Flowers white, regular, perfect, 5-parted, about 6 mm across, in large corymb-like cymes at the tips of the branches, blooming in early to midsummer. Fruit a dark purple berry about 0.5 cm in diameter, ripening in late summer.

DISTRIBUTION IN IOWA Native throughout the state.

When it blooms in early to midsummer, the common elderberry is a conspicuous sight in ditches, in low woods, along shorelines, and in other moist habitats across Iowa. Its flowers are individually very small but are grouped in showy clusters of up to several hundred blossoms. The purplish berries that follow are much enjoyed by birds.

Elderberry is a good choice for conservation plantings and shrub borders, mixing well with other tall shrubs such as dogwoods and viburnums. Regular pruning is needed to keep it vigorous and attractive.

Sambucus pubens Michx., Red Elderberry

SYNONYM *S. racemosa* L. subsp. *pubens* (Michx.) House

DISTINGUISHING CHARACTERISTICS Medium-size to large shrub. Leaves pinnately compound, opposite; leaflets 5 or sometimes 7 in number, elliptic to oblong, tapered to a slender tip, 7 to 14 cm long, toothed. Flowers and fruits similar to *S. canadensis* except cymes tall and paniclelike; flowers blooming in spring; fruits red.

DISTRIBUTION IN IOWA Native in the northeastern corner of the state south to Jackson County.

This tall northern shrub just reaches Iowa, inhabiting cool woods in our northeast corner. It is not hard to grow and, if you like native plants, it is well worth trying in a naturalistic garden or landscape. Its bright red fruits are quite attractive in late summer and easily distinguish it from the common elderberry then.

Shepherdia

This is a genus of three North American species, easily recognized by their foliage. One species is native in western Iowa.

Shepherdia argentea (Pursh) Nutt., Buffaloberry

DISTINGUISHING CHARACTERISTICS Large colonial shrub, often thorny. Leaves simple, opposite; blades elliptic to oblong with blunt or rounded tips, 2.5 to 6.5 cm long, entire, coated with minute silver and brown scales beneath, dotted with minute silver scales above. Flowers yellowish, regular, apetalous, about 4 mm across, with 4 petal-like sepals united at their base and minutely scaly on the outside, unisexual with the staminate and the pistillate on separate plants, in small clusters from overwintering buds, blooming in spring. Fruit a red drupe about 7 mm long, ripening in summer.

DISTRIBUTION IN IOWA Native in the Loess Hills from Harrison County north to Plymouth County. There is also a small native population in Estherville in Emmet County.

This distinctive shrub reaches the east edge of its range in Iowa and is considered a threatened species here. Most of our native plants occur in the Loess Hills, whose dry slopes provide an environment similar to the western prairies where the species is more common. Individual plants often resemble small trees, though they typically spread laterally via suckers. The male and the female flowers occur on different plants, so only some bear the bright red berries that are a hallmark of the species.

When cultivating buffaloberry, it is best to provide a sunny well-drained location. It is not the easiest species to manage in a landscape, with its often thorny branches and tendency to colonize.

Smilax

This is a large and widely distributed genus with both woody and herbaceous species. Three are native in Iowa, including the following woody vine.

Smilax tamnoides L. var. *hispida* Fern., Greenbrier

SYNONYM *S. hispida* Muhl. ex Torr.

DISTINGUISHING CHARACTERISTICS Prickly vine with green stems, climbing by means of coiling tendrils developed from the leaf stipules. Leaves simple, alternate; blades broadly ovate to nearly round, mostly 6 to 12 cm long, entire, with the main veins meeting in a common point at the base. Flowers greenish, regular, 6-parted, about 0.5 cm wide, unisexual with the staminate and the pistillate on separate plants, in long-stalked umbels from the axils of the leaves, blooming in late spring or early summer. Fruit a blackish berry about 1 cm in diameter, ripening in late summer or autumn.

DISTRIBUTION IN IOWA Native throughout the state.

This vine is a familiar sight in Iowa woodlands, especially in bottomlands. With its bright green prickly stems, it is easy to recognize even in winter. Its small greenish flowers are unisexual, with the male and the female on different plants. Female plants develop grapelike berries in characteristic round umbels. The fruits are eaten by catbirds, robins, thrushes, raccoons, opossums, and other wildlife.

Greenbrier is noteworthy as our only woody member of the monocots, a large group of flowering plants that have parallel-veined leaves and woody bundles rather than typical wood inside their stems. Other familiar monocots are the grasses, sedges, lilies, and palms.

Solanum

Solanum is a very large genus of both woody and herbaceous plants, most of them indigenous to warmer parts of the world. One species, the potato, is an important crop; some others are notoriously poisonous. Iowa's flora includes three native herbs and the following woody vine, which was introduced from the Old World.

Solanum dulcamara L., Bittersweet Nightshade

DISTINGUISHING CHARACTERISTICS Vine climbing by twisting stems, without tendrils or aerial roots, emitting a distinctive unpleasant odor when bruised. Leaves simple or appearing compound, alternate; blades ovate, often deeply lobed at the base with 1 or 2 pairs of lobes smaller than the rest of the blade, 6 to 8 cm long, their margins entire. Flowers purple, regular, perfect, 5-parted, 1 to 1.5 cm long, with swept-back petals and a cone of yellow stamens, in small cymes at the tips of the shoots or in the axils of the leaves, blooming in summer. Fruit a red berry about 1 cm long, ripening in summer or autumn.

DISTRIBUTION IN IOWA Naturalized locally.

This introduced plant is barely woody, its ropy stems usually sprawling on the ground, at other times climbing on low objects such as shrubs and fences. Birds disperse it from place to place by feeding on its bright red berries, which are reputedly poisonous to people. Once established, the plants spread by sending up new stems from their wide-spreading roots. When uprooted or disturbed, they emit a characteristic foul odor.

Bittersweet nightshade is sometimes called the European bittersweet, although it is not related to the true bittersweets, which belong to the genus *Celastrus*. It is potentially invasive and should be removed from natural areas when found.

Spiraea, Spirea

This is a genus of about a hundred species, found worldwide in north temperate areas but especially diverse in Asia. Most are small to medium-size shrubs. In central Asia they are a characteristic component of the shrub-steppe, a prairie-like habitat of grasses, wildflowers, and dwarf shrubs, filling the same ecological niche as leadplant, New Jersey tea, and wild roses on our own prairies.

Spireas are among the most useful woody plants for landscaping: attractive, easy to grow, and fitting well in small spaces. A sunny site is best. Most produce white flowers in spring, though some are summer-blooming, including a few with purplish flowers. To keep them compact and tidy, give them an annual renewal pruning and heading back in early spring.

Spiraea alba Du Roi, Meadowsweet

DISTINGUISHING CHARACTERISTICS Small to medium-size shrub. Leaves simple, alternate; blades narrowly elliptic, 3 to 7 cm long, toothed. Flowers white, regular, perfect, 5-parted, 5 to 7 mm across, in dense upright panicles at the tips of the stems, blooming in mid to late summer. Fruit a brown follicle 2 to 3 mm long, arranged in a compact sessile cluster of 4 to 6 (usually 5) fruits at the end of each branch of the panicle, each cluster resembling a small capsule; follicles each splitting open along 1 seam, persisting on the twigs in winter.

DISTRIBUTION IN IOWA Native locally in north, east, and central Iowa.

Our only native spirea is easily mistaken for an herbaceous plant, with its slender wandlike stems resembling those of goldenrod and its penchant for growing with grasses, sedges, and wildflowers in moist open places. It is most easily spotted in summer, when its attractive clusters of tiny white flowers appear. Though seldom cultivated, it could be tried in naturalistic landscapes, wetland restorations, and pollinator gardens.

Staphylea, Bladdernut

The bladdernuts are a small genus of Eurasian and North American species, recognizable by their trifoliate or pinnate leaves and curious bladderlike pods. One species is native in Iowa.

Staphylea trifolia L., Bladdernut

DISTINGUISHING CHARACTERISTICS Large colonial shrub. Leaves compound, opposite; leaflets 3, oval to elliptic, 4 to 10 cm long, finely toothed, the terminal (middle) one long-stalked. Flowers greenish white, bell-shaped, regular, perfect, 5-parted, about 1 cm long, in drooping panicles at the ends of short leafy shoots in spring. Fruit a drooping bladderlike capsule with papery walls, brown when ripe, about 4 cm long, persisting on the branches into winter.

DISTRIBUTION IN IOWA Native across most of the state.

Bladdernut is one of those native shrubs that is common but not well known, perhaps because it frequents deep woods and is rarely planted. Look for it in cool, moist habitats such as ravines, the lower parts of north- and east-facing slopes, and terraces. Once you know it, you can easily find it even in winter, as its green twigs, white-streaked purplish branchlets, and persistent seed pods are distinctive.

In May bladdernut produces small, bell-shaped, green and white flowers, which are followed by inflated papery pods that change from green to brown as they mature. Inside are brown seeds resembling small popcorn kernels, which often break loose and rattle when the pods are shaken. Seeds collected and stratified in the fall will germinate in their second spring.

Where its colonizing isn't a concern, bladdernut is a nice shrub for naturalistic landscaping and woodland restoration. A site that is moist throughout the growing season is best. Bladdernut can grow quite tall, and if you don't mind removing suckers when they appear, it can be trained as a small tree.

Symphoricarpos

This is a genus of low-growing colonial shrubs, closely related to the honeysuckles (*Lonicera*) and with very similar foliage. As their common names suggest, some have very colorful berries. All but one of the species is indigenous to North America. Three are native in Iowa.

Our native *Symphoricarpos* are all easy to grow and, in the right setting, useful for conservation plantings and landscaping. While small in height, all spread horizontally by suckering, eventually covering a larger area than might have been anticipated. Their berries are eaten by grouse, quail, robins, and other birds.

Symphoricarpos albus (L.) Blake, Snowberry (not illustrated)

DISTINGUISHING CHARACTERISTICS Similar to *S. occidentalis* except leaves smaller with petioles 3 mm long or less, fruits white.

DISTRIBUTION IN IOWA Native in Allamakee and Clayton counties, occasionally escaped from cultivation elsewhere.

Snowberry is a wide-ranging northern and western species that is named for its showy fruit. It just reaches the northeast corner of Iowa, where it inhabits rocky ledges and bluffs. Plants that grow in western North America, var. *laevigatus* (Fern.) Blake, have especially attractive berries and are usually preferred for landscaping.

Symphoricarpos occidentalis Hooker, Wolfberry

DISTINGUISHING CHARACTERISTICS Small colonial shrub; pith of twigs usually hollow. Leaves simple, opposite; blades oval, 3.5 to 7 cm long, their margins entire or with a few large blunt to rounded teeth. Flowers pinkish white, slightly irregular, perfect, 5-parted, the petals united at their base, 1 to 1.5 cm across, in small, short-stalked clusters from the axils of the upper leaves, blooming in early to midsummer. Fruit a greenish white berry, eventually turning black and remaining on the shrub through winter.

DISTRIBUTION IN IOWA Native in northern and western Iowa, occasionally seen elsewhere.

This is a common shrub of the prairie-forest border, often forming large colonies. It is a good choice for planting on dry sunny sites, for example, to cover a bank or fill a bed. In nature it is quite dwarf, but in the more favorable conditions of cultivation it can reach shoulder-high. As with other *Symphoricarpos*, it should be planted only where its suckering can be contained or ignored.

Symphoricarpos orbiculatus Moench, Coralberry

DISTINGUISHING CHARACTERISTICS Small colonial shrub; pith of twigs solid. Leaves simple, opposite; blades oval, mostly 2.5 to 5 cm long, entire. Flowers yellowish white or purplish, bell-shaped, perfect, 5-parted, the petals united at the base and 3 to 4 mm long, in small dense clusters from the axils of the upper leaves, blooming in late summer. Fruit a pink or red berry 3 to 4 mm in diameter, ripening in autumn and persisting in winter.

DISTRIBUTION IN IOWA Native in southern and central Iowa and in the Loess Hills north to Woodbury County.

Coralberry is named for its bright red to coral fruits, which easily distinguish it from our other native *Symphoricarpos*. It grows in a variety of open to partly shaded habitats, including banks, clearings, wooded pastures, old fields, edges, prairies, and rights-of-way. In naturalistic settings it is a good shrub for landscaping.

Taxus, Yew

The yews are a small but widespread genus of evergreen shrubs and trees, long valued as ornamentals because of their beautiful foliage. Their most distinctive feature is their seed, which is borne in a red fleshy, cuplike structure on the female plants. Otherwise they can be easily mistaken for one of the cone-bearing trees such as hemlock or fir.

One species of yew is native in Iowa. Most cultivated plants are nonnatives, such as the Japanese yew, *T. cuspidata* Sieb. & Zucc., and its hybrid with the English yew, *T. baccata* L. The foliage of all species is reputedly poisonous, although deer browse them preferentially and don't seem any worse for the experience. Children should not have access to the seeds, which contain a potent alkaloid that affects the heart (Kingsbury 1965).

Taxus canadensis Marsh., Canada Yew

DISTINGUISHING CHARACTERISTICS Low shrub with wide-spreading branches. Leaves simple, alternate, evergreen; blades linear, 1.5 to 2 cm long, entire, abruptly tapered to a slender point. Reproductive parts in small unisexual cones that appear in the axils of the leaves in spring, the male and the female on separate plants; male cones yellowish, falling soon after shedding their pollen; female cones greenish at first, later bright red, fleshy, cup-shaped, 0.5 to 1 cm long, with a single dark seed visible in the opening.

DISTRIBUTION IN IOWA Native in east Iowa.

If you know yews as landscape plants, you might be surprised when meeting this one in the wild. Cultivated *Taxus* are often tall, substantial shrubs, even small trees. Canada yew is a spreader, growing only a few feet high but many times that wide.

To see this handsome shrub in Iowa, you will need to explore rugged wooded terrain in the eastern part of the state. Unfortunately its populations were healthier in the past than they are today, because of browsing by our now much larger deer herd. In some locales it is limited to rocky ledges where the deer can't reach.

Though not commonly cultivated in Iowa, Canada yew is a nice groundcover in moist, cool, shady locations. Well-drained soil is a must, and there is no point in planting it where deer are known to roam.

Toxicodendron

It is unlikely that any genus of plants has caused as much misery as this one, at least in North America, where it is distributed the most widely. It is often considered part of the genus *Rhus*, but it is certainly appropriate to list it separately, as it differs in both its whitish fruits and its noxious qualities.

The "poison" in *Toxicodendron* is a skin-irritating substance called urushiol. People get it on their skin by either touching the plants or contacting something else that has, such as dogs, tools, boots, clothing, or even the smoke of burning plants. Though everyone is not equally affected, a person's seeming immunity can vanish with increased exposure, so it is best not to take chances with these plants.

Two species of the genus are native in Iowa, both called poison ivy. Two others occur to our east and south: poison sumac, *T. vernix* (L.) Kuntze, which comes as close as Minnesota and Wisconsin, and poison oak, *T. quercifolium* Greene, which grows in the southeast. Reports of the latter in Iowa are most certainly cases of mistaken identity, resulting from the sometimes oaklike shape of poison ivy leaves.

Because *Toxicodendron* species are harmful to us, we instinctively regard them as bad and do our best to eradicate them. Their absence would be unfortunate for wildlife, however, which uses them to a greater extent than most people realize. Their fruits persist into winter and are eaten by many kinds of birds, including pheasants, quail, woodpeckers, chickadees, bluebirds, juncos, and native sparrows. Some animals even browse their twigs and foliage!

Toxicodendron radicans (L.) Kuntze subsp. *negundo* (Greene) Gillis, Poison Ivy

DISTINGUISHING CHARACTERISTICS Plant with one of two growth forms: (1) vine climbing with aerial rootlets or (2) large colonial shrub; in both forms with long, often horizontal branches. Otherwise similar to *T. rydbergii.*

DISTRIBUTION IN IOWA Native across much of the state; see the following discussion.

People are sometimes surprised to learn that the poison ivies are woody plants that can be encountered year round. This species grows as a high-climbing vine or tall upright shrub, in either case producing long horizontal branches. When climbing it adheres tightly to the trunks of trees, using rootlets growing out of the stem. Though found in diverse habitats, it tends to be associated with established woods and is thus more prevalent in the south, east, and central parts of the state where that habitat occurs.

Toxicodendron rydbergii (Small) Greene, Western Poison Ivy (not illustrated)

DISTINGUISHING CHARACTERISTICS Dwarf shrub often forming large patches on the ground; stems growing up to about waist-high, either unbranched or with a few short branches. Leaves compound, alternate; leaflets 3, broadly ovate or oval to nearly round, sometimes asymmetric, 4 to 20 cm long, the terminal (center) 1 on a much longer stalk than the other 2, the margins entire or with a few large teeth. Flowers similar to those of sumacs (*Rhus*) but in more open panicles, blooming in early summer. Fruit a yellowish white drupe about 0.5 cm in diameter, ripening in late summer to early autumn and persisting in winter.

DISTRIBUTION IN IOWA Native, especially northward.

This species is a true dwarf, seldom growing more than knee-high. Unlike the preceding species, it is very sparsely branched, and any branches present are very short. Incredibly adaptable and tough, it grows in all kinds of habitats. Like its close relatives the sumacs, it often forms large patches by sprouting from underground stems.

Vaccinium

This is a large genus found all around the Northern Hemisphere, mostly in cool regions but extending into lower latitudes on mountain chains. It is part of the large and distinctive heath family, Ericaceae, which also includes the rhododendrons, azaleas, and heathers. In an interesting ecological twist, plants in the family share more than just their botanical features: they also need acid soils. This limits their distribution to certain geographic regions and habitats, for example, sandy areas and sphagnum bogs. In such places they are often dominant plants.

Vaccinium species are diverse in growth form and size, ranging from dwarf trailing shrubs to small trees. Some, such as the cranberry and blueberries, are important economically. Two species are native in Iowa, though rare.

The fruits of these native blueberries are very small, in keeping with the diminutive size of the plants themselves. Most of the blueberries sold in stores come from the so-called highbush blueberries, which are cultivars and hybrids of *V. corymbosum* L., a species native to the eastern U.S. These can be cultivated in Iowa but it does take a special effort, as they are more particular about soil than other small fruits. For more information on how to grow them, see Jauron 2013.

Vaccinium angustifolium Aiton, Lowbush Blueberry

DISTINGUISHING CHARACTERISTICS Dwarf colonial shrub; twigs slender, dotted with numerous tiny warts (seen with magnifying glass). Leaves simple, alternate; blades elliptic, 2 to 4 cm long, their margins with tiny inconspicuous teeth (best seen with magnifying glass), their veins dividing and forming a network near the margin. Flowers white or light pink, urn-shaped, regular, perfect, 5-parted, the petals united for most of their length and about 0.5 cm long, in small dense racemes from overwintering buds, blooming when the leaves are partly grown in spring. Fruit resembling cultivated blueberries but smaller, ripening in summer.

DISTRIBUTION IN IOWA Native in Allamakee, Clayton, and Jones counties.

This is the common blueberry of the North Woods, much appreciated among those who reside in or visit that region. It just barely ranges into the state of Iowa, inhabiting sandy woods in three of our eastern counties. It seems ironic that a plant so abundant in Minnesota could be listed by our state as threatened.

Vaccinium myrtilloides Michx., Velvetleaf Blueberry

DISTINGUISHING CHARACTERISTICS Similar to *V. angustifolium* except margins of leaf blades entire and hairy.

DISTRIBUTION IN IOWA Native in Allamakee and Clayton counties.

This is another northern blueberry that just reaches Iowa's northeast corner. It closely resembles *V. angustifolium*, often grows with it, and is also listed by our state as threatened.

Viburnum

This genus is remarkably diverse, as suggested by its many common names: arrowwood, blackhaw, cranberry-bush, nannyberry, wayfaring tree, and wild raisin, among others. There are more than a hundred species worldwide, distributed over a wide area in both the Old World and the New. Most are very attractive shrubs and, being easy to grow, they are excellent choices for landscaping.

A common feature of the viburnums is their small white flowers, which appear in showy branched clusters at the ends of the branches in spring. Their foliage is more varied, with some species having lobed leaves resembling maples, others producing roundish leaves edged with large teeth, and still others having finely toothed oval leaves like those of cherries or plums. The leaves can be very colorful in autumn, often turning late in the season. Shades of purple and purple-red predominate, sometimes mixed with yellow. If you frequent the outdoors in fall, you may also note the distinctive foxy odor that some species produce.

The fruits of viburnums are attractive in autumn, too: blue, bright red, or nearly black, depending on the species. Each has a single large seed inside. These are eaten and dispersed by birds including grouse, pheasants, cardinals, robins, starlings, waxwings, and thrushes.

Viburnums can be divided into several groups based on characteristics of their leaves, buds, and fruits. The four groups described below each have at least one wild species in Iowa. Additional viburnum groups are represented here by cultivated species only.

The leatherleaf viburnums have thick leathery leaves that are often evergreen or persistent in winter and not obviously toothed. Tiny star-shaped hairs are present on their twigs and foliage, and their buds are naked. Their fruits are nearly black when ripe, though sometimes red in their earlier stages. There is one species in Iowa, *V. lantana.*

The highbush-cranberries, also called cranberry-bushes, have lobed leaves and two-scaled buds. Their bright red fruits add much color to the winter landscape and, because they are not preferred by birds, often persist through much of the season. Species in Iowa are *V. opulus* and *V. trilobum.*

The arrowwoods are a large group, and in some cases their taxonomy is problematic. The leaves are lobed or coarsely toothed, with the veins running straight into the tips of the teeth. The buds have four scales, and the fruits are blue to nearly black. Species include *V. acerifolium, V. dentatum, V. molle,* and *V. rafinesquianum.*

The blackhaws have finely toothed leaves with the veins dividing and forming a network near the margin. Their buds have two scales, and their fruits are nearly black. Species in Iowa are *V. lentago* and *V. prunifolium.*

Viburnum acerifolium L., Mapleleaf Viburnum (not illustrated)

DISTINGUISHING CHARACTERISTICS Medium-size to large shrub; buds with 4 scales, the outer pair much shorter than the inner. Leaves simple, opposite; blades 3-lobed and maplelike, 4 to 9 cm long, toothed. Flowers and fruits similar to *V. rafinesquianum.*

DISTRIBUTION IN IOWA Wild and presumably native in Allamakee County.

Mapleleaf viburnum is a characteristic shrub of eastern U.S. woodlands but was only recently discovered in Iowa. We don't know why no one noticed it here before; possibly it was overlooked because it is rare and its leaves are similar to other species. Or perhaps birds dispersed it here only recently.

Viburnum dentatum L., Southern Arrowwood (not illustrated)

DISTINGUISHING CHARACTERISTICS Similar to *V. rafinesquianum* except petioles longer relative to the blades, stipules usually absent.

DISTRIBUTION IN IOWA Planted and sometimes escaping (see below).

This is a variable viburnum and one of the most frequently planted. It is naturalizing in some Iowa localities, including the Ames area and around Lake of Three Fires State Park in Taylor County (Mark Widrlechner, personal communication).

V. dentatum is sometimes listed as native in southern Iowa, but most specimens are a closer fit with *V. rafinesquianum* and are perhaps better regarded as that species.

Viburnum lantana L., Wayfaring Tree (not illustrated)

DISTINGUISHING CHARACTERISTICS Large shrub; buds naked; twigs coated with minute star-shaped hairs (seen with magnifying glass). Leaves simple, opposite; blades oval to ovate, 5 to 14 cm long, with tiny inconspicuous teeth along the margin, softly hairy on both surfaces with tiny star-shaped hairs, the veins or their branches running into the teeth. Flowers similar to *V. lentago*. Fruit a subglobose to ellipsoid drupe 8 to 10 mm long, turning from red to blackish as it ripens late in the growing season.

DISTRIBUTION IN IOWA An occasional escape from cultivation.

Wayfaring tree is more often a shrub than a tree, though it can grow quite tall. Indigenous to Europe and west Asia, it was introduced to Iowa for landscaping.

Viburnum lentago L., Nannyberry

DISTINGUISHING CHARACTERISTICS Large shrub or small tree, sometimes forming colonies by suckering; buds with 2 valvate scales. Leaves simple, opposite; blades oval to elliptic, tapered to a slender tip, 5 to 15 cm long, finely toothed, the veins dividing and forming a network near the margin; petioles often slightly winged. Flowers white, very slightly irregular, perfect, 5-parted, about 0.5 cm wide, in large umbel-like cymes at the ends of short leafy shoots from the tips of last year's twigs, blooming in late spring. Fruit a subglobose to ellipsoid drupe a little more than 1 cm long, nearly black when ripe in late summer or autumn, often persisting in winter.

DISTRIBUTION IN IOWA Native throughout the state.

Nannyberry grows in a variety of habitats around Iowa, from prairies and fens to bottomland and upland woods. It is well suited to conservation plantings but less desirable for landscaping, as it can grow very large and forms colonies by suckering. Also, individual plants may become unsightly in summer because of mildew on their leaves.

Viburnum prunifolium L., Blackhaw

DISTINGUISHING CHARACTERISTICS Large shrub or small tree; branchlets often bearing short, stiff, nearly perpendicular side twigs; buds with 2 valvate scales. Leaves simple, opposite; blades oval to elliptic, rounded or pointed at the tip, 3 to 8 cm long, finely toothed, their veins dividing and forming a network near the margin. Flowers and fruits similar to *V. lentago.*

DISTRIBUTION IN IOWA Native locally in southeast, east central, and central Iowa, also reported from Taylor County.

Blackhaw is our most arborescent viburnum and one of the most attractive, useful for shrub borders or trained as a small specimen tree. It produces short, stiff twigs that project from the branchlets at a wide angle, a characteristic feature. Native plants grow locally in woods and along edges, particularly in southeast Iowa.

Viburnum molle Michx., Kentucky Viburnum

DISTINGUISHING CHARACTERISTICS Medium-size to large shrub with peeling birchlike bark; buds with 4 scales. Leaves simple, opposite; blades nearly round, usually with heart-shaped bases, 7 to 14 cm long and about as wide, 3 to 4 times longer than the petioles, the margins commonly with 20 to 26 teeth on each side, the veins or their forks running into the teeth. Flowers and fruits similar to *V. rafinesquianum*.

DISTRIBUTION IN IOWA Native in Des Moines, Lee, Henry, Jefferson, and Van Buren counties, also reported from Pottawattamie and Tama counties.

Kentucky viburnum inhabits wooded ridges and slopes in a few of our southeastern counties. Though not commonly cultivated, it has attractive peeling bark and is well worth trying in naturalistic gardens.

Viburnum rafinesquianum Schult., Downy Arrowwood

DISTINGUISHING CHARACTERISTICS Medium-size to large shrub; buds with 4 scales. Leaves simple, opposite; blades oval, ovate or somewhat rounded, 4 to 7 cm long, 5 to 15 (rarely 4) times longer than the petioles, with 6 to 12 teeth on each side, the veins or their forks running into the teeth; petioles often bearing linear stipules at their base. Flowers white, very slightly irregular, perfect, 5-parted, about 4 mm across, in umbel-like cymes at the ends of short leafy shoots from the tips of last year's twigs, blooming in spring or early summer. Fruit a blackish drupe, ripening in late summer or autumn.

DISTRIBUTION IN IOWA Native throughout all but extreme western Iowa.

This is our most widespread arrowwood, growing in upland woods and along edges across much of Iowa, especially eastward. It is a desirable shrub for conservation plantings and landscaping, though perhaps too big for smaller gardens.

Viburnum opulus L., Eurasian Highbush-Cranberry

DISTINGUISHING CHARACTERISTICS Large shrub; buds with 2 fused scales. Leaves simple, opposite; blades palmately 3-lobed and veined, 4 to 10 cm long and about as wide, coarsely toothed; petioles bearing conspicuous oval or bean-shaped glands with concave tips. Flowers white, very slightly irregular, 5-parted, of 2 distinct types: (1) sterile flowers about 2 cm wide around the perimeter of the inflorescence and (2) much smaller, more numerous perfect flowers in the center; arranged in large umbel-like cymes at the ends of 4-leaved shoots in late spring. Fruit a red drupe about 8 mm long, ripening in late summer and persisting through winter.

DISTRIBUTION IN IOWA Escaped from cultivation.

As Iowans have learned, exotic shrubs with berrylike fruits can become a nuisance. This species seems less aggressive than buckthorns and honeysuckles, but it does escape from cultivation in Iowa and should be monitored as potentially invasive (Farrar 2001). It has a very broad natural range, from Europe east to the Altai Mountains of central Asia.

Viburnum trilobum Marsh., American Highbush-Cranberry

SYNONYM *V. opulus* L. subsp. *trilobum* (Marsh.) R. T. Clausen

DISTINGUISHING CHARACTERISTICS Similar to *V. opulus* except glands on petiole club-shaped and flat-topped.

DISTRIBUTION IN IOWA Native in Allamakee, Clayton, Delaware, Dubuque, Fayette, Mitchell, and Winneshiek counties.

This attractive shrub is almost identical to *V. opulus* and often considered a subspecies of it. It is native throughout the northeastern U.S. and adjacent Canada, just reaching Iowa's northeast corner. Look for it on cool wooded slopes there.

Petiole glands of *V. opulus* (left) and *V. trilobum*.

Vitis, Grape

Wild grapes grow throughout the Northern Hemisphere, numbering several dozen species. There are more species in Iowa than you might expect, though only one species is common. Their fruits are eaten by many birds and mammals including bluebirds, cardinals, woodpeckers, blue jays, orioles, tanagers, kingbirds, robins, thrushes, waxwings, grouse, quail, pheasants, turkeys, opossums, raccoons, skunks, foxes, and squirrels.

Vitis aestivalis Michx., Summer Grape (not illustrated)

DISTINGUISHING CHARACTERISTICS Similar to *V. riparia* except lower surface of leaves pale or whitened (glaucous) with persistent reddish hairs; partitions in pith much thicker (3 to 4 mm).

DISTRIBUTION IN IOWA Native in Allamakee, Clayton, Fayette, Dubuque, Jackson, Jones, Lee, and Louisa counties.

This species can be distinguished from our other wild grapes by the pale lower surface of its leaves. It ranges from the U.S. East Coast to just west of the Mississippi River, inhabiting woods and clearings in some of Iowa's eastern counties.

Vitis cinerea Engelm., Fox Grape (not illustrated)

DISTINGUISHING CHARACTERISTICS Similar to *V. riparia* except leaves sometimes not lobed, their lower surface persistently gray-hairy.

DISTRIBUTION IN IOWA Native in extreme southern Iowa, reported from Decatur, Des Moines, Fremont, Jefferson, Lee, Muscatine, and Page counties.

This southeastern grape is rare in Iowa, growing in low, especially sandy woods and other habitats in a few of our southern counties.

Vitis riparia Michx., Riverbank Grape

DISTINGUISHING CHARACTERISTICS Large vigorous vine, climbing with tendrils; pith of twigs brown, bearing partitions (diaphragms) less than 1 mm thick at the nodes; tendrils opposite the leaves, forked at the tip into 2 branches. Leaves simple, alternate; blades palmately lobed and veined, up to 14 cm long and nearly equal in width, toothed, green and glabrous beneath except for hairs along the veins. Flowers green, regular, unisexual, with minute sepals and deciduous petals, 3 to 4 mm long, in elongate panicles opposite the leaves in late spring or early summer. Fruit similar to cultivated grapes but much smaller, about 1 cm in diameter, partly to mostly coated with a thin white waxy material (glaucous), ripening in late summer.

DISTRIBUTION IN IOWA Native throughout the state.

As its name suggests, this species is most common in bottomland woods, but it is an adaptable species that will grow almost anywhere, even on prairies. It can be very weedy in shrub plantings, completely covering its supporting hosts with its rapidly growing stems and distinctive large leaves.

Vitis vulpina L., Frost Grape (not illustrated)

DISTINGUISHING CHARACTERISTICS Similar to *V. riparia* except partitions in pith much thicker (2 to 6 mm), fruit shiny and not glaucous.

DISTRIBUTION IN IOWA Native locally.

Frost grape is at the west edge of its range in Iowa and not very common. It resembles riverbank grape and is thus easily overlooked in the woodsy places where it grows.

Zanthoxylum

This is a moderately large genus of spiny shrubs and trees, most of which are indigenous to tropical or subtropical areas of the world. The few temperate-zone species are found mostly in east and central Asia. One species grows across most of the east and central U.S. including all of Iowa.

Zanthoxylum americanum P. Miller, Prickly-Ash

DISTINGUISHING CHARACTERISTICS Large colonial shrub or small tree; twigs bearing paired spines at the nodes. Leaves pinnately compound, alternate; leaflets 7 to 11, ovate to elliptic, 2 to 6 cm long, finely and obscurely toothed, nearly sessile, dotted with tiny glands (seen with magnifying glass). Flowers greenish, regular, 4- or 5-parted, the petals 2 to 3 mm long, unisexual with the staminate and the pistillate on separate plants, in small sessile clusters from overwintering buds, blooming before the leaves appear in spring. Fruit a red follicle about 0.5 cm long, leathery, citrus-scented, splitting open to reveal a single black seed that often hangs from the follicle on a slender thread.

DISTRIBUTION IN IOWA Native statewide.

This peculiar shrub forms thickets in open woods and clearings across Iowa, in both upland and bottomland sites. Individual stems often resemble small crooked trees. The male and the female flowers appear on separate plants, so some colonies bear the tiny red fruits while others do not.

Prickly-ash is not a true ash but a member of the citrus family. If you examine (and smell) its fruits, you will understand the relationship, even though the fruits are much smaller than oranges, lemons, and other cultivated citrus.

They produce an odd numbing sensation when placed in the mouth and before modern dentistry were often used as a remedy for toothache.

As the northernmost representative of its family, prickly-ash is in most parts of Iowa the only larval food source for the giant swallowtail butterfly. One would probably never plant this shrub in a landscape, but because of its usefulness to the caterpillars, it is certainly worth conserving in wild places.

Key to Shrubs and Vines Using Winter Twigs

THE FOLLOWING KEY will identify common native and naturalized species when no leaves are present. A few rarer species that are conspicuous in winter are also included.

To use the key, read the two descriptions in step 1 and select the one that matches your specimen. The number at the end of that description will tell you the step to go to next. Proceed in this way, step by step, until the key gives you a name.

Once you have identified a specimen with the key, we suggest you check your identification by comparing the specimen to the descriptions and images of that species. If you do not know the meaning of a botanical term, see "How to Identify Shrubs and Vines" or the glossary.

1. Vine: 2
1. Shrub: 13
2. Stems spiny: greenbrier, *Smilax tamnoides* var. *hispida*
2. Stems not spiny: 3
3. Leaf scars opposite: 4
3. Leaf scars alternate: 6
4. Climbing by means of roots that grow out of the stem; fruit a large woody, cigar-shaped pod: trumpet creeper, *Campsis radicans*
4. Climbing by twining; fruit, if present, not podlike: 5
5. Climbing by means of twining leafstalks, which persist on the twigs and cover the leaf scars; seeds (achenes) with long fuzzy tails, clustered in moplike heads: virgin's bower, *Clematis virginiana*. Leatherflower, *C. pitcheri*, which is native in eastern, southern, and central Iowa, and purple clematis, *C. occidentalis*, which is rare in northeastern Iowa, will also key here. Seeds of *C. pitcheri* do not have long fuzzy appendages.
5. Climbing by means of twining main stems; fruit, if present, a red berry: wild honeysuckle, *Lonicera dioica* var. *glaucescens*, and grape honeysuckle, *L. reticulata* (not easily distinguished in winter). Japanese honeysuckle, *L. japonica*, with persisting green leaves and black fruits, has escaped from cultivation in some parts of Iowa.
6. Vine climbing with tendrils and/or aerial roots: 7
6. Vine climbing by twining (coiling) stems: 10

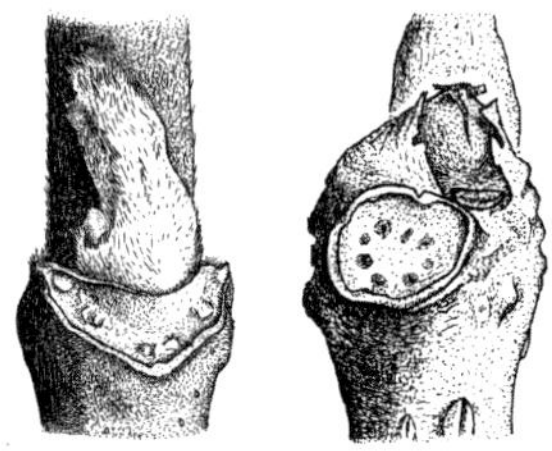

A B

FIG. 31

7. Leaf scars V-shaped; buds stalked, naked (fig. 31a): poison ivy, *Toxicodendron radicans* subsp. *negundo*
7. Leaf scars half-round or roundish; buds sessile, with overlapping scales (fig. 31b): 8

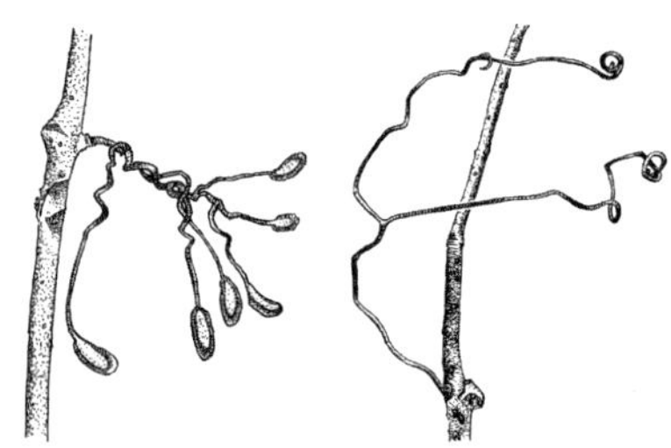

A B

FIG. 32

8. Vine climbing with aerial roots or short, highly branched tendrils, the tendril branches tipped by small adhesive disks (fig. 32a): Virginia creeper, *Parthenocissus quinquefolia*
8. Vine climbing by long tendrils forked into no more than 2 or 3 branches, usually without adhesive disks (fig. 32b): 9

9. Bark of stems peeling into thin strips; pith of twigs brown: riverbank grape, *Vitis riparia*. Other grapes are native in eastern and southern Iowa; they are not keyed here.

9. Bark not peeling; pith white: woodbine, *Parthenocissus vitacea*

10. Twigs green; leaf scars roundish, concave: moonseed, *Menispermum canadense*

10. Twigs gray or brown; leaf scars crescent-shaped to half-round: 11

11. Weak, barely woody vine with hollow twigs, emitting a distinctive unpleasant odor when bruised: bittersweet nightshade, *Solanum dulcamara*

11. Vigorous woody vine; twigs with solid pith: 12

A B

FIG. 33

12. Fruits in elongated racemelike panicles from the tips of the branches (fig. 33a): American bittersweet, *Celastrus scandens*

12. Fruits in small clusters attached to the twig between the buds and the leaf scars (fig. 33b): Oriental bittersweet, *Celastrus orbiculatus*

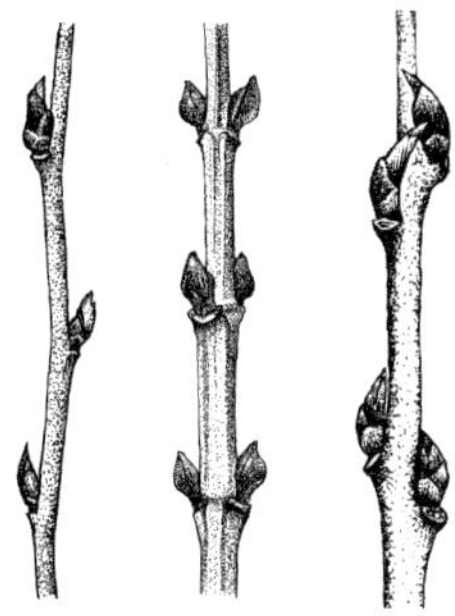

A B C

FIG. 34

13. Leaf scars alternate (fig. 34a): 14

13. Leaf scars opposite (fig. 34b), subopposite (fig. 34c), or in whorls of 3: 58

14. With spines, prickles, or catkins: 15

14. Without these structures: 30

15. With spines or prickles: 16

15. With catkins: 26

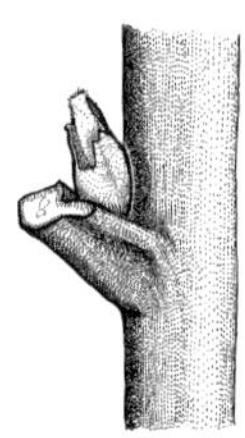

FIG. 35

16. Bases of most leafstalks remaining on the twig through winter, covering the leaf scars (fig. 35): 17

16. Leafstalks deciduous, not covering the leaf scars (the scars may be very small or narrow and hard to see; look carefully for them immediately below the buds): 20

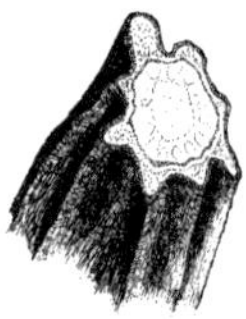

FIG. 36

17. With grooves running lengthwise down the twigs (fig. 36); buds and leaf scars crowded on short spur shoots: Japanese barberry, *Berberis thunbergii*
17. Twigs not grooved; no spur shoots present: 18
18. Stems either trailing on the ground or with their tips curving downward and touching the ground, rooting at the tips: 19
18. Stems erect or arching, not rooting at the tips: Allegheny blackberry, *Rubus allegheniensis*. Several other, less common *Rubus* species will also key here.
19. Stems trailing on the ground: dewberries, *Rubus*
19. Stem tips curving downward and often touching the ground, purplish with a white waxy coating: black raspberry, *Rubus occidentalis*
20. Fruit a hip (red berrylike fruit with the remnants of the flower attached to the end opposite the stem, as in an apple or a pear): 21
20. Fruit absent or, if present, then not a hip: 23

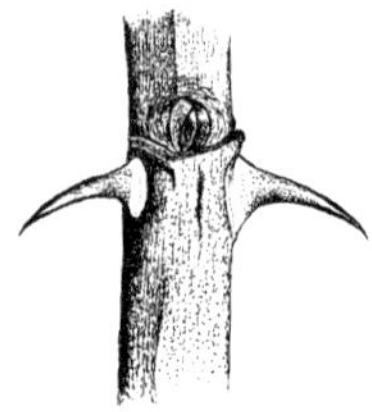

FIG. 37

21. Large shrub with at least some of the prickles stout and curved (fig. 37): multiflora rose, *Rosa multiflora*, and prairie rose, *R. setigera* (see descriptions on page 192)
21. Low to medium-size shrub with straight needlelike prickles: 22
22. Shrub growing knee-high or lower with the twigs very prickly; at least some of the fruits occurring at the end of stems that sprouted from the ground the previous spring: sunshine or wild rose, *Rosa arkansana*, and pasture rose, *R. carolina* (not easily distinguished in winter)
22. Low to medium-size shrub with few or no prickles on the last season's growth; fruits on side branches of the main stems: smooth wild rose, *Rosa blanda*

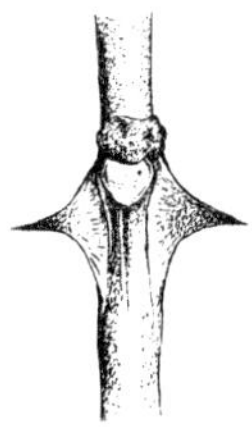

FIG. 38

23. Twig with 2 stout spines on either side of each leaf scar and no spines or prickles between the nodes; buds round, red, with a bumpy surface, lacking distinct scales (fig. 38): prickly-ash, *Zanthoxylum americanum*
23. Without these characteristics: 24

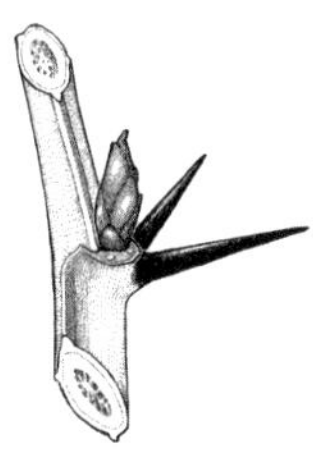

FIG. 39

24. Twigs with lines or ridges running downward from each leaf scar (fig. 39): Missouri gooseberry, *Ribes missouriense*, and prickly gooseberry, *R. cynosbati* (not easily distinguished in winter)
24. Twigs not lined: 25
25. With scattered to dense prickles between the nodes: roses, go back to step 21
25. With solitary spines or short thorn-tipped twigs: 48
26. Buds covered by the leaf scar and thus apparently absent: fragrant sumac, *Rhus aromatica*
26. Buds plainly visible on the twig above the leaf scar: 27
27. Shrub of wetlands in northeast and north central Iowa; fruit resembling a miniature cone, 1 to 2 cm long: 28
27. Shrub of woods, edges, or fencerows; fruit, if present, a nut enclosed by a papery husk: 29
28. Bud enclosed by 2 scales that meet along the edges without overlapping: speckled alder, *Alnus rugosa*
28. Bud with overlapping scales: bog birch, *Betula pumila*

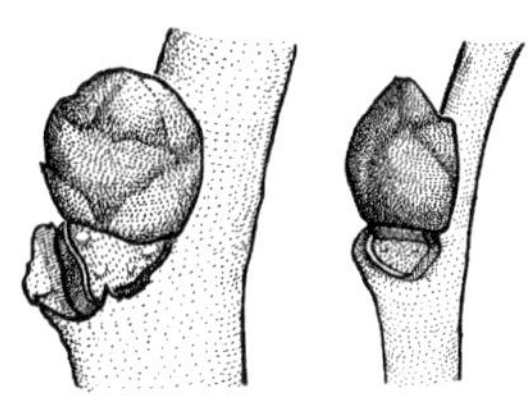

A B

FIG. 40

29. Buds about as long as wide, blunt or rounded (fig. 40a); catkins stalked, mostly 1.5 or more cm long: American hazelnut, *Corylus americana*
29. Buds longer than wide, pointed (fig. 40b); catkins nearly sessile, less than 1.5 cm long: beaked hazelnut, *Corylus cornuta*

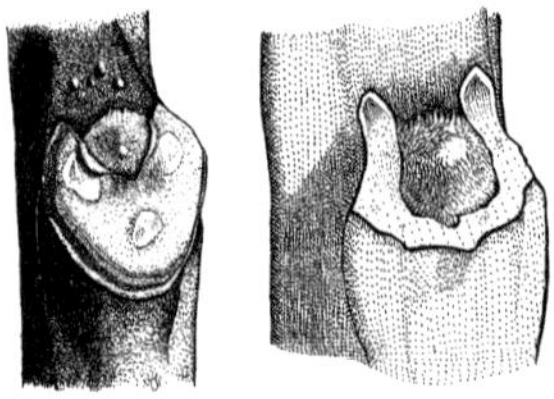

A B

FIG. 41

30. Leaf scar partly to completely covering or encircling the bud (fig. 41a, b): 31
30. Leaf scar in the normal position immediately below the bud: 35
31. Twig stout with thick spongy pith: 32
31. Twig slender: 33
32. Twig densely hairy: staghorn sumac, *Rhus typhina*
32. Twig smooth: smooth sumac, *Rhus glabra*
33. Bud covered and obscured by the leaf scar: fragrant sumac, *Rhus aromatica*
33. Bud visible: 34
34. Leaf scar U-shaped with 3 bundle scars, sometimes partly covering the bud (see fig. 41a in step 30); fruit a round samara with the seed in the center, often persisting in winter: hoptree, *Ptelea trifoliata*
34. Leaf scar ringlike and nearly encircling the bud, with 5 or more bundle scars (see fig. 41b in step 30); fruit not persisting: leatherwood, *Dirca palustris*
35. Bud naked or single-scaled: 36
35. Bud with 2 or more scales: 40
36. Bud naked: 37
36. Bud single-scaled: 38
37. Leaf scar small, half-round; fruit a woody pod (capsule) with shiny black seeds: witch-hazel, *Hamamelis virginiana*. Glossy buckthorn, *Rhamnus frangula,* has similar twig features, but its fruits are dark purple berries. It is invasive in states to the east of Iowa and should be watched for here.
37. Leaf scar prominent, V-shaped (see fig. 31a in step 7); fruit if present an off-white or yellowish berry: poison ivy, *Toxicodendron radicans* subsp. *negundo,* and western poison ivy, *T. rydbergii* (see descriptions on page 194)
38. Buds averaging more than 5 mm long: pussy willow, *Salix discolor.* Several other native willows will key here; they are not easily distinguished in winter.
38. Buds averaging less than 5 mm long: 39
39. Twig glabrous to sparsely hairy; thicket-forming shrub or small tree with polelike stems: sandbar willow, *Salix interior*
39. Twig densely hairy; low prairie shrub: prairie willow, *Salix humilis*
40. Small seed pods present in clusters at the ends of the branches: 41
40. No seed pods present: 45

41. Fruits deciduous in autumn but with tiny cuplike receptacles remaining (see fig. 44 in step 49): 50
41. Pods (follicles or legumes) present: 42
42. Seed pods in corymbs; bark of the main stems papery and peeling as on a birch tree: ninebark, *Physocarpus opulifolius*
42. Seed pods in large racemes or panicles; bark not peeling: 43

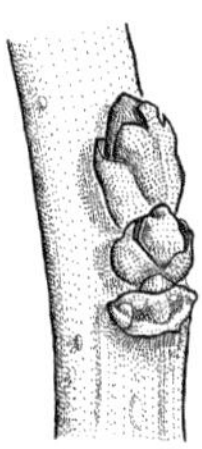

FIG. 42

43. Buds in pairs at some of the nodes, one above the other (fig. 42); tall shrub of wet places: indigo bush, *Amorpha fruticosa*
43. Buds solitary at the nodes; low shrub: 44
44. Twig densely coated with soft gray hairs; shrub of dry prairies: leadplant, *Amorpha canescens*
44. Twig glabrous to sparsely hairy; shrub of moist open places: meadowsweet, *Spiraea alba*

FIG. 43

45. Leaf scar elongated into a narrow crescent (fig. 43): 46
45. Leaf scar some other shape: 48
46. Bud flattened on the twig side; shrub grown agriculturally for its dark purple berries, rarely wild: aronia berry or chokeberry, *Aronia*
46. Bud not flattened; native species: 47
47. Shrub forming colonies by suckering: low serviceberry, *Amelanchier humilis*
47. Shrub with multiple stems from 1 crown, not colonial: roundleaf serviceberry, *Amelanchier sanguinea*. Other serviceberries grow to be small trees, and young specimens of those species will key here. They are not distinguishable from *A. sanguinea* in winter.
48. Each leaf scar with 1 bundle scar: 49
48. Each leaf scar with 3 bundle scars: 53

FIG. 44

49. Dwarf shrub of upland prairies; fruits deciduous in autumn but their supporting stalks (pedicels) often persist in winter, each tipped by a tiny cuplike structure (fig. 44): 50
49. Tall shrub; fruits otherwise: 51
50. Fruit clusters terminating on long leafless stalks arising from below the branch tips: New Jersey tea, *Ceanothus americanus*
50. Fruit clusters terminating on short stalks at the ends of the branches: redroot, *Ceanothus herbaceus*
51. Twig and buds coated with minute brown and silver scale-like structures (best seen with magnifying glass): autumn olive, *Elaeagnus umbellata*
51. Twig and buds not scale-coated: 52
52. Buds solitary; fruits purple when present: buckthorn, *Rhamnus*
52. Buds superposed in pairs at many of the nodes; fruits bright red when present: winterberry, *Ilex verticillata*
53. Bud with 2 scales that meet along the edge without overlapping; twigs green or purple: pagoda or alternate-leaf dogwood, *Cornus alternifolia*
53. Bud with 3 or more overlapping scales; twigs gray, brown, or reddish: 54

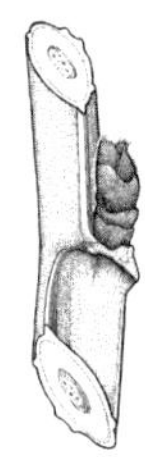

FIG. 45

54. Lines or ridges running down the twigs from each leaf scar (fig. 45); tiny scattered yellow dots often present on twigs (use magnifying glass): wild black currant, *Ribes americanum*. Northern black current, *R. hudsonianum*, which is rare in northeastern Iowa, will also key here.
54. Twigs not lined; yellow dots absent: 55
55. Terminal bud present: 56
55. Terminal bud absent; twig tipped by a lateral bud or sometimes a sharp thornlike point: 57

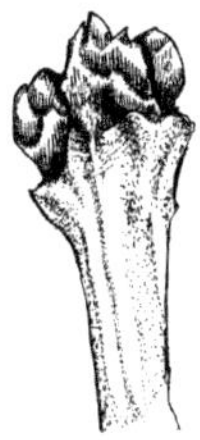

FIG. 46

56. Buds ovoid-elongate, bicolored with brown and tan scales: choke cherry, *Prunus virginiana*
56. Buds ovoid, brown or reddish brown, the terminal often clustered with several lateral buds at the twig tip (fig. 46): pin cherry, *Prunus pensylvanica.* Dwarf chinkapin oak, *Quercus prinoides,* will also key here. It is native in the southern part of Iowa, where it is not common, while *Prunus pensylvanica* grows primarily in northern and central Iowa.

FIG. 47

57. Buds often collateral (fig. 47); short thorn-tipped twigs often present: American plum, *Prunus americana*
57. Buds solitary at the nodes; shrubs not thorny: lanceleaf buckthorn, *Rhamnus lanceolata.* Alderleaf buckthorn, *R. alnifolia,* a low colonial shrub that is rare in northeastern Iowa, will also key here.

FIG. 48

58. Fruit a hard brown ball 1.5 to 2.5 cm in diameter; leaf scars conspicuous, roundish, sometimes in whorls of 3, each with a single C-shaped bundle scar (fig. 48): buttonbush, *Cephalanthus occidentalis*
58. Fruit and leaf scars not as described above: 59
59. Fruit an elongated brown pod about 1 cm long, in clusters at the tips of the stems: 60
59. Fruit absent or, if present, then not as described above: 61
60. Each leaf scar with 1 bundle scar; short side shoots often present on twig: shrubby St. John's–wort, *Hypericum prolificum*
60. Each leaf scar with 3 bundle scars; twig lacking short side shoots: bush honeysuckle, *Diervilla lonicera*

FIG. 49

61. Fruits winged, key-shaped, in clusters at the tips of the twigs (fig. 49): 62
61. Fruits absent or, if present, then not winged: 63
62. Buds with 3 or more overlapping scales; cultivated shrub, sometimes escaping: Amur maple, *Acer ginnala*
62. Buds with 2 scales that meet along the edges without overlapping; native in extreme northeastern Iowa: mountain maple, *Acer spicatum*
63. Bud with 2 scales that meet along the edges without overlapping, as in a duck's bill: 64
63. Bud with 3 or more overlapping scales: 71
64. Twig and bud scales densely coated with tiny scalelike structures that give them a silvery sheen (individual scalelike structures best seen with magnifying glass); each leaf scar with 1 bundle scar: buffaloberry, *Shepherdia argentea*
64. Twig and bud scales not scale-coated; each leaf scar with 3 bundle scars: 65

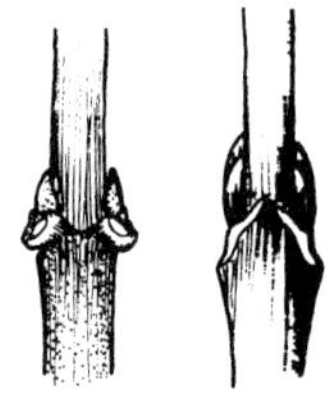

A B

FIG. 50

65. Leaf scars raised above twig on the persisting bases of the petioles (fig. 50a): 66
65. Leaf scars not raised (fig. 50b): 68
66. Bark of entire shrub bright red or purple-red: red-osier dogwood, *Cornus stolonifera*
66. Bark of main stems some other color; twigs reddish or not: 67
67. Twigs and branchlets dark purple or green flecked with purple: roundleaf dogwood, *Cornus rugosa*
67. Twigs and branchlets brown, gray, or purple-red: gray dogwood, *Cornus racemosa*, roughleaf dogwood, *C. drummondii*, and silky dogwood, *C. obliqua* (see descriptions on pages 199–200)
68. Twig green or purple; fruit a bladderlike pod: bladdernut, *Staphylea trifolia*
68. Twig gray or brown; fruit berry-like if present: 69

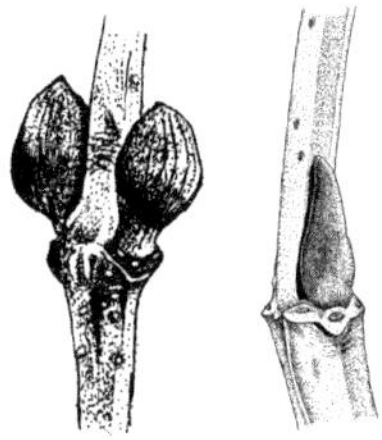

A B

FIG. 51

69. Buds subglobose to short-ovoid (fig. 51a); fruits red: Eurasian highbush-cranberry, *Viburnum opulus*, and American highbush-cranberry, *V. trilobum* (not distinguishable in winter)
69. Buds elongated (fig. 51b); fruits dark purple: 70
70. With short, stiff side twigs projecting from the branchlets at wide angles; southeastern Iowa only: blackhaw, *Viburnum prunifolium*
70. Without short, stiff side twigs; widely distributed: nannyberry, *Viburnum lentago*
71. Twigs green or purple: 72
71. Twigs light brown, reddish brown, or gray: 74

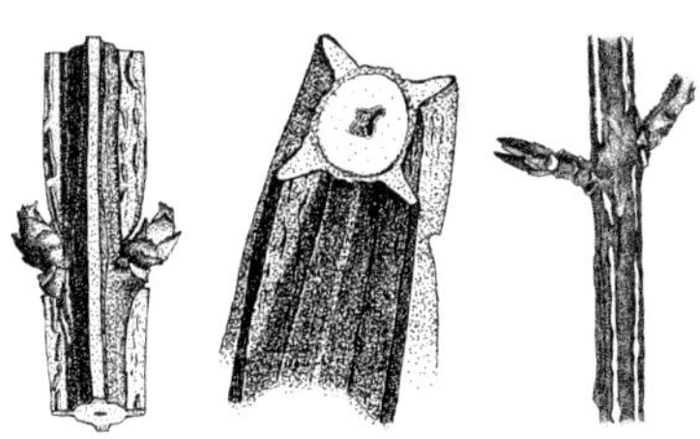

A B C

FIG. 52

72. Leaf scar with 1 crescent-shaped bundle scar; twig often bearing 4 lines or wings running downward from the leaf scars (fig. 52a–c); fruit red and berrylike when present: 73
72. Leaf scar with 3 or more dotlike bundle scars; twig not lined or winged; fruit a brown bladderlike pod: bladdernut, *Staphylea trifolia*
73. Twigs with corky wings (fig. 52a, b): burning bush, *Euonymus alatus*
73. Twigs lacking corky wings but often lined (fig. 52c): wahoo, *Euonymus atropurpureus*

FIG. 53

74. Leaf scar large and broadly crescent-shaped to heart-shaped or shield-shaped (fig. 53): 75
74. Leaf scar half-round to triangular in shape, small: 76
75. Pith white: common elderberry, *Sambucus canadensis*
75. Pith brown: red elderberry, *Sambucus pubens*
76. Leaf scars subopposite (see fig. 34c in step 13); twig tips often sharp and thornlike: common buckthorn, *Rhamnus cathartica*
76. Leaf scars opposite; twig tips not thornlike: 77

FIG. 54

77. Bud scales from previous winter persisting at the twig bases (fig. 54): 78
77. Bud scales not persisting: 80

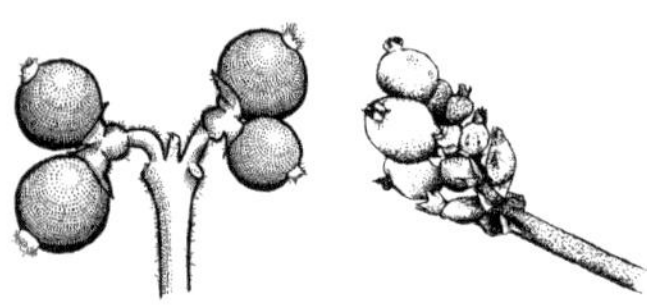

A B

FIG. 55

78. Tall shrub with berries in stalked pairs along the twigs (fig. 55a): honeysuckle, *Lonicera*
78. Low shrub with berries in small, compact, nearly sessile clusters from the upper nodes (fig. 55b): 79
79. Berries red; twig with solid pith: coralberry, *Symphoricarpos orbiculatus*
79. Berries white, often turning darker in winter; twig usually hollow: wolfberry, *Symphoricarpos occidentalis*
80. Each leaf scar with 1 bundle scar: privet, *Ligustrum*
80. Each leaf scar with 3 bundle scars: 81
81. Bark of main stems papery and peeling as on a birch tree: Kentucky viburnum, *Viburnum molle*
81. Bark not papery and peeling: downy arrowwood, *Viburnum rafinesquianum*. Mapleleaf viburnum, *V. acerifolium*, which is rare in northeastern Iowa, and southern arrowwood, *V. dentatum*, which occasionally escapes, will also key here. *V. dentatum* often has angled, ridged twigs, which when present will distinguish it from *V. rafinesquianum*.

Shrubs and Vines in Winter

THE WINTER TWIGS of native and naturalized shrubs and vines are described and illustrated in the following pages. To facilitate identification, we have grouped species with similar winter twigs together with their descriptions and images. All but a few uncommon species are included. For more information, see the descriptions of these species in "Native and Naturalized Shrubs and Vines."

The differences between woody plants in winter are more subtle than when the plants are in leaf, so you may find it difficult to identify twigs by just looking at the images. If so, we suggest you use the winter key first, then check your identification using the descriptions and images of that species.

Please be aware that twig color and the shapes of leaf scars can vary within a species, so some specimens you find may not exactly match the images in the plates. The images show the relative diameters of the species' twigs but are not exactly to scale.

PL. 1, left to right: *Campsis radicans, Celastrus scandens, Clematis virginiana, Lonicera dioica* var. *glaucescens, Menispermum canadense, Parthenocissus quinquefolia, Parthenocissus vitacea, Smilax tamnoides* var. *hispida, Toxicodendron radicans* subsp. *negundo, Vitis riparia.*

Plate 1. Vines

Campsis radicans. Trumpet creeper. Climbing against surfaces often using aerial roots. Twigs moderate to rather stout, pale yellow to light brown. Leaf scars opposite, roundish, large, with 1 ring-shaped or C-shaped bundle scar. Buds solitary above each leaf scar, squat, with 2 or 3 pairs of brown scales.

Celastrus scandens. American bittersweet. Climbing with twining stems. Twigs moderate, gray or brown. Leaf scars alternate, roundish, small, with 1 elongated or curved, often indistinct bundle scar. Buds solitary, subglobose, pointing away from the twig at a right angle, with several brown scales. Oriental bittersweet, *C. orbiculatus*, is similar except in fruit.

Clematis virginiana. Virgin's bower. Climbing with twining petioles. Twigs slender, brown. Leaf scars opposite, obscured by the base of the petiole, which remains on the twig in winter. Buds solitary above each leaf scar, ovoid, small, with a few often indistinct scales, hairy.

Lonicera dioica var. *glaucescens*. Wild honeysuckle. Climbing with twining stems. Twigs slender, light brown or gray, hollow in center, with the scales from last winter's bud persisting at their base. Leaf scars opposite, triangular to crescent-shaped, the 2 scars of each opposing pair connected by the remnant of the leaf base, with 3 bundle scars. Buds solitary above each leaf scar, ovoid to ovoid-elongate, with 2 or more pairs of scales. Grape honeysuckle, *L. reticulata*, is similar.

Menispermum canadense. Moonseed. Climbing with twining stems. Twigs slender to moderate, green. Leaf scars alternate, ovate to round, concave, with 3 to several often indistinct bundle scars. Buds superposed in 2s or 3s, the lowest one usually covered by the leaf scar and the upper one(s) partly embedded in the twig, small, brown, indistinctly scaly.

Parthenocissus quinquefolia. Virginia creeper. Similar to *P. vitacea* except its tendrils are short and each is divided into several branches bearing small adhesive disks at the end. Rootlike outgrowths often develop when the vine is growing on tree trunks.

Parthenocissus vitacea. Woodbine. Climbing with coiling tendrils. Twigs slender to rather stout, light brown or gray, with white pith. Leaf scars alternate, round or roundish, conspicuous, often concave, with half a dozen or more often indistinct bundle scars that are either scattered or arranged in a circular pattern. Buds small, brown, scaly, sometimes collateral, the single or paired buds covered by 2 chaffy outer scales that form a squat conical structure; outer scales sometimes breaking partly or completely off. Tendrils long, once- or twice-branched, the branch tips swollen or tightly coiled when the vine is growing on tree bark.

Smilax tamnoides var. *hispida*. Greenbrier. Climbing with coiling tendrils produced from the tips of the leaf stipules. Twigs slender to moderate, green, prickly. Leaf scars alternate, covered by the persisting bases of the petioles. Buds solitary or superposed, pointing away from the twig, irregularly shaped, each with 1 leaflike scale whose edges overlap.

Solanum dulcamara. Bittersweet nightshade (not illustrated). Climbing by twining stems. Twigs slender, hollow in center, pale yellow or light brown.

Leaf scars alternate, raised, half-round, with 1 bundle scar (sometimes divided into 3). Buds solitary, small, subglobose, few-scaled.

Toxicodendron radicans subsp. *negundo*. Poison ivy. Climbing with aerial roots. Twigs moderate, light brown or gray. Leaf scars alternate, V-shaped or crescent-shaped, with several bundle scars. Buds solitary, stalked, elongate, naked, pale yellow-brown.

Vitis riparia. Riverbank grape. Climbing with coiling tendrils. Twigs slender to moderate, brown, with brown pith. Leaf scars alternate, small, variably shaped, with several often indistinct bundle scars. Buds solitary or collateral, small, subglobose to ovoid, with 2 brown outer scales that are often parted or broken at the tip, revealing the pale hairs within. Tendrils long, each forking once.

PL. 2, left to right: *Berberis thunbergii, Elaeagnus umbellata, Ribes missouriense, Rosa arkansana, Rosa multiflora, Rubus allegheniensis, Rubus occidentalis, Zanthoxylum americanum.*

Plate 2. Thorny Shrubs with Alternate Leaf Scars

Berberis thunbergii. Japanese barberry. Twigs slender, grooved, dark purple-brown, spiny at the nodes. (Spines usually 1 per node but sometimes more, sometimes branched.) Leaf scars covered by the persisting bases of the petioles, clustered with the buds on short spur shoots arranged alternately on the twig. Buds subglobose, small, with several scales colored like the twigs.

Elaeagnus umbellata. Autumn olive. Twigs slender, often spiny at some nodes, coated with tiny brown, silver-edged scales (best seen with magnifying glass). Leaf scars small, half-round, with 1 bundle scar. Buds subglobose and usually solitary, with 3 or 4 thick brown scales.

Ribes missouriense. Missouri gooseberry. Twigs slender, pale gray, armed with 1 to 3 dark spines at each node, prickly or not between the nodes. Leaf scars crescent-shaped or U-shaped, with 3 bundle scars. Buds solitary, elongate, with several brown scales, sessile on the twigs, raised on short spur shoots on the branchlets. Prickly gooseberry, *R. cynosbati*, is similar.

Rosa arkansana. Sunshine rose or wild rose. Twigs slender, dark red or reddish purple, prickly. Leaf scars curved and very narrow, almost linelike, with 3 bundle scars. Buds solitary, ovoid, with 3 to 5 visible scales colored like the twigs. The pasture rose, *R. carolina*, and the smooth wild rose, *R. blanda*, are similar except the twigs of *R. blanda* are unarmed or very sparsely prickly.

Rosa multiflora. Multiflora rose. Twigs slender to moderate, green or purplish, with stout, broad-based, straight or curved prickles at the nodes and between the nodes. Leaf scars curved and very narrow, almost linelike, with 3 bundle scars. Buds solitary, subglobose to short-ovoid, with about 3 reddish scales. The prairie rose, *R. setigera*, is similar except its buds are sometimes longer with more numerous scales.

Rubus allegheniensis. Allegheny blackberry. Canes erect, arching at the end but not tip-rooting, with strong, broad-based prickles. Leaf scars and buds similar to *R. occidentalis*.

Rubus occidentalis. Black raspberry. Twig a long cane that arches downward and roots where it touches the soil, its surface purple, glaucous, and prickly. Leaf scars covered and obscured by the persisting petioles. Buds superposed, the lower one much smaller and covered by the petiole, the upper ovoid to ovoid-elongate with several scales, sometimes with another smaller bud at its base.

Rubus species. Dewberry (not illustrated). Canes slender, prickly, trailing on the ground. Leaf scars and buds similar to other *Rubus* species.

Zanthoxylum americanum. Prickly-ash. Twigs slender to moderate, brown, with 2 spines at each node. Leaf scars mostly heart-shaped, with 3 bundle scars. Buds solitary or superposed, globose, red, with a bumpy, cauliflowerlike surface, the scales indistinct.

PL. 3, left to right: *Dirca palustris, Hamamelis virginiana, Ptelea trifoliata, Rhus aromatica, Rhus glabra, Rhus typhina, Salix discolor, Salix interior.*

Plate 3. Leaf Scars Alternate; Buds Naked, One-scaled or Indistinctly Scaly

Dirca palustris. Leatherwood. Twigs moderate, brown, usually glabrous, somewhat swollen at the tip. Leaf scars raised, ringlike and nearly encircling the buds, with 5 or more bundle scars. Buds short-conical, pale, rather indistinctly scaly. Branches very flexible, with tough outer bark.

Hamamelis virginiana. Witch-hazel. Twigs rather slender, brown or gray. Leaf scars small, half-round to triangular or heart-shaped, with 3 bundle scars. Buds stalked, elongate, often in pairs with the 2 buds lying alongside one another, each with 2 scales that fall early and leave the bud naked; brown in color but often appearing light gray or tan through a coating of tiny hairs.

Ptelea trifoliata. Hoptree. Twigs slender to moderate, dark brown, glabrous. Leaf scars small, more or less U-shaped, with 3 bundle scars. Buds superposed in pairs, the lower often covered by the leaf scar and the upper partly so, coated with pale silky hairs that obscure the scales.

Rhus aromatica. Fragrant sumac. Twigs slender, light brown, often bearing small catkins at the tip. Leaf scars small, raised, round, with several bundle scars, covering and obscuring the buds.

Rhus glabra. Smooth sumac. Twigs stout, light to dark brown or reddish brown, with thick spongy pith, often somewhat glaucous, glabrous. Leaf scars ringlike, nearly encircling the buds, with about a dozen bundle scars often aggregated into 3 groups. Buds solitary, globose to conical, the scales obscured by a covering of pale hairs.

Rhus typhina. Staghorn sumac. Similar to *R. glabra* except twigs densely covered with golden brown hairs, the branches thus resembling a stag's antlers in velvet.

Salix discolor. Pussy willow. Twigs moderate, brown, hairy or glabrous. Leaf scars crescent-shaped with 3 bundle scars. Buds solitary, ovoid, with 1 glossy reddish scale, of 2 distinct sizes, the larger ones (flower buds) 7 to 15 mm long.

Salix humilis. Prairie willow (not illustrated). Twigs slender, brown, finely gray-hairy. Leaf scars crescent-shaped with 3 bundle scars. Buds solitary, ovoid, single-scaled, about 4 mm long.

Salix interior. Sandbar willow. Twigs very slender, light brown or reddish, usually glabrous. Leaf scars crescent-shaped with 3 bundle scars. Buds solitary or collateral in pairs, ovoid to ovoid-elongate, single-scaled, 2 to 5 mm long.

Toxicodendron. Poison ivy. See plate 1. *T. radicans* subsp. *negundo* is an often tall shrub with long branches; western poison ivy, *T. rydbergii,* is a dwarf colonial shrub whose stems are unbranched or sparsely branched.

PL. 4, left to right: *Amelanchier* species, *Aronia melanocarpa, Physocarpus opulifolius, Prunus americana, Prunus pensylvanica, Prunus virginiana, Ribes americanum, Spiraea alba.*

Plate 4. Leaf Scars Alternate; Buds with Several Overlapping Scales

Amelanchier. Serviceberry. Twigs slender, brown or reddish brown. Leaf scars linear to crescent-shaped, with 3 bundle scars. Buds solitary, ovoid to elongate, with several dark purplish scales. Low serviceberry, *A. humilis,* spreads by rhizomes to form small colonies. Roundleaf serviceberry, *A. sanguinea,* has its stems arising from a single crown.

Aronia. Aronia berry or black chokeberry. Twigs slender, reddish brown. Leaf scars crescent-shaped to U-shaped, with 3 bundle scars. Buds solitary, ovoid-elongate, flattened on the twig side, with about 5 purplish scales.

Physocarpus opulifolius. Ninebark. Twigs slender, light brown the first year, then gray, appearing angled because of lines running down from the nodes, glabrous. Leaf scars small, raised above the surface of the twig on cushionlike structures, triangular to broadly crescent-shaped, with 3 or 5 bundle scars. Buds solitary, ovoid to elongate, with several to many dark brown scales.

Prunus americana. American plum. Twigs rather slender, brown to reddish brown or gray, glabrous or pubescent, the shorter side twigs often thorny at the tip. Leaf scars raised above the surface of the twig on cushionlike structures, half-round, with 3 bundle scars. Buds small, solitary or collateral in pairs, with several brown or reddish brown scales; terminal bud absent.

Prunus pensylvanica. Pin cherry. Twigs slender, dark purplish brown or red. Leaf scars raised above the surface of the twig on cushionlike structures, half-round or roundish, with 3 bundle scars. Buds small, ovoid, with several scales colored like the twig, the terminal bud and a few laterals often in a cluster at the twig tip, otherwise solitary.

Prunus virginiana. Choke cherry. Twigs slender, light brown or gray. Leaf scars slightly raised above the surface of the twig, half-round, with 3 bundle scars. Buds solitary, ovoid to ovoid-elongate, with several bicolored brown and tan scales.

Ribes americanum. Wild black currant. Twigs slender, tan or light gray, with lines running downward from the nodes, finely hairy, dotted with tiny amber-colored glands (see with magnifying glass). Leaf scar slightly raised, V-shaped, with 3 bundle scars. Buds solitary, ovoid, sometimes slightly stalked, with several brown scales often dotted like the twig.

Spiraea alba. Meadowsweet. Twigs slender to moderate, brown, appearing somewhat angled because of lines running downward from the nodes, glabrous to sparsely hairy. Leaf scars small, raised, triangular, with 1 bundle scar. Buds solitary, globose to subglobose, with several to many brown scales.

PL. 5, left to right: *Alnus rugosa*, *Amorpha canescens*, *Amorpha fruticosa*, *Betula pumila*, *Ceanothus americanus*, *Cornus alternifolia*, *Corylus americana*, *Ilex verticillata*, *Rhamnus lanceolata*.

Plate 5. Leaf Scars Alternate; Buds with Two to Several Scales

Alnus rugosa. Speckled alder. Twigs slender, brown to dark purple-brown, often bearing dark purple catkins at the end. Leaf scars small, half-round, with 3 bundle scars. Buds solitary, stalked, elongate, with 2 or sometimes 3 purplish scales.

Amorpha canescens. Leadplant. Twigs slender to moderate, densely and softly gray-hairy. Leaf scars small, half-round to somewhat triangular, with 3 often indistinct bundle scars. Buds solitary, very small (about 2 mm), subglobose with rounded tips, with 2 or 3 pairs of brown scales.

Amorpha fruticosa. Indigo bush. Twigs slender to moderate, gray or light brown, glabrous to finely hairy, tipped by the slender stems of last summer's racemes or sometimes by spindle-shaped insect galls. Leaf scars small, half-round to somewhat triangular, with 3 often indistinct bundle scars. Buds subglobose to ovoid, with 2 to 4 pairs of brown scales, often superposed in pairs, with the upper bud larger.

Betula pumila. Bog birch. Twigs slender, gray or dark brown, finely hairy, more or less dotted with tiny scalelike glands, bearing short, dark purple-brown catkins. Leaf scars small, half-round, with 3 bundle scars. Buds solitary, ovoid, with 3 or 4 dark purple-brown scales.

Ceanothus americanus. New Jersey tea. Twigs slender, olive green or brown, finely hairy. Leaf scars small, half-round, with 1 or sometimes 3 bundle scars. Buds solitary, ovoid, small, covered with fine hairs and more or less enclosed by the persisting scalelike stipules. Cup-shaped receptacles of the fruits persisting in small clusters; clusters raised on long stalks emanating from nodes well below the tip of the twig (receptacles 3 to 4 mm across). Redroot or narrowleaf New Jersey tea, *C. herbaceus,* is similar except its fruit clusters have short stalks emanating from the ends of the twigs.

Cornus alternifolia. Pagoda or alternate-leaf dogwood. Twigs slender, green or purple, the internodes often very long with buds and leaf scars only near the tip of the twig, often bearing short side shoots ending in a terminal bud. Leaf scars raised above the surface of the twig on cushionlike structures, crescent-shaped to somewhat triangular, with 3 bundle scars. Buds solitary, the terminals ovoid-elongate and much larger than the laterals, with 2 or 3 green or purplish scales.

Corylus americana. American hazelnut. Twigs slender, light brown or gray, finely hairy to nearly glabrous, bearing stalked light beige catkins mostly longer than 1.5 cm. Leaf scars small, triangular or half-round, with 3 or more often indistinct bundle scars. Buds solitary, subglobose, with blunt or rounded tips and several brown scales. Beaked hazelnut, *C. cornuta,* is similar except its buds are ovoid and pointed, its catkins nearly sessile and shorter than 1.5 cm.

Ilex verticillata. Winterberry. Twigs slender, brown or greenish. Leaf scars roundish, small, with 1 bundle scar. Buds superposed in pairs, subglobose, with about 4 brown scales.

Rhamnus lanceolata. Lanceleaf buckthorn. Similar to common buckthorn, *R. cathartica* (see pl. 8), except twigs lacking thorny tips, leaf scars mostly alternate, and buds usually small (2 to 3 mm), subglobose to ovoid, appearing banded with light and dark brown.

PL. 6, left to right: *Cephalanthus occidentalis, Cornus obliqua, Cornus racemosa, Cornus rugosa, Cornus stolonifera, Shepherdia argentea, Viburnum lentago, Viburnum opulus, Viburnum prunifolium.*

Plate 6. Leaf Scars Opposite, Subopposite, or Whorled; Buds Mostly Valvate or Indistinctly Scaly

Acer spicatum. Mountain maple (not illustrated). Twigs rather slender, greenish or purplish. Leaf scars V-shaped or crescent-shaped with 3 bundle scars. Buds solitary, oblong, valvate, with greenish or reddish scales.

Cephalanthus occidentalis. Buttonbush. Twigs slender to rather stout, brown or gray, encircled at each node by linelike stipule scars connecting the tops of the leaf scars. Leaf scars opposite or in whorls of 3, shield-shaped, conspicuous, each with a single C-shaped bundle scar. Buds solitary, very small, partly embedded in the twig with only their tips visible, indistinctly scaly.

Cornus. Dogwood. Iowa's native dogwoods share the following features. Twigs slender to moderate. Leaf scars small, raised above the surface of the twig on the persisting bases of the petiole, often (but not always) V-shaped, U-shaped, or crescent-shaped, with 3 bundle scars. Buds solitary, slender, valvate. The species can often be distinguished by twig color and habitat as described below, but these features vary within species and overlap between species, so winter identification is not always certain.

Cornus obliqua. Silky dogwood. Twigs purple-red, with brown pith. Bark of main stems gray. Usually in lowland habitats.

Cornus racemosa, gray dogwood, and *C. drummondii*, roughleaf dogwood. Not easily distinguished in winter. Twigs brown or purple-red. Usually in upland habitats, in or near woods.

Cornus rugosa. Roundleaf dogwood. Twigs dark purple, reddish, or green flecked with purple. Moist wooded slopes and bluffs.

Cornus stolonifera. Red-osier dogwood. Twigs, branchlets, and stems bright red or purple-red (bright yellow in some cultivated plants). Pith of twigs white. Opposing leaf scars connected by a straight or a curved line on each side of the twig. Usually in lowland habitats.

Shepherdia argentea. Buffaloberry. Twigs rather slender, coated with tiny silvery scales. Leaf scars small, half-round, with 1 bundle scar. Buds stalked, valvate, coated with tiny brown and silver scales, of 2 types: oblong leaf buds and ovoid flower buds, the former mostly solitary, the latter in clusters of 2 or 3 that have short thick stalks. Branchlets often bearing short side twigs that are thorny at the tip.

Viburnum lentago. Nannyberry. Twigs moderate, brown or gray. Leaf scars V-shaped to crescent-shaped, with 3 bundle scars. Buds solitary, elongate, either narrow (leaf buds) or with their lower half swollen and bulbous (flower buds), valvate, with brown or gray scales.

Viburnum opulus. Eurasian highbush-cranberry. Twigs moderate to somewhat stout, light brown or gray. Leaf scars crescent-shaped with 3 bundle scars. Buds ovoid with a narrow stalklike base, with 2 red or reddish scales. (Seam between the scales may be indistinct, so the bud appears 1-scaled.) American highbush-cranberry, *V. trilobum*, is similar.

Viburnum prunifolium. Blackhaw. Similar to *V. lentago* except that it produces many short, stiff side twigs that project from the branchlets at wide angles. It is found in southeastern Iowa only.

PL. 7, left to right: *Diervilla lonicera, Hypericum prolificum, Lonicera maackii, Sambucus canadensis, Symphoricarpos occidentalis, Symphoricarpos orbiculatus, Viburnum molle, Viburnum rafinesquianum.*

Plate 7. Leaf Scars Opposite, Subopposite, or Whorled; Buds with Overlapping Scales

Diervilla lonicera. Bush honeysuckle. Twigs slender to moderate, pale brown, with 2 or 4 lengthwise lines, with scales from last winter's bud persisting at their base. Leaf scars triangular, with 3 bundle scars; opposing leaf scars connected by a fine line on each side of the twig. Buds solitary or superposed, when superposed the lower much smaller, ovoid-elongate, with several pairs of brown scales.

Hypericum prolificum. Shrubby St. John's–wort. Twigs very slender, light brown, angled, often bearing short side branches above leaf scars. Leaf scars very small, triangular to diamond-shaped, with 1 bundle scar. Buds tiny, solitary, with several often leaflike scales.

Lonicera. Honeysuckle. Twigs slender, brown or gray, with scales from the previous winter's bud persisting at their base; branchlets hollow. Leaf scar small, variously shaped, raised on the persisting and often uneven bases of the petioles, often partitioned into an outer scar and a smaller inner scar containing the 3 bundle scars. Buds solitary or superposed, when superposed the lowest bud largest, with several scales, often pointing at right angles from the twig. Stalks of fruit cluster, when present, inserted between the leaf scars and the buds, often persisting as broken stubs between the two.

Sambucus canadensis. Common elderberry. Twigs moderate to stout, light gray, with thick, soft white pith; branchlets often bearing conspicuous raised lenticels. Leaf scars large, broadly crescent-shaped to heart-shaped or sometimes shield-shaped, usually with 5 bundle scars; opposing leaf scars connected by a short line on each side of the twig. Buds solitary or sometimes collateral or superposed with 1 large bud and 1 or more smaller ones, subglobose, with several brown scales. Red elderberry, *S. pubens*, is similar except the pith of its twigs is brown.

Symphoricarpos occidentalis. Wolfberry. Twigs slender, brown, usually hollow, with scales from the previous winter's bud persisting at their base. Leaf scars raised and crescent-shaped, with 1 often indistinct bundle scar, often obscured by the persisting bases of the petioles; opposing leaf scars connected by a raised line on each side of the twig. Buds solitary or sometimes collateral, subglobose to short-ovoid, with 2 or more pairs of brown keeled scales.

Symphoricarpos orbiculatus. Coralberry. Similar to *S. occidentalis* except twigs not hollow (i.e., pith present). The red to coral fruits of *S. orbiculatus* will also distinguish it when they are present.

Viburnum molle. Kentucky viburnum. Similar to *V. rafinesquianum* except bark of main stems papery and peeling.

Viburnum rafinesquianum. Arrowwood. Twigs slender, brown or gray. Leaf scars V-shaped or crescent-shaped with 3 bundle scars. Buds solitary, ovoid, usually with 4 brown scales.

PL. 8, left to right: *Acer ginnala*, *Euonymus alatus*, *Euonymus atropurpureus* (two images), *Ligustrum* species, *Rhamnus cathartica*, *Staphylea trifolia*.

Plate 8. Leaf Scars Opposite, Subopposite, or Whorled; Buds with Overlapping Scales (continued)

Acer ginnala. Amur maple. Twigs slender, brown. Leaf scars crescent-shaped to somewhat V-shaped, raised on a short extension of the twig, with 3 bundle scars. Buds small, solitary, subglobose, with 2 or 3 pairs of visible scales. Branchlets often bearing short side twigs, each tipped by a fruit cluster or its broken stalk.

Euonymus alatus. Burning bush. Twigs slender to moderate, green, with 4 brown corky wings. Leaf scars small, crescent-shaped, each with a single elongated bundle scar near its upper margin. Buds solitary, ovoid, with 4 or 5 pairs of brown scales.

Euonymus atropurpureus. Wahoo. Twigs rather slender, green or purple, often with 4 lines. Leaf scars small, crescent-shaped or half-round, each with a single curved bundle scar near its upper margin. Buds solitary, ovoid to ovoid-elongate, colored like the twig, with 2 or more pairs of somewhat spreading scales.

Ligustrum. Privet. Twigs slender, gray. Leaf scars small, half-round, with a single elongated and sometimes indistinct bundle scar. Buds usually solitary, ovoid, with about half a dozen dark scales.

Rhamnus cathartica. Common buckthorn. Twigs rather slender, gray, often tipped by a short thorn. Leaf scars half-round, slightly raised, usually subopposite but sometimes opposite or alternate; 3 or more bundle scars in a short line. Buds solitary, ovoid to ovoid-elongate, with 4 or more dark purple-brown scales.

Staphylea trifolia. Bladdernut. Twigs slender to moderate, green; branchlets dark purple-brown with prominent white lenticels. Leaf scars variably shaped but usually somewhat half-round, with 3 or more bundle scars. Buds solitary, subglobose to short-ovoid, with 2 to 4 dark purple scales.

Shrubs and Vines in Nature

MORE THAN 130 SPECIES of shrubs and vines were growing naturally in Iowa when European Americans arrived. Additional species are growing here now, most of which were introduced by people. Where are shrubs and vines distributed in Iowa, and why?

First, it is important to remember that some species of shrubs and vines have existed in Iowa much longer than others. Those that preceded European Americans are said to be native, while those brought here from other places are introduced. When the seeds of introduced species disperse to a wild area and grow into new plants, we say they have escaped. If these escaped plants begin to reproduce and spread, mimicking a native species, they are called naturalized. Nonnative species evolved in climates, habitats, and communities different from ours, which sometimes makes it hard to understand why they grow where they do in Iowa.

Some native species are common throughout Iowa, growing in a variety of environments. Others are confined to a particular region, locality, or habitat. Their patterns of distribution are determined both by their inherent features and by historical factors. Some of the latter include glaciation, climate change, fire suppression, and the conversion of natural land to agriculture and other uses.

Iowa's Changing Vegetation

Before people changed the landscape of Iowa, nature often did. In the distant past, shallow seas occupied much or all of Iowa, leaving deposits that later became the bedrock of our state (Prior 1976). Later, during the Pleistocene Ice Age, great glaciers alternately advanced into Iowa and then melted. The glaciers both eroded and deposited materials, leaving a completely changed landscape when they departed.

Land newly freed from melting glaciers may have been occupied by a narrow band of tundralike vegetation similar to that in the Arctic today. This was soon replaced by a forest of northern coniferous and broadleaf trees as the postglacial climate became warmer and drier. Eventually this vegetation disappeared, too, except in northeast Iowa and a few other places where cooler conditions allowed some of its species to survive. Today, nearly 20 percent of the shrub and vine species in Iowa are remnants of this once extensive northern or boreal forest.

Over most of Iowa, the boreal forest was replaced by a temperate forest of oaks and other deciduous trees. Later, as the climate continued to warm, prairie gained the upper hand, replacing the forest over most of Iowa. Eventually somewhat cooler and moister conditions returned, allowing forest to spread north and west along Iowa's river valleys, slowly encroaching upon the prairie.

Frequent prairie fires favored the prairie in this forest-prairie dynamic, killing invading trees except in areas protected by firebreaks such as large bodies of water, steep rocky slopes, and moist ravines. Thus, at the time European Americans arrived, the landscape was in many places a mosaic of prairie and woodland. Shrubs often occurred in the boundary between the two.

Because of Iowa's climate history and its location between different climatic and vegetational regions, many of our native shrubs and vines range into Iowa from the north, east, south, or west. Some of these just barely make their way into the state, for example, fox grape in the southern part of the state, buffaloberry in the west, and witch-hazel along our eastern border. Often these species grow very well when planted outside their natural range, so why they are not more widely distributed in nature is an interesting question. Each has different tolerances to drought, heat, cold, and other environmental conditions, and these tolerances can interact with one another in complex ways.

Some Special Habitats

Topography creates special habitats in some parts of Iowa. One of the most interesting is in northeast Iowa, where carbonate bedrock lies close to the surface. Water infiltrates through cracks in this rock, gradually dissolving it to create crevices and caves. The walls of these spaces become very cold in winter as frigid air sinks in. During spring melt, water flowing into the crevices freezes when it contacts the supercooled rocks. In summer, warmer air enters the crevices and

PL. 9. Buttonbush grows along the edges of wetlands in many parts of Iowa.

is chilled by the slowly melting ice around it. The chilled air then drains downward, emerging through openings in the rock onto steep, rocky slopes below, creating cool conditions favoring northern plants.

Shrubs and vines that thrive on these cold-air or algific slopes include the mountain maple, alderleaf buckthorn, purple clematis, northern black currant, and prickly wild rose. These species have probably survived there since they became established as part of a boreal forest shortly following deglaciation.

Another unusual habitat is the fen, a wetland fed by mineral-rich water that seeps out of the ground, often on the side of a hill where the slope intercepts an impermeable layer in the soil. Bog birch, bog willow, and sage willow are characteristic shrubs of this very interesting environment.

Other wetlands occur in basins left by glaciers or in cut-off stream channels called *oxbows*. Shrubs often found in and around these habitats include silky dogwood, indigo bush, buttonbush, wild black currant, and various willows (see pl. 9).

The Loess Hills in western Iowa are another special habitat. The sunny, west-facing slopes there are drier than most other places in Iowa, favoring western species such as yucca and buffaloberry. When people first visit this unusual landform, they are often surprised by the beautiful prairies and scenic views it offers.

How Shrubs Grow

Shrubs differ from trees in both their size and their tendency to form multiple stems. Some species produce clumps of stems from a single crown and increase in size mainly by growing taller. Others remain modest in height and use underground stems to grow horizontally, producing new aboveground stems at some distance away from the original plant. Still other species combine these two methods of growth.

Like all green plants, shrubs require light for photosynthesis and water and nutrients from the soil. Given their need for light, one might expect them to grow best in open areas free of taller vegetation, and that is where most of them are found. Before European American settlement, open areas were abundant on Iowa's prairies, dry ridges, and rock faces, in marshes, and along woodland edges. Today, Iowa landscapes provide these and additional habitats such as fencerows, utility corridors, former pastureland, and thousands of miles of roadsides. Thanks to their resprouting ability (see below), shrubs adapt well to periodic clearing practices that prevent their habitat from being overgrown by trees.

When not maintained, most of these habitats revert eventually to forest. What then becomes of the shrubs? Species adapted to the high light intensity of open areas, if they survive, struggle under a closed canopy of trees, often unable to produce fruit except on the forest edge (see pl. 10). Within the forest, struggling individuals can occasionally find themselves in a gap in the canopy created by tree fall or other disturbance, where they can get enough sunlight to fruit. Other species of shrubs are shade-tolerant, adapted to completing their growth and reproduction within the shade of canopy trees, but these species, too, often grow more vigorously and fruit more prolifically in a more lighted environment.

Being shorter than trees, shrubs are more vulnerable to browsing by animals. They respond to this challenge by vigorously resprouting when their terminal growth is removed. The new growth appears from buds either lower on the stem or at the shrub's crown, in the latter case forming new stems. People take advantage of this adaptation when using shrubs for clipped hedges and formal landscaping.

PL. 10. The shrub border between forests and open areas is a habitat favored by many kinds of wildlife.

This resprouting ability also benefited shrubs in the past when the prairie-forest border was a prime habitat for them. Being slender and thin-barked, their aboveground stems were easily injured or killed in a prairie fire. However, the shrubs themselves could survive by forming new stems after the fire, especially if their colonies were large and the fire occurred when they were dormant.

Though the prairie is mostly gone, shrubs are still common along the edges of woods. Fire is less of a threat now, so they can grow unimpeded and invade uncultivated areas nearby. In places where prairies do survive, such as the Loess Hills, some of these colonizing shrubs can become a nuisance for those seeking to perpetuate the prairie.

How Vines Grow

Vines behave much like shrubs except that they have a special advantage: they do not have to support their own stems. Thus a greater percentage of their resources can be placed in stem elongation and leaf production. In open areas they can quickly cover open soil or clamber over surrounding vegetation. Some, like wild grapes and Virginia creeper, can climb steep cliff faces and tall trees to reach a light-filled canopy without investing in a massive woody stem.

Vines have a number of ingenious adaptations to hold fast to the structures on which they are growing. One way is by twining, that is, by coiling around the stem of the host plant. Usually the main stem of the vine is the twining part but, in some vines, other organs serve this function (see below). Large vigorous vines sometimes damage small trees by twining around their trunks and restricting their growth.

Other vines climb using special outgrowths of their stems called aerial roots or tendrils. Vines with aerial roots, such as trumpet creeper and poison ivy, grow tightly appressed to the trunks of trees. Vines with tendrils, including woodbine and wild grape, tend to climb trees more loosely or clamber on shrubs and fences. Their tendrils may or may not be forked, depending on the species. In Virginia creeper, the tips of the tendrils develop small adhesive pads that help them hold fast to their support. In other vines, the tendrils probe into cracks in the bark or other irregularities, expanding at their tip to hold the vine in place.

Two Iowa vines have unique methods of producing tendrils: by twining petioles (clematis) or by the elongated and twining tips of their stipules (greenbrier). Unlike most woody plants, they cannot shed their leaves by forming an abscission zone where their petioles join the twig, or they would lose their attachment to supporting structures.

Spreading from Place to Place

More than two-thirds of native shrub and vine species have fleshy fruits that are eaten by animals, primarily birds. The plants in effect hitch a ride by offering the animals free food, hiding their seeds inside. In many cases the fruits are brightly colored or borne on colorful stalks, which increases their visibility. When an animal eats them, the seeds pass unharmed through its digestive tract and germinate where the animal deposits them. It is no surprise that many of our most common invasive species disperse by this method.

The remaining shrub and vine species disperse their seeds in various ways. Witch-hazel forcibly ejects its seeds from small woody pods. Willows, maples, and hoptree use the wind. Hazelnuts produce nuts that are gathered and buried by squirrels and chipmunks; they depend upon the animals losing track of some of them. Other species, such as bladdernut, use water or gravity to move their seeds from place to place.

The fruits of most species ripen late in the growing season. In most cases, the seeds of these late-maturing species will not germinate until they have been chilled for several months. This ensures that the seedlings appear in spring, rather than summer or fall, giving them as much time as possible to establish before winter.

Rare, Threatened, and Endangered Species

A surprising number of Iowa's shrubs and vines are rare. As of 2014, the Iowa Department of Natural Resources, which keeps track of these plants, lists thirty-seven species as endangered, threatened, or of special concern, representing nearly 30 percent of the shrubs and vines native in Iowa.

How are these degrees of rarity defined? Endangered species are those in danger of extinction throughout all or a significant part of their range, while threatened species are likely to become endangered in the foreseeable future. Special concern plants are suspected to have conservation problems, but the DNR has not been able to fully document their status. See the DNR's website for more information about Iowa's endangered, threatened, and special concern species, both plant and animal, at http://www.iowadnr.gov/Environment/ThreatenedEndangered/NaturalAreasInventory.aspx.

It is important to note that plants considered endangered, threatened, or of special concern in Iowa may not be rare through their entire range. For example, the lowbush blueberry is common in Minnesota and other northern states, but in Iowa it grows in only a few places. It is listed as threatened here because if its numbers were to be reduced, it would be in danger of extirpation from Iowa.

Plants become rare for different reasons. As noted above, some species just barely range into Iowa and were probably never common during our current climatic period. Others have become scarce because of habitat destruction, changes in land management, or competition with invasive species. Some rare plants are widely distributed in a particular region of Iowa but occur in low numbers, while others are fairly common in a special habitat that itself is rare.

Why should we preserve rare plants? One reason is that they make outdoor Iowa a more diverse and interesting place. Another is that they support native wildlife, for instance, the many insects hosted by indigo bush as described elsewhere in this book. Rare plants may also someday prove useful to people, providing new foods and medicines or genes to improve crop plants. An example is the aronia berry, a once-obscure shrub now cultivated for the health benefits its fruits confer. Rare species can also be indicators of a healthy environment. Like a canary in a mine, their loss may be an early warning of problems that may in time affect common species.

Even if a species is abundant elsewhere, its rare populations in Iowa are worth conserving. Many Iowa plants are at the edge of their range, and these peripheral populations may have unique genetic traits that allow them to survive conditions marginal for their species. At a time of rapid climate change, such populations may be essential to keeping species alive.

State parks and preserves are important refuges for endangered, threatened, and special concern plants. These plants are also protected on other public lands, including those managed by the federal government and county conservation boards, on preserves owned by nonprofit organizations such as The Nature Conservancy, and on private property.

Invasive Species

Anyone who farms and gardens is familiar with weeds. Most of these unwanted plants were accidentally introduced from the Old World and, being adapted to disturbance by people, thrived in the highly modified environment that characterizes most of Iowa. Others that are well behaved in their native lands may spread unimpeded in Iowa, where they find themselves free of the competitors and pests that held them in check where they naturally occur.

Invasive plants are weeds that aggressively colonize natural areas, pastures, roadsides, and other places, often excluding native plants. Many were intentionally introduced by people who did not realize their invasive potential; these species later spread to the wild. Over time they can become so abundant that they are easily mistaken for a native species.

During the past few decades, invasive shrubs have become a terrible problem in Iowa's woods and open lands. Most were introduced for landscaping or conservation and, producing berries that are attractive to birds, have spread beyond the places they were planted. Their names unfortunately are now all too familiar: common buckthorn, honeysuckles, multiflora rose, autumn olive, Oriental bittersweet. And their impact continues to grow.

These problem species illustrate the importance of being very careful about plant introductions, especially shrubs that are easy to grow and that produce fruits dispersed by birds or wind. When planting shrubs as ornamentals or to attract birds, it is best to use native species or introduced ones that have been cultivated for many years and have not escaped to the wild.

For more information about invasive woody plants in Iowa and a discussion of how we might anticipate invasiveness, see the articles by Farrar (2001) and Widrlechner (2001) cited in the bibliography.

Shrubs, Vines, and Wildlife

It would be hard to overestimate the importance of shrubs and vines to wildlife. The animals using them range from insects to birds to small and large mammals, often as part of complex interactions as noted elsewhere in this book.

Studies in Iowa and elsewhere have shown that many of our favorite birds, especially migrating species that winter farther south, key on shrub density and diversity in choosing their nesting territories here (Norris et al. 2003). Other studies have indicated that the diversity of wildlife species in a given place correlates well with the diversity in plant structure (forms and sizes of plants). Diversity in plant structure depends in turn on having a variety of plant species present.

In Iowa as elsewhere, wildlife species differ in where they choose to live. Some prefer the solitude and plant structure of deep forest interiors, others the broad expanses of grasslands with scattered shrubs and vines. The edges between plant communities, often dominated by shrubs and vines, are often particularly rich in wildlife.

Another valuable habitat is the savanna, once prevalent in Iowa but now rare. Managers who restore savannas often try to completely clear the understory of tree saplings, shrubs, and vines. However, a recent study by Mabry (2013) showed that maintaining a 10 to 35 percent cover of shrubs benefited shrub-dependent, declining bird species such as willow flycatcher, Bell's vireo, field sparrow, brown thrasher, common yellowthroat, and yellow-billed cuckoo while still retaining the open character desired in a savanna.

Narrow vegetation corridors are still another important habitat because they allow wildlife to travel between larger sanctuaries. When we think "corridors," we automatically picture fencerows, small stream channels, and roadsides lined with shrubs, vines, and small trees. It's instructive to walk along one of these corridors on a winter morning after an overnight snowfall. You can hear the bustling twitter of foraging songbirds and see the tracks of mammals and large birds, here and there venturing out of the corridor into crop fields to forage for waste grain, then scurrying back to a secure thicket of shrubs and vines. A sense of their dependence on and appreciation of the tangle of shrubs and vines is palpable.

Does it matter to wildlife what species of shrubs are present in an area? Many habitats in Iowa are dominated by exotic shrubs that were introduced because it was thought they would be useful for wildlife. While these do provide food, their prevalence does have drawbacks. Studies have shown that the specific architecture of shrubs' stems and branches makes a difference to nesting and foraging birds, and the birds often do not choose exotic species such as buckthorn and honeysuckle (Schmidt and Whelan 1999; Woods 1993). Moreover, exotic shrubs are often invasive and create a cover thicker than some birds prefer while outcompeting native plant species and thus reducing diversity. Thus it is always best to plant native species.

For more information about the value of shrubs and vines to wildlife, we recommend *American Wildlife and Plants: A Guide to Wildlife Food Habits* (Martin et al. 1951). This older but still relevant book lists which plants are most used for food by individual wildlife species based on the analysis of stomach contents. Among the woody plants, twenty-two of the top thirty-five genera in the United States (excluding Alaska and Hawaii) are shrubs or vines. The most important genera in Iowa include *Rubus* (blackberries and raspberries), *Prunus* (wild cherries and plums), *Cornus* (dogwoods), *Vitis* (grapes), *Toxicodendron* (poison ivy), *Juniperus* (junipers and eastern redcedar), and *Sambucus* (elderberries). Other notable genera in the top thirty-five include *Rhus* (sumacs), *Salix* (willows), *Symphoricarpos* (snowberry and coralberry), *Smilax* (greenbriers), and *Parthenocissus* (Virginia creeper and woodbine).

American Wildlife and Plants makes special note of the time of year that different plant foods are available. It is easy to imagine the smorgasbord of plant foods available in summer and fall, but consider how many of those remain by late winter and early spring when wildlife is no less in need of food. This is the time of year when rabbits and deer browse the twigs and stem bark of shrubs, squirrels and turkeys eat buds (especially pollen-rich catkins), and the persistent fruits of poison ivy, sumac, coralberry, and wild roses become lifesavers to fruit-eating wildlife.

Growing Shrubs and Vines

When people move to a new place, they often take their favorite plants with them. Such was the case when European Americans migrated to Iowa; they introduced trees, shrubs, grasses, crops, and ornamental plants that had not grown here previously.

Today our gardens and landscapes are dominated by such introduced plants as lilacs, Norway maples, and hydrangeas. Our own Iowa-native plants are often overlooked, though they have much to offer: winter hardiness, resistance to drought and climatic extremes, and usefulness to native wildlife and pollinators. Many natives are ornamental as well, providing attractive flowers, bright autumn color, and winter interest from colorful stems or fruits.

Of course, you don't have to use native plants exclusively; you can mix them with your favorite introduced plants. Your goal should be a landscape that is sustainable, authentic to place, and satisfying to you. The value of native plants is that they make this goal much easier to attain.

Selecting the Right Plants for the Site

Our native shrubs and vines have varied uses. The tougher, more adaptable species are valuable for such conservation purposes as erosion control, stream buffers, and components of windbreaks. Large shrubs are useful for screens and masses in informal, naturalistic landscapes or as focal points in smaller, more structured settings. In Iowa, large shrubs are also commonly planted along highways, where they serve as windbreaks and also provide colorful stems and foliage as well as food and habitat for wildlife. Dwarf shrubs can be mixed with perennials and ornamental grasses in garden beds and borders. Vines can be trained on trellises to add color and texture to a landscape or grown on arbors to provide shade.

Always select species that are well suited to your site, based on either previous experience or consideration of where the plants grow in nature. For instance, sites that are sunny most of the day are best planted with species from well-lit habitats, while shady places are best planted with woodland shrubs.

Another important consideration is a plant's ultimate size. Native shrub species vary from dwarf to very large, so there is a suitable species for nearly every situation. Where space is limited, it is better to plant a small species than a larger one that will have to be constantly pruned to keep it in bounds. Likewise, plants that form colonies are not the best choices for small gardens.

Keep in mind that plants native in one part of Iowa may not be suitable for cultivation everywhere. For example, the mountain maple grows in northeast Iowa on algific slopes and in other cool environments. It is certainly worth trying in other parts of the state, but most likely it would not survive in a suburban landscape or along an expressway in Des Moines.

In contrast, plants from disturbed habitats are often very adaptable in cultivation. Thus, species that grow naturally in bottomlands, an environment prone to flooding, usually grow well in both lowland and upland sites. Upland species are adapted to a more stable environment with well-aerated soils, and they do not necessarily thrive when planted in lowlands, especially where water stands for very long.

Within a species, the geographic origin or provenance of plants can make a difference to success in cultivation. Plants grown from native Iowa seed will probably prove more satisfactory than the same species grown from seed collected in Tennessee, because the Iowa plants are adapted to local conditions. When planting natives, try to obtain locally sourced material whenever possible.

As an aid to plant selection, we offer two tables of native shrubs and vines suited to various uses. These are intended as a guide only, not as an exclusive list of what will grow in Iowa. We would not discourage anyone from experimenting with other native shrubs and vines. Species in table 2 are less adapted to general use than those in table 1 and are not easily found in nurseries, but they are worth trying in naturalistic gardens and landscapes.

TABLE 1. Native Shrubs and Vines Useful for Planting

Plant Type	Conservation, Wildlife, and Naturalistic Landscaping	Home Landscaping
Large shrub	Speckled alder* Indigo bush* Buttonbush* Silky dogwood* Gray dogwood Red-osier dogwood* American hazelnut Wahoo Ninebark American plum Smooth sumac Pussy willow* Sandbar willow* Common elderberry* Nannyberry Blackhaw Downy arrowwood American highbush-cranberry	Pagoda or alternate-leaf dogwood Red-osier dogwood* Witch-hazel Ninebark Blackhaw Downy arrowwood American highbush-cranberry
Medium shrub	Low serviceberry Black chokeberry (aronia berry) Fragrant sumac Wild black currant* Smooth wild rose Prairie willow Meadowsweet* Wolfberry Coralberry	Fragrant sumac Clove or buffalo currant Prairie willow Coralberry
Small shrub	Leadplant New Jersey tea Bush honeysuckle (*Diervilla*) Sunshine or wild rose Pasture rose Black raspberry	Leadplant New Jersey tea Bush honeysuckle (*Diervilla*) Creeping juniper Shrubby cinquefoil
Vine	American bittersweet Virginia creeper Woodbine	American bittersweet Virgin's bower Wild honeysuckle Grape honeysuckle

*These species are especially tolerant of wet places.

TABLE 2. Native Shrubs and Vines Recommended for Trial Plantings

Plant Type	Species
Large shrub	Bog birch Roundleaf dogwood Winterberry Pin cherry Bebb's willow Red elderberry Bladdernut Kentucky viburnum
Medium shrub	Leatherwood Shrubby St. John's–wort Dwarf or sand cherry
Small shrub	Bearberry
Vine	Leather flower

Types of Nursery Stock

Nurseries offer plants in various ways. Bare-root plants are typically used for large-scale plantings such as windbreaks and habitat restoration. These are available in early spring when the plants are still dormant and, as their name suggests, come with no soil attached to the roots. They must be planted almost immediately upon arrival.

Container-grown plants have been grown for a time in a plastic or biodegradable pot. They can be planted almost anytime, although spring and fall are best. We particularly recommend late September and October, as the soil is still warm and thus favorable for root growth, while the weather is cool and thus less stressful on the plants.

Larger shrubs may be available balled and burlapped or B&B as they are known in the nursery trade. These have been grown in the field and are dug so the roots are enclosed in a ball of natural soil, which is then wrapped with burlap to hold it together. If you purchase plants in this way, be sure to follow the nursery's planting instructions.

Growing Plants from Seed

Unfortunately, many nurseries have a very limited selection of native plants. If you can't find the species you want, you can always try growing them from seed. Many native shrubs and vines are easy to propagate this way, and growing them yourself can be a very satisfying hobby.

Begin by collecting your seeds when their fruits are ripe, which for most species is in the fall. Remove them from their pulp or pod and sow them outdoors in the place you want them to be or, if you plan to grow them in containers the next year, store them over the winter as described below.

Most woody plant seeds must undergo several weeks of cool, moist conditions before they can germinate, in effect mimicking the conditions they experience naturally over the winter. One way to accomplish this is to place the cleaned seeds in a plastic bag with a little potting soil, peat, or sand and keep them in a refrigerator. Or you can plant the seeds in pots and store the pots in a garage over the winter. The soil should be kept slightly moist but not so wet that the seeds mold.

Depending on the species, your seeds will germinate either the spring you plant them or the following spring. For more information on the germination requirements of different species, see *Seeds of Woody Plants in North America* (Young and Young 1992).

How to Plant

After you purchase or propagate your plants, there are several measures you can take to ensure their success. Proper planting is perhaps the most important of these.

First, dig a hole that will accommodate the plant's roots without crowding. Ideally the hole should be wider than the root ball but no deeper, to prevent the crown of the shrub from settling in the hole and becoming buried.

If the plant is in a container, carefully remove the container by grasping the crown of the plant and gently lifting. If the roots are tightly bound or encircling the container, carefully remove some of the potting soil and tease the roots out of the mass, so they can more easily grow into the soil.

Next, place the plant in the hole and gently spread the roots outward. Backfill with the same soil you dug from the hole, tamped lightly but not so firmly that you compact the soil. Water thoroughly, prune any branches that were damaged during planting, and mulch.

Caring for Shrubs and Vines

Most native shrubs and vines are relatively care-free. As with other plants, you can enhance their health, vigor, and appearance through cultural practices such as watering, mulching, and pruning.

Watering is especially important during a plant's first year or two in the ground, but during drought it can benefit plants of all ages. Plants should be watered when the soil feels dry.

Mulching is the application of material to the soil surface beneath a plant, to reduce weeds and to help maintain a favorable environment for root growth. Wood chips or a similar organic material are best. Maintain mulch at a depth of 2 to 3 inches, pulling it back from the crown of the plant.

Pruning is both an art and a science. It is sometimes done for the wrong reason, for example, to reduce the size of a plant that is really too big for its location and needs to be replaced with something smaller. Better reasons are to keep the plant vigorous and maintain its natural form. Pruning techniques include renewal, heading back, and rejuvenation.

Renewal pruning is the selective removal of individual stems by cutting them off at the ground. Its goals are to maintain the natural size and shape of a plant while encouraging new vigorous growth from the base. Renewal pruning can also be used to gradually reduce the size of overgrown plants, although as noted above you might consider whether such plants are appropriate for the site. Renewal is best performed in early spring while the plant is still dormant, as it is easier to see its structure then. In the case of spring-blooming plants, it can be delayed until just after flowering if desired. Remove about one-third of the stems at a time.

Heading back is reducing the length of a stem by cutting it back to a bud. It accomplishes the same purpose as shearing (see below), except it is a more finessed approach that helps maintain a plant's natural appearance. It is most effective when combined with renewal pruning. In garden settings, dwarf shrubs such as *Potentilla*, *Spiraea*, and *Diervilla* should be both renewal-pruned and headed-back each year in late winter or early spring.

Rejuvenation is a quick way to restore a plant that has become overgrown or misshapen: cutting all its stems off at the ground. Because it is so drastic, it

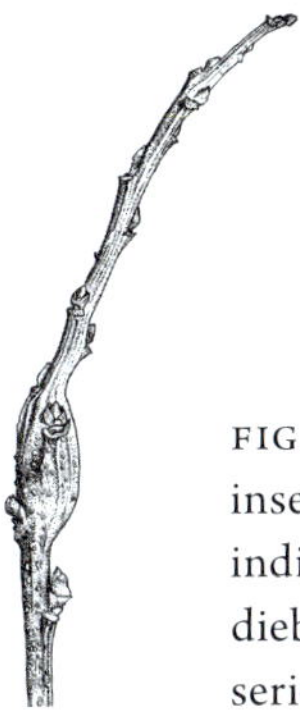

FIG. 56. Stem galls caused by insects, such as this one on indigo bush, may cause minor dieback but usually do not seriously harm plants.

should be performed only on healthy plants while they are dormant. The resulting new growth will be extremely vigorous and may grow so long that it becomes floppy. Thus, rejuvenation often needs to be followed by other methods of pruning.

A final method of pruning, called shearing, is appropriate for hedges and topiary in formal gardens, but we do not recommend it for native shrubs in most landscapes, as it prevents the plants from attaining their natural form and proportions. If not properly performed, shearing causes dense growth at the top of plants whose shade prevents new growth at the bottom. Over time, this leads to an unattractive plant that is bare of foliage for most of its height.

Insects and Diseases

Most native shrubs and vines do not suffer serious insect and disease problems. A few species are prone to mildew, which can mar their foliage late in the season but usually does no serious harm to the plant. Others may suffer minor damage from insect larvae that chew the foliage, mine the green tissue inside leaves, or form galls on the leaves or stems (fig. 56). By viewing these insects as a part of nature rather than as pests and accepting that plants don't have to be perfect to be beautiful, you can turn a problem into an opportunity to learn about some very interesting creatures.

Wildlife Damage

Deer and other animals can at times be very destructive of woody plants. Deer rub their antlers on stems during autumn and early winter, sometimes breaking or girdling them. Near rivers and streams, beavers cut stems to the ground. Deer and rabbits may browse plants so severely that they become stunted or unsightly.

You can try to minimize browsing by choosing so-called wildlife-resistant plants, but in our experience this strategy does not always work. If hungry enough, animals will eat whatever food is available, including plants they might normally leave alone.

In existing landscapes, wildlife damage can sometimes be reduced by applying chemical repellents or by setting out soap or human hair. Unfortunately, you cannot rely on such remedies to work indefinitely. In smaller landscapes, the best defense is a sturdy wire cage around individual plants. A well-maintained electric fence can be very effective in excluding deer from larger areas.

Using Vines Creatively

When we think of vines in the landscape, the first image that often comes to mind is of ivy climbing walls. Vines are versatile plants, however, that can be put to several other uses.

If you would like to create a shady spot in your landscape and don't have room for a tree, consider an arbor planted with American bittersweet or virgin's bower. If you need to cover a dry shady spot where grass doesn't want to grow, try a groundcover of woodbine. If you would like something tall to serve as a focal point or to screen an unwanted view, build a trellis planted with wild honeysuckle or one of the vines noted above. If you want to benefit wildlife but don't have much space, plant Virginia creeper at the base of a shade tree and allow it to grow up onto the trunk.

You can either purchase arbors and trellises or make them yourself. To create a trellis for stronger vines, construct a frame of treated 4-by-4 posts and staple sturdy wire mesh to it. Or for smaller species such as clematis, use the cut stems of large shrubs to create a framework held together with screws. Use your imagination and be creative! Above all, enjoy the natural beauty these plants provide and the wildlife they attract.

GLOSSARY

achene: a small dry single-seeded fruit.
acuminate: tapered to a slender tip.
acute: pointed.
algific (slope): cold-air.
alternate: occurring singly at each node on the twig. See figure 1.
anther: the pollen-bearing sac at the tip of the stamen.
apetalous: lacking petals.
ascendate (inflorescence): few-flowered with the lower flowers on long stalks.
axil (of leaf): the junction of the petiole and the twig.

berry: a fleshy fruit with seeds suspended in the flesh.
bisexual (flower): having both male and female parts.
bract: a very small leaflike structure.
branchlet: a small branch consisting of a twig and one or several years' previous growth.
bud: a shoot or flower cluster in its initial stage, before environmental conditions are such that it can fully expand and develop; typically small, somewhat egg-shaped, and enclosed by protective scales.
bundle scar: a small dot or line within a leaf scar, marking the place where a vascular bundle of the leaf entered the twig.

calyx: a collective term for the sepals of a flower.
capsule: a podlike fruit with more than one internal chamber, usually splitting open along two or more seams.
carpel: the female part of a flower, often united into a flask-shaped structure called the pistil with a narrow neck or style and a swollen tip or stigma.
catkin: a cylindrical cluster of small, closely spaced, usually imperfect, and apetalous flowers, often long, drooping, and tail-like, also known as an ament.
chaffy: dry and papery in texture, like the chaff of grains.
chambered (pith): consisting of thin cross walls with no tissue in between.
collateral (bud): side by side.
compound (leaf): divided into two or more separate blades.
cordate: heart-shaped.

corolla: a collective term for all the petals of an individual flower.
corymb: a branched inflorescence with a flat or convex top. See figure 4.
corymbose: resembling a corymb.
cultivar: a cultivated variety of a species with features that make it desirable horticulturally and that is propagated in such a way that these features are maintained from one generation to the next.
cyme: a flat or convex inflorescence whose central or terminal flowers bloom first.

deciduous (leaf): separating from the stem and dropping in autumn.
decumbent (stem): trailing on the ground with the tip pointing upward.
diaphragmed (pith): solid with cross walls at regular intervals.
dioecious: having male and female flowers on separate plants, so individual plants are either male or female.
drupe: a fleshy fruit with a single large hard seed (stone) in the middle (cherry, plum, olive).

ellipsoid (fruit): about twice as long as it is in diameter and tending to be widest near the middle.
elliptic: about twice as long as wide and widest near the middle. See figure 1.
entire (leaf margin): not toothed. See figure 1.
escaped (species): growing in a wild place after its seeds were dispersed there from cultivated plants.

fascicle: a small, bunched cluster of flowers, fruits, or leaves.
filament: the stalklike base of a stamen, bearing anthers at its tip.
filiform: threadlike.
floricane: the second-year flowering and fruiting cane of a raspberry or a blackberry.
follicle: a podlike fruit with a single chamber.

glabrous: lacking hairs.
gland: a small dotlike or lumplike secretory structure.
glaucous: with a pale waxy coating.
globose: ball-shaped. See figure 3.

herbaceous (plant or stem): not woody, that is, dying back entirely to the ground every winter.

imperfect (flower): having either male or female parts but not both.
inferior (ovary): having the petals at its top (compare to superior).

inflorescence: flower cluster.
internode: the elongated portion of a twig between successive nodes.
introduced (species): imported into an area by people.
irregular (flower): having petals of different sizes and shapes.

keeled: folded with a lengthwise ridge in the middle, as in the hull of a ship.

lanceolate: several times longer than wide with the base wider than the tip; the opposite of oblanceolate. See figure 1.
lateral bud: one of the buds located along the side of a twig; if located at the tip of the twig, differing from a terminal bud in being the same size as the other lateral buds and in having the broken-off twig tip or scar above its base.
leaflet: an individual blade of a compound leaf.
leaf scar: a small impression on a winter twig, marking the place where a leaf was attached during the previous growing season.
legume: a beanlike fruit with a single chamber and two seams.
lenticel: a pore in the bark of a twig or young stem, usually dotlike or linelike in shape and sometimes much different in color than the bark.
linear: long and narrow with nearly parallel sides. See figure 1.

moderate (twig): for purposes of this book, a twig whose internodes average 3 to 4 mm in diameter.
monoecious: having male and female flowers on the same plant.

naked (bud): lacking scales.
native (species): growing naturally in an area before it was settled by people and not introduced by them either deliberately or accidentally.
naturalized (species): escaped from cultivation and reproducing successfully in the wild as if native.
node: the place on a twig where a leaf is attached.
nutlet: a small nutlike fruit.

oblanceolate: several times longer than wide with the tip wider than the base; the opposite of lanceolate.
oblong: two to three times longer than wide with nearly parallel sides. See figure 1.
obovate: egg-shaped in outline with the tip wider than the base; the opposite of ovate. See figure 1.
opposite: occurring in pairs at each node on the twig, one on either side. See figure 1.
orbicular: round.

oval: slightly longer than wide and widest near the middle. See figure 1.
ovate: egg-shaped in outline with the base wider than the tip; the opposite of obovate. See figure 1.
ovoid: egg-shaped. See figure 3.
ovoid-elongate: narrowly egg-shaped.

palmately: with the leaflets, lobes, or veins arranged around a common point, like the spokes of a wheel or the spread fingers of a hand. See figure 1.
panicle: a branched inflorescence whose top is not flat. See figure 4.
pedicel: the stalk of a flower or fruit.
perfect (flower): having both male and female parts.
petiole: the stalk of a leaf.
pilose: bearing soft hairs
pinnately compound (leaf): with the leaflets arranged along either side of a central stem. See figure 1.
pistil: the female part of a flower, centrally located and usually flasklike in shape and consisting of one or more united carpels.
pistillate (flower): female.
pith: the center core of a twig.
plicate: with lengthwise folds, like corrugated cardboard.
polygamous: having both perfect and imperfect flowers on one individual plant.
pome: a fleshy fruit with more than one seed, the seeds confined to a separate section in the middle, and the remnants of the flower located on the end opposite the stem (apple, pear).
prickle: a sharply pointed outgrowth from the surface of a twig or leaf petiole.
primocane: the first-year nonflowering and nonfruiting cane of a raspberry or a blackberry.
pubescent: hairy.
pyramidal: pyramid-shaped.

raceme: an inflorescence consisting of a single unbranched stem with stalked flowers. See figure 4.
racemose: resembling a raceme.
rachis: the axis of a pinnate leaf along which the leaflets are arranged.
receptacle: the base of the flower where the carpels, stamens, petals, and sepals are attached; in most cases it is noticeably thicker than the stalk that supports the flower.
regular (flower): with all petals of the same size and shape.
rhombic: diamond-shaped.

samara: a dry winged fruit with the seed at one end or in the middle.
sepals: the outer whorl of flower parts, usually green and leafy in appearance.
serrate: bearing regularly spaced teeth.
sessile: not stalked.
simple (leaf): with a single blade, not divided into leaflets. See figure 1.
sinus: the space between two leaf lobes.
slender (twig): for purposes of this book, a twig whose internodes are less than 3 mm in diameter.
solitary (bud): occurring by itself above the leaf scar, that is, not superposed or collateral.
spatulate: spoon-shaped with the narrow part at the base.
spike: an inflorescence consisting of a single upright, unbranched stem with unstalked flowers. See figure 4.
spine: a leaf or stipule that has become woody, sharp, and thornlike.
spur shoot: a short, stubby twig with closely spaced leaves and leaf scars.
stamen: the male part of a flower, consisting of a slender stalk or filament and a pollen-bearing sac called the anther.
staminate (flower): male.
stellate: star-shaped.
stipule: a small leafy structure usually occurring in pairs at the node and leaving a small linelike scar on the twig when it falls.
stout (twig): for purposes of this book, a twig whose internodes are 5 mm or more in diameter.
subglobose: nearly ball-shaped, slightly longer than it is wide or thick. See figure 3.
subopposite: associated in pairs but not exactly opposite one another.
subtended (by): bearing some other structure at its base.
style: the slender necklike portion of a pistil.
superior (ovary): having the petals at its base (compare to inferior).
superposed (buds): arranged one above the other.

tendril: in vines, a usually coiling outgrowth of the stem used for grasping an object or surface on which the vine is climbing.
terminal bud: a bud that occupies the tip of the twig and is not a lateral bud.
thorn: a sharply pointed, modified twig.
tomentose: bearing dense matted hairs.
toothed: bearing small toothlike projections along the margin. See figure 1.
torus: in the genus *Rubus*, the dome-shaped or thimblelike structure (receptacle) to which the fruit is attached.
trifoliate (leaf): divided into three leaflets, as in the leaf of clover or poison ivy.

truncate: with the end leveled off as if it were cut away, not pointed or rounded.
twig: the terminal portion of a woody stem, bearing leaves or, in the winter, leaf scars.

umbel: an inflorescence with multiple stems of similar length radiating from a common point, like the ribs of an umbrella. See figure 4.
unisexual (flower): having either male or female parts but not both.

valvate: covered by two scales that meet along the edges without overlapping.
vascular bundle: a strand of tissue that transports water and nutrients within a plant.

whorled: having three or more leaves, buds, or leaf scars at each node.

BIBLIOGRAPHY

Bailey, L. H. 1941. Species *batorum*. The genus *Rubus* in North America. *Gentes Herbarum* 5: 1–64.

Brandhorst, C. T. 1962. The microcommunity associated with the gall of *Walshia amorphella* (Lepidoptera: Cosmopterygidae) on *Amorpha fruticosa*. *Annals of the Entomological Society of America* 35 (4): 476–479.

Cronquist, A. 1978. Once again, what is a species? In *Biosystematics in Agriculture*, ed. L. V. Knutson, pp. 3–20. Allanheld, Osmun, Montclair, N.J.

Eilers, L. J., and D. M. Roosa. 1994. *The Vascular Plants of Iowa: An Annotated Checklist and Natural History*. University of Iowa Press, Iowa City.

Farrar, D. R. 2001. Exotic and invasive woody plant species in Iowa. *Journal of the Iowa Academy of Science* 108 (4): 154–157.

Fernald, M. L. 1950. *Gray's Manual of Botany*. 8th ed. D. Van Nostrand, New York.

Gleason, H. A. 1952. *The New Britton and Brown Illustrated Flora of the Northeastern United States and Adjacent Canada*. Hafner Press, New York.

Iowa Department of Natural Resources. 2013. State Forest Nursery 2013–2014 seedling catalog. Des Moines.

———. 2014. Iowa Natural Areas Inventory (INAI) interactive website. http://www.iowadnr.gov/Environment/ThreatenedEndangered/NaturalAreasInventory.aspx.

Iowa General Assembly. 2014. Iowa Code Chapter 317. Weeds. http://www.legis.iowa.gov/law.

Jauron, R. 2013. Growing blueberries in Iowa. Iowa State University Extension RG 503 (rev.). Iowa State University, Ames.

Johnson-Groh, C. L., and D. R. Farrar. 1985. Flora and phytogeographical history of Ledges State Park, Boone County, Iowa. *Proceedings of the Iowa Academy of Science* 92 (4): 137–143.

———, D. Q. Lewis, and J. F. Shearer. 1987. Vegetation communities and flora of Dolliver State Park, Webster County, Iowa. *Proceedings of the Iowa Academy of Science* 94 (3): 84–88.

Kingsbury, J. M. 1965. *Deadly Harvest: A Guide to Common Poisonous Plants*. Holt, Rinehart and Winston, New York.

Klots, A. B. 1951. *A Field Guide to the Butterflies of North America East of the Great Plains*. Houghton Mifflin, Boston.

Lammers, T. G. 1980. The vascular flora of Starr's Cave State Preserve. *Proceedings of the Iowa Academy of Science* 87 (4): 148–158.

Mabry, C. 2013. Optimal shrub density for bird habitat in the midwestern United States. *Ecological Restoration* 31 (1): 63–68.

McCormick, L. E. 2000a. Plant inventory of Lamson Woods State Preserve, Jefferson County, Iowa. Unpublished report.

———. 2000b. Plant inventory of Woodthrush Woods State Preserve, Jefferson County, Iowa. Unpublished report.

Mader, E., M. Shepherd, M. Vaughan, S. Black, and G. LeBuhn. 2011. *Attracting Native Pollinators.* Storey Publishing, North Adams, Mass.

Maloy, O. C. 2001. White pine blister rust. Plant Health Progress doi:10.1094/PHP-2001-0924-01-HM. American Phytopathological Society, St. Paul, Minn.

Martin, A. C., H. S. Zim, and A. L. Nelson. 1951. *American Wildlife and Plants: A Guide to Wildlife Food Habits.* McGraw-Hill, New York. Reprint, Dover Publications, New York, 1961.

Morton Arboretum staff. 1990. *Woody Plants of the Morton Arboretum.* Morton Arboretum, Lisle, Ill.

Neal, M. C. 1965. *In Gardens of Hawaii.* Bernice P. Bishop Museum Special Publication 50. Bishop Museum Press, Honolulu.

Nekola, J. C. 1990. Rare Iowa plant notes from the R. V. Drexler Herbarium. *Journal of the Iowa Academy of Science* 97 (1): 55–73.

Norris, W. R., L. M. Hemesath, D. M. Debinski, and D. R. Farrar. 2003. Does bird community composition vary along a disturbance gradient in northeast Iowa, USA, forests? *Natural Areas Journal* 23: 262–273.

———, D. Q. Lewis, M. P. Widrlechner, J. D. Thompson, and R. O. Pope. 2001. Lessons from an inventory of the Ames, Iowa, flora (1859–2000). *Journal of the Iowa Academy of Science* 108 (2): 34–63.

Novacek, J. M., D. M. Roosa, and W. P. Pusateri. 1985. The vegetation of the Loess Hills landform along the Missouri River. *Proceedings of the Iowa Academy of Science* 92 (5): 199–212.

Peattie, D. C. 1953. *A Natural History of Western Trees.* Bonanza Books, New York.

Petrides, G. A. 1972. *A Field Guide to Trees and Shrubs.* 2d ed. Houghton Mifflin, Boston.

Preston, R. J. 1989. *North American Trees.* 4th ed. Iowa State University Press, Ames.

Prior, J. 1976. *A Regional Guide to Iowa Landforms.* Iowa Geological Survey Educational Series 3. Iowa Geological Survey, Iowa City.

Pusateri, W. P., D. M. Roosa, and D. R. Farrar. 1993. Habitat and distribution of plants special to Iowa's Driftless Area. *Journal of the Iowa Academy of Science* 100 (2): 29–53.

Rehder, A. 1940. *Manual of Cultivated Trees and Shrubs.* 2d ed. Macmillan, New York.

Rohrer, J. R. 2000. The sand cherry in Wisconsin and neighboring states. *Michigan Botanist* 39: 59–69.

Roosa, D. M., L. J. Eilers, and S. Zager. 1991. An annotated checklist of the vascular plant flora of Guthrie County, Iowa. *Journal of the Iowa Academy of Science* 98 (1): 14–30.

Rosendahl, C. O. 1955. *Trees and Shrubs of the Upper Midwest*. University of Minnesota Press, Minneapolis.

Schmidt, K. A., and C. J. Whelan. 1999. Effects of exotic *Lonicera* and *Rhamnus* on songbird nest predation. *Conservation Biology* 13: 1502–1506.

Smith, W. R. 2008. *Trees and Shrubs of Minnesota*. University of Minnesota Press, Minneapolis.

Swink, F., and G. Wilhelm. 1994. *Plants of the Chicago Region*. 4th ed. Indiana Academy of Science, Indianapolis.

Thompson, J. D. 2007. An inventory of the vascular flora of Hamilton County, Iowa (2001–2004). *Journal of the Iowa Academy of Science* 114 (1): 1–27.

———. 2010. The vascular flora of Boone County, Iowa (2005–2008). *Journal of the Iowa Academy of Science* 117 (1–4): 9–46.

Trelease, W. 1931. *Winter Botany*. 3d ed. Reprint, Dover Publications, New York, 1967.

van der Linden, P. J., and D. R. Farrar. 2011. *Forest and Shade Trees of Iowa*. 3d ed. University of Iowa Press, Iowa City.

van Gelderen, D. M., P. C. de Jong, and H. J. Oterdoom. 1994. *Maples of the World*. Timber Press, Portland, Ore.

Voss, E. G. 1985. *Michigan Flora*. Part 2. Cranbrook Institute of Science Bulletin 59. Ann Arbor.

———. 1996. *Michigan Flora*. Part 3. Cranbrook Institute of Science Bulletin 61. Ann Arbor.

Watson, W. C. 1989. The vascular flora of Pilot Knob State Preserve. *Journal of the Iowa Academy of Science* 96 (1): 6–13.

Widrlechner, M. P. 1998. The genus *Rubus* L. in Iowa. *Castanea* 63: 415–465.

———. 2001. The role of environmental analogs in identifying potentially invasive woody plants in Iowa. *Journal of the Iowa Academy of Science* 108 (4): 158–165.

———, and R. K. Rabeler. 1991. *Rubus parvifolius* (Rosaceae), naturalized in Illinois and Iowa. *Michigan Botanist* 30: 23–30.

Wilson, B. L. 1992. Checklist of the vascular flora of Page County, Iowa. *Journal of the Iowa Academy of Science* 99 (1): 23–33.

Woods, K. D. 1993. Effects on invasion by *Lonicera tatarica* L. on herbs and tree seedlings in four New England forests. *American Midland Naturalist* 130: 62–74.

Young, J. A., and C. G. Young. 1992. *Seeds of Woody Plants in North America*. Dioscorides Press, Portland, Ore.

INDEX

OTHER BUR OAK TITLES OF INTEREST

The Butterflies of Iowa
Dennis W. Schlicht, John C. Downey, and Jeffrey C. Nekola

A Country So Full of Game: The Story of Wildlife in Iowa
James J. Dinsmore

The Emerald Horizon: The History of Nature in Iowa
Cornelia F. Mutel

Field Guide to Wildflowers of Nebraska and the Great Plains
Jon Farrar

Forest and Shade Trees of Iowa
Peter J. van der Linden and Donald R. Farrar

Grasses in Your Pocket: A Guide to the Prairie Grasses of the Upper Midwest
Anna B. Gardner, Michael Hurst, Deborah Lewis, and Lynn G. Clark

The Guide to Oklahoma Wildflowers
Patricia Folley

An Illustrated Guide to Iowa Prairie Plants
Paul Christiansen and Mark Müller

Landforms of Iowa
Jean C. Prior

Mushrooms and Other Fungi of the Midcontinental United States
D. M. Huffman, L. H. Tiffany, G. Knaphus, and R. A. Healy

A Practical Guide to Prairie Restoration
Carl Kurtz

Prairie: A North American Guide
Suzanne Winckler

Prairie in Your Pocket: A Guide to Plants of the Tallgrass Prairie
Mark Müller

The Tallgrass Prairie Center Guide to Prairie Restoration in the Upper Midwest
Daryl Smith, Dave Williams, Greg Houseal, and Kirk Henderson

The Tallgrass Prairie Center Guide to Seed and Seedling Identification in the Upper Midwest
Dave Williams and Brent Butler

The Tallgrass Prairie Reader
John T. Price

Trees in Your Pocket: A Guide to Trees of the Upper Midwest
Thomas Rosburg

The Vascular Plants of Iowa: An Annotated Checklist and Natural History
Lawrence J. Eilers and Dean M. Roosa

Wetlands in Your Pocket:
A Guide to Common Plants and
Animals of Midwestern Wetlands
Mark Müller

Where the Sky Began:
Land of the Tallgrass Prairie
John Madsen

Wildflowers and Other Plants
of Iowa Wetlands
Sylvan T. Runkel and Dean M. Roosa

Wildflowers of Iowa Woodlands
Sylvan T. Runkel and Alvin F. Bull

Wildflowers of the Tallgrass Prairie:
The Upper Midwest
Sylvan T. Runkel and Dean M. Roosa

Woodland in Your Pocket:
A Guide to Common Woodland
Plants of the Midwest
Mark Müller